Juridicum – Schriftenreihe zum Wirtschafts-, Unternehmens- und Bankrecht / Series on Business, Corporate and Banking Law

Die Schriftenreihe zum **Wirtschafts-, Unternehmens- und Bankrecht / Series on Business, Corporate and Banking Law** bietet ein Forum für aktuelle und herausragende wissenschaftliche Beiträge aus den genannten Rechtsgebieten. Veröffentlicht werden vor allem Dissertationsschriften, daneben auch ausgewählte Sammelbände zu aktuellen und rechtswissenschaftlich interessanten Fragestellungen. Der Fokus liegt vor allem auf dem deutschen und deutschsprachigen Recht, typischerweise jedoch mit europäischen und internationalen Bezügen. Die Reihe zeichnet sich auch ansonsten durch ihre internationale Ausrichtung aus: Publikationen sind sowohl in deutscher als auch in englischer Sprache möglich. Herausgegeben wird sie von renommierten Wissenschaftlerinnen und Wissenschaftlern aus Deutschland, der Schweiz und Italien, die damit einen grenzüberschreitenden wissenschaftlichen Dialog im Wirtschafts-, Unternehmens- und Bankrecht fördern möchten.

Salih Tayfun İnce

Artificial Intelligence and Corporation Management

A Comparative Legal Analysis

Springer

Salih Tayfun İnce
Fatih Sultan Mehmet Vakif University
Istanbul, Türkiye

This doctoral thesis was submitted to and successfully defended at the Faculty of Law, Philipps-Universität Marburg, where it received the highest distinction (summa cum laude) and was approved for publication.

ISSN 3091-5384 ISSN 3091-5392 (electronic)
Juridicum – Schriftenreihe zum Wirtschafts-, Unternehmens- und Bankrecht / Series on Business, Corporate and Banking Law
ISBN 978-3-658-52671-9 ISBN 978-3-658-52672-6 (eBook)
https://doi.org/10.1007/978-3-658-52672-6

This Springer imprint is published by the registered company Springer Fachmedien Wiesbaden GmbH, part of Springer Nature.
The registered company address is: Abraham-Lincoln-Str. 46, 65189 Wiesbaden, Germany

To my beloved wife, Zeynep Aşıgül İnce,
with love and gratitude

Preface

This work was accepted as a doctoral dissertation by the Faculty of Law at Philipps-Universität Marburg in the summer semester of 2026. The oral examination took place on 27 April 2026. The literature and case law are current as of the end of February 2026.

First and foremost, I would like to express my deepest gratitude to my doctoral supervisor, Professor Dr. Florian Möslein, LL.M. (London). He inspired the topic of this dissertation and supported me throughout my doctoral studies with exceptional dedication, academic generosity, and constant encouragement. His profound expertise, pioneering academic approach, intellectual openness, and the academically free environment he provided were invaluable to the completion of this work. Having Professor Möslein as my *Doktorvater* has been one of the greatest privileges of my academic life, for which I am profoundly thankful.

I am also sincerely grateful to Professor Dr. Sebastian Omlor, LL.M. (NYU), LL.M. Eur., for serving as a member of my doctoral examination committee, for his careful written evaluation, and for his thought-provoking questions during the oral examination. I also wish to thank Professor Dr. Tobias Helms for chairing the examination committee.

I would like to express my gratitude to Istanbul Fatih Sultan Mehmet Vakif University, where I served as a research assistant during my doctoral studies. I am particularly thankful to Professor Dr. Ersin Çamoğlu and Assistant Professor Dr. Bünyamin Gürpınar, with whom I had the opportunity to work in the Department of Commercial Law during that period, for their support and for the collegial academic environment they fostered.

During the course of my doctoral research, I had the valuable opportunity to be invited to participate as a speaker in the Geneva Digital Law Research Colloquium. I would like to thank its distinguished organisers and participants for providing an inspiring forum for academic exchange and discussion of my work.

I owe a special debt of gratitude to my family. My mother, Aysel İnce, my father, Necati İnce, and my sister, Hazal Burcu İnce, have accompanied me throughout this journey with their presence, patience, and unconditional support. I remain truly grateful to them and fully aware that I owe much of who I am today to their love, guidance, and encouragement.

This dissertation is dedicated to my beloved wife, Attorney-at-Law Zeynep Aşıgül İnce, my companion in life and my greatest source of strength. Throughout my doctoral studies and the writing of this dissertation, as in every part of my life, she believed in me, encouraged me, motivated me, and stood by me with unwavering support. Without her support, compassion, and patience, I could not have completed this work.

İstanbul
June 2026

Salih Tayfun İnce

Competing Interests The author has no competing interests to declare that are relevant to the content of this manuscript.

Contents

Abbreviations

AGI	Artificial General Intelligence
AI	Artificial Intelligence
AktG	*Aktiengesetz*, German Stock Corporation Act
Art.	Article
BGB	*Bürgerliches Gesetzbuch,* German Civil Code
BGH	*Bundesgerichtshof,* Federal Court of Justice
BGHZ	*Entscheidungen des Bundesgerichtshofes in Zivilsachen,* Decisions of the Federal Court of Justice in Civil Matters
BJR	Business Judgment Rule
BMJV	*Das Bundesministerium der Justiz und für Verbraucherschutz*, the Federal Ministry of Justice and Consumer Protection
CAIO	Chief Artificial Intelligence Officer
CDO	Chief Digitalisation Officer
CDR	Corporate Digital Responsibility
CEO	Chief Executive Officer
Cf.	*Confer*, compare
CSR	Corporate Social Responsibility
DCGK	*Der deutsche Corporate Governance Kodex*, the German Corporate Governance Codex
ed.	edition
Ed.	Editor
e.g.	*exempli gratia*, for example
ESG	Environmental Social Governance
et al.	*et alia*, and others
etc.	*et cetera*, and other similar things
EU	European Union

EU AI Act	European Union Artificial Intelligence Act
ff.	following (paragraphs, pages)
fn.	footnote
GDPR	General Data Protection Regulation
GOFAI	Good Old-Fashioned AI
i.e.	*id est*, that is
KVKK	*Kişisel Verileri Koruma Kanunu*, Turkish Personal Data Protection Law
ML	Machine Learning
n.d.	no date
No.	Number
OECD	Organisation for Economic Co-operation and Development
OWiG	*Gesetz über Ordnungswidrigkeiten*, (German) Act on Regulatory Offences
p.	page
para.	paragraph
PLD	Product Liability Directive
pp.	pages
§	Section
subpara.	subparagraph
TCC	*Türk Ticaret Kanunu*, Turkish Commercial Code
TCO	*Türk Borçlar Kanunu*, Turkish Code of Obligations
WpHG	*Wertpapierhandelsgesetz*, German Securities Trading Act

Introduction 1

1.1 In General

Technological advancement is a central force in shaping entire human history. Certain technological advancements are classified as disruptive due to their profound socioeconomic and environmental ramifications. These technologies eliminate and replace products, markets, or value networks that preceded them.[1] As one of these disruptive technologies, artificial intelligence (AI)[2] is exerting a disruptive influence on domains traditionally considered exclusive to human cognitive capabilities. AI, which can simulate human decision-making processes, albeit to a limited extent for now, can replicate outcomes typically associated with human intelligence, especially in data-driven domains. There is virtually no field in which AI has not been used or considered for use. Especially medicine, law, and engineering, where human intelligence has played a dominant role for centuries, are starting to be dominated by AI systems. The integration of AI enables more accurate medical diagnoses,[3] facilitates more in-depth and comprehensive

---

[1] Rahman et al. (2017), Perintis eJournal, p. 112.

[2] While scholarly discourse often distinguishes between 'AI' as an intangible algorithmic model and an 'AI system' as its tangible implementation, this study employs the terms 'AI' and 'AI system' interchangeably.

[3] Max Planck Society (2025, June 20). "Human–AI Collectives Make The Most Accurate Medical Diagnoses." Available at: https://www.mpg.de/24908163/human-ai-collectives-make-the-most-accurate-medical-diagnoses. (Last accessed: 25.12.2025).

S. T. İnce, *Artificial Intelligence and Corporation Management*, Juridicum – Schriftenreihe zum Wirtschafts-, Unternehmens- und Bankrecht / Series on Business, Corporate and Banking Law,
https://doi.org/10.1007/978-3-658-52672-6_1

legal research,[4] and generates more efficient engineering solutions.[5] Moreover, the unprecedented speed at which AI can execute such tasks, far surpassing human capabilities, is one of its most transformative benefits.

All these opportunities provided by AI have created a competitive environment for the creation and use of these systems. Countries and corporations are making significant investments to keep up with the AI race. For example, Türkiye prepared the National Artificial Intelligence Strategy in 2021.[6] Furthermore, Türkiye's Industry and Technology Strategy for 2030 frames AI not only as a technological advancement but also as a strategically and economically significant field.[7] Similarly, Germany prepared its National AI Strategy in 2018 and revised it in 2020.[8] In addition to determining strategy, governments are advancing legal frameworks for AI. In the European Union (EU), including Germany, the European Union Artificial Intelligence Act (EU AI Act)[9] was recently adopted, creating a binding regulatory regime tailored to AI systems. Although Türkiye has not yet enacted a specific law on AI, the Medium-Term Plan[10] outlines an intention to harmonise Turkish law with the EU AI Act in the 2026–2028 period.

Beyond governmental prioritisation, corporations, as key market players, are also striving to integrate AI systems into all their organisational structures and workflows. Industrial operations are increasingly becoming AI-based. Similarly,

[4] Kelly Griffith (2025, October 7). "How To Effectively Use AI For Legal Research," Thomson Reuters Legal Solutions Blog. Available at: https://legal.thomsonreuters.com/blog/how-to-effectively-use-ai-for-legal-research/. (Last accessed: 25.12.2025).

[5] Hayden Horner (2025, May 12). "How Engineers Use AI To Work Smarter, Prototype Faster, And Stress Less," Engineering Institute of Technology. Available at: https://www.eit.edu.au/how-engineers-use-ai-to-work-smarter-stress-less/. (Last accessed: 25.12.2025).

[6] The Presidential Circular No. 2021/18 regarding the "National Artificial Intelligence Strategy 2021–2025," Official Gazette dated 20/08/2021 and numbered 31574.

[7] Republic of Türkiye Ministry of Industry and Technology, "2030 Industry and Technology Strategy," p. 46. Available at: https://www.sanayi.gov.tr/assets/pdf/plan-program/2030IndustryAndTechnologyStrategyENG.pdf?1751241600107. (Last accessed: 25.12.2025).

[8] Artificial Intelligence Strategy of the German Federal Government 2020 Update. Available at: https://www.ki-strategie-deutschland.de/files/downloads/Fortschreibung_KI-Strategie_engl.pdf. (Last accessed: 25.12.2025).

[9] Regulation (EU) 2024/1689 of the European Parliament and of the Council of 13 June 2024 laying down harmonised rules on artificial intelligence and amending Regulations (EC) No 300/2008, (EU) No 167/2013, (EU) No 168/2013, (EU) 2018/858, (EU) 2018/1139 and (EU) 2019/2144 and Directives 2014/90/EU, (EU) 2016/797 and (EU) 2020/1828 (Artificial Intelligence Act).

[10] The Presidential Decision regarding 2026–2028 Medium-Term Plan, No. 10376, Official Gazette dated 07/09/2025 and numbered 33010-Duplicate Issue, p. 24 and 72.

corporations' ongoing initiatives and future roadmaps for AI integration into management are accelerating. Within this direction, integrating AI systems into corporate boards,[11] where strategic and complex management decisions are made, is also seen as crucial for effective management.[12] The use of AI in administrative tasks, such as data and document management, record keeping, and scheduling, is a subject of significant contemporary discussion in corporate management, as these repetitive, non-creative tasks can be handled effectively by AI.[13] The next step is to implement AI in more complex tasks, such as predictive market analysis, merger and acquisition due diligence, dynamic resource allocation and the development of long-term corporate strategy. As AI systems grow more sophisticated with the advancement of generative AI tools based on Large Language Models, such as GPT Series, Gemini, Mistral and Llama, etc., fundamental questions are emerging about their role in corporate management. These questions range from AI's use as advisory tools for corporate boards and the delegation of specific tasks to them, to the more profound possibility of AI systems achieving formal membership on corporate boards.[14] This study will examine these questions through a legal lens, analysing the potential regulatory and governance implications in Turkish and German corporate law.

1.2 Terminology and Technical Understanding

1.2.1 Brief Historical Background of AI

1.2.1.1 From Ancient Times to World War II

Throughout history, various philosophers, authors,[15] and scientists have contributed to the field of AI in different ways and to varying degrees. Especially, efforts to develop computational reasoning paved the way for AI. In this context, Aristotle's inventions of formalism and syllogism provided a basis for the

[11] In this comparative study, unless otherwise specified as 'supervisory board', the term 'board' refers to the 'board of directors' in Turkish law and the 'management board' in German law.

[12] Möslein (2022), p. 74.

[13] Petrin (2019), Colum. Bus. L. Rev., p. 971 and 993; Dönmez Canseven (2021), pp. 93–94; Petrin (2024), Sing JLS, p. 93.

[14] For actual examples of AI systems being appointed as board members to corporations' boards in various ways, see 2.1.2.1.

[15] Literary fictions played a guiding role for the development of artificial life idea. For examples of these fictions, see McCorduck (2004), p. 18; Nilsson (2010), p. 19 ff.

computation of reasoning. He studied rationality as an inseparable element of the mind. His idea of formalism, which distinguishes matter and form in the process of data abstraction,[16] can be considered his most important contribution to AI. This distinction, which enabled validating thought patterns not in terms of their contents but of their forms, is currently used in computational theory of mind and AI.[17] In the same vein, he developed syllogisms to formulate proper reasoning. This system provides a very useful form or template for reasoning.[18]

The attempt to formalise reasoning continued with the construction of calculators as specialised machines for computation. As an early example of these attempts, Ramon Lull claimed that machines could carry out reasoning. He created *Ars Magna* (Great Art),[19] a set of paper discs. Specific rotations of the discs generated answers to some theological questions.[20] In the same vein, Leonardo da Vinci drew plans of a mechanical calculator but did not construct it. Wilhelm Schickard built the first calculating machine around 1623. Soon afterwards, Blaise Pascal introduced his calculator in 1642. Gottfried Wilhelm Leibniz attempted to construct a mechanical reasoning structure based on a new language (*lingua characteristica*) capable of formulating all knowledge. According to this projection, a *calculus ratiocinator (*calculus of reasoning) operating in *the lingua characteristica* would give the correct answers to the questions posed in this technical language.[21]

Later, Charles Stanhope invented a box that was like an analogue computer, capable of providing answers to basic problems in logic and probability. 'Stanhope's box' (later called 'The Stanhope Demonstrator') is considered the first logic machine to operate in practice.[22] At the end of the eighteenth century, Baron von Kempelen developed a thinking machine called 'The Turk'. Although there was a small, experienced chess player in the box, this machine led many people to think they were playing chess with the machine.[23]

Computing machines became more complex in the nineteenth century. Charles Babbage designed a calculator called the 'Difference Engine' in 1822. Later,

---

[16] Lucci and Kopec (2016), p. 26.

[17] Arkoudas and Bringsjord (2014), p. 36.

[18] Nilsson (2010), pp. 27–28.

[19] McCorduck (2004), p. 11.

[20] Nilsson (2010), p. 20.

[21] Nilsson (2010), pp. 28–29.

[22] Nilsson (2010), pp. 29–31; Lucci and Kopec (2016), p. 27.

[23] Lucci and Kopec (2016), p. 28 and 501.

he designed a general computation machine called the 'Analytical Engine.'[24] Babbage discussed the possibility of a chess-playing machine in his book 'The Life of a Philosopher' in 1845.[25]

The contribution of epistemological and ontological thoughts to AI should not be neglected. These philosophical inquiries accelerated during and after the Enlightenment. For instance, the confirmation theory, which seeks to acquire knowledge from elementary experiences, is among the first modern theories to treat the mind as a computational process.[26]

1.2.1.2 From World War II to Today

As early as 1947, Alan Turing was giving lectures about AI.[27] Besides, he published his essay "*Computing Machinery and Intelligence*" in 1950.[28] Although this publication could be considered the beginning of modern AI research,[29] the official birthplace of AI is accepted as the Summer Workshop held at Dartmouth College in 1956.[30] Although Allen Newell and Herbert A. Simon introduced their program, 'Logic Theorist', which could prove elementary theorems of propositional calculus,[31] this workshop did not yield breakthroughs for the field. Still, it brought together pioneers of the field and gave the field its name.[32] John McCarthy proposed using 'artificial intelligence' as the name of the field,[33] and it was first used in the proposal for this summer workshop. By this name, he sought to differentiate this field from previous studies of automata.[34] Besides, he wanted to avoid association with 'cybernetics.'[35] On the contrary, Newell and Simon continued to refer to their study as 'complex information processing' for

[24] Lucci and Kopec (2016), p. 27.

[25] Nilsson (2010), p. 123.

[26] Russell and Norvig (2010), p. 6. For more information on philosophical contributions to the AI, see Russell and Norvig (2010), pp. 5–7.

[27] Russell and Norvig (2010), p. 17.

[28] Alan Mathison Turing, (1950). Computing machinery and intelligence. Mind, 59 (236), 433–460.

[29] Mainzer (2020), p. 10.

[30] Franklin (2014), p. 18; Buxmann and Schmidt (2019), p. 4; Haddadin and Knobbe (2020), p. 7.

[31] Arkoudas and Bringsjord (2014), p. 40.

[32] Russell and Norvig (2010), pp. 17–18.

[33] Franklin (2014), p. 18; Haddadin and Knobbe (2020), p. 7.

[34] McCorduck (2004), pp. 114–115.

[35] Nilsson (2010), p. 78.

years.[36] Today, although its borders remain unclear, the term AI is commonly accepted.

After this summer school, the dominant programming language for the following 30 years, Lisp, was created by McCarthy in 1958. In the same year, he introduced his hypothetical program, 'Advice Taker', as a so-called 'complete AI system'. This program differed from others in its approach to using general knowledge. While it is operating, this program could accept new axioms by manipulating the knowledge representation with the deductive process. This new feature provided it with general competencies in other areas without being programmed.[37]

In 1959, the 'General Problem Server'(GPS) was introduced by Allen Newell, John Clifford Shaw, and Herb Simon to mechanise problem-solving.[38] First time in the field, GPS took the 'thinking humanly' approach and imitated human problem-solving protocols. After the success of GPS, Newell and Simon developed their physical symbol system hypothesis. According to this hypothesis, manipulating data structures composed of symbols is necessary for the operation of intelligent systems.[39] It was a new approach for the creation of symbolic AI systems.

During the 1950s, the field of AI continued to attract state funds. However, in most cases, AI systems failed. The main reason for this failure was methodological. AI systems that successfully worked on simple examples failed when tested on more complex problems. The researchers believed that all they needed to overcome these failures was faster hardware and greater memory capacity. Then, they understood that these concrete facilities are necessary but not sufficient to handle the 'combinatorial explosion' in which the possible states are impractically high.[40] They had to explore different methods, such as machine learning and new neural network techniques.

After failures with these methods, researchers focused on other methods that leverage domain-specific knowledge and narrow areas of expertise. In this way, knowledge-intensive systems emerged as expert systems. 'R1' was the first expert system to become commercially successful. 'DENDRAL' was one of the early

---

[36] McCorduck (2004), p. 115.

[37] Russell and Norvig (2010), p. 19.

[38] Nilsson (2010), p. 121.

[39] Russell and Norvig (2010), p. 18.

[40] Lucci and Kopec (2016), p. 18.

examples of these systems.[41] 'MYCIN' was another example of an expert system in medical diagnosis.[42]

Despite gradual advancement, there were two periods known as the AI winters. The first AI winter began with the publication of the 'Lighthill Report' in 1973 and continued through 1980. Later, the second AI winter occurred between 1987 and 1993.[43] The underlying reason for these stagnation periods was the withdrawal of funding from AI research due to the unfulfillment of the expectations regarding AI.[44]

Over the last two winters, AI technologies have consolidated thanks to the accessibility and expansion of databases, the development of the World Wide Web, and the decline in computer prices.[45] Today, other important reasons for the rise in AI include the availability of big data, cheaper storage options, faster processors, ubiquitous connectivity, cloud solutions, progress in algorithms, the creation of new techniques, openness of code, increased knowledge sharing and funding.[46] With all these capabilities in place, the concept of generative adversarial networks emerged in 2014. In 2022, OpenAI introduced the GPT Series, a set of generative AI systems combining large language models. Subsequently, dozens of applications, such as Gemini, Mistral, Llama and Bing AI, were developed and released as alternatives. These applications are now used in every aspect of life. Today, AI technology is being taken a step further with 'Agentic AI[47]'. The next stage will be the development and widespread adoption of 'physical AI[48]'.

---

[41] Lucci and Kopec (2016), p. 30.

[42] Russell and Norvig (2010), p. 23; Lucci and Kopec (2016), p. 15 and 212.

[43] Burgess (2018), p. 12.

[44] Burgess (2018), p. 12; Delipetrev et al. (2020), p. 8.

[45] Nilsson (2010), p. 589.

[46] Pan (2016), Engineering, pp. 410–411; Stone et al. (2016), p. 14; Burgess (2018), pp. 13–19; Craglia et al. (2018), p. 16; Iafrate (2018), pp. 38–39; Buxmann and Schmidt (2019), p. 4; The Royal Society (2019), p. 5; Delipetrev et al. (2020), p. 12; DIN e.V. & DKE. (2020), p. 64.

[47] "*Agentic AI is an artificial intelligence system that can accomplish a specific goal with limited supervision. It consists of AI agents—machine learning models that mimic human decision-making to solve problems in real time. In a multiagent system, each agent performs a specific subtask required to reach the goal and their efforts are coordinated through AI orchestration.*" IBM (n.d.). "What is agentic AI?," IBM Think Topics. Available at: https://www.ibm.com/think/topics/agentic-ai. (Last accessed: 25.12.2025).

[48] "*Physical AI refers to artificial intelligence systems that enable machines to autonomously perceive, understand, reason about, and interact with the physical world in real time.*" Jim Rowan, Tim Gaus, Franz Gilbert and Caroline Brown (2025, December 24). "AI goes physical: Navigating the convergence of AI and robotics."

Concerning winters and acceleration periods of AI, one of the best summaries of the history of AI belongs to Russell and Norvig: "*The history of AI has had cycles of success, misplaced optimism, and resulting cutbacks in enthusiasm and funding. There have also been cycles of introducing new creative approaches and systematically refining the best ones.*"[49]

1.2.2 Predictions

Although some AI forecasts raised public expectations and later disappointed, predictions from field experts offer a sense of future developments in AI. In the early days of modern AI research, some leading researchers of the field, made bold predictions about AI.[50] Since these predictions were not materialised as quickly as predicted timeline, they are used against the entire idea of AI. As has happened before, the future of the AI field may be very different from what is forecasted today.[51] This approach, which illustrates the difficulty of predicting the future of AI, is known as Amara's Law. This law dictates, "*We tend to overestimate the effect of a technology in the short run and underestimate the effect in the long run.*"[52]

As is the case with other emerging fields, there are optimists, pessimists, and pragmatists regarding AI's current status and future.[53] The creation of human-level AI is the benchmark for the future AI debate, as this achievement is the ultimate aim of AI. In this respect, it is claimed that the production of intelligent, complex robots capable of engaging in human interaction is not feasible in the near future.[54] In the same vein, after arguing the inadequacy of AI in terms of creativity in general, Boden states, "*AGI* [Artificial General Intelligence] *is as far as ever.*"[55] From another perspective, Nilsson predicts that humans will create machines more intelligent than humans, an inevitable outcome of scientific

---

Deloitte Insights. https://www.deloitte.com/us/en/insights/topics/technology-management/tech-trends/2026/physical-ai-humanoid-robots.html. (Last accessed: 25.12.2025).

[49] Russell and Norvig (2010), p. 30.

[50] Delipetrev et al. (2020), p. 7.

[51] Arkoudas and Bringsjord (2014), p. 58.

[52] Rodney Brooks (2017, September 7). "The Seven Deadly Sins of Predicting the Future of AI." Available at: http://rodneybrooks.com/the-seven-deadly-sins-of-predicting-the-future-of-ai/. (Last accessed: 25.12.2025)

[53] Turner (2019), pp. 32–34.

[54] Haddadin and Knobbe (2020), p. 25.

[55] Boden (2016), p. 72.

progress and economic necessity.[56] However, he does not predict when it will happen.

There are scientific surveys of researchers' predictions for AI. According to a survey, AI experts foresee that AI systems will reach overall human ability by 2040–50 with a probability of more than 50%, and by 2075 with a probability of 90%. Besides, they assume that achieving superintelligence will take 2 to 30 years, with 10% and 75% probability, respectively, from reaching human intelligence.[57] In another recent survey, researchers forecast that the likelihood that AI will outperform humans across all tasks in 45 years is 50%. They assign a 10% probability for the occurrence of said outperformance in 9 years.[58] The same respondents believe there is a 50% chance of full automation of labour in 122 years. They assign 10% probability for full automation of labour in 20 years.[59]

In 2016, philosopher Jim Moor asked some participants of the 1956 Dartmouth Workshop whether human-level AI would be achieved within the next 50 years. John McCarthy and Marvin Minsky replied in the affirmative, Trenchard Moore gave a negative answer, and Ray Solomonoff qualified the AI as the light at the end of the tunnel against the self-destruction of humanity.[60]

In one of his later articles, McCarthy states that some researchers believe that creating large numbers of programs representing vast knowledge bases is enough to achieve human-level intelligence. However, he indicates that most researchers in the field believe that existing techniques are inadequate and that breakthroughs are needed to achieve human-level intelligence. Hence, it is not possible to forecast when human-level intelligence will be achieved.[61] Concerning Amara's law and prospective breakthroughs in the field, this study agrees with McCarthy that it is not possible to predict the future of AI in terms of its content and timeline. However, the inevitable progress in the field of AI will create new challenges, such as the replacement of humans by machines in specific professions,[62] the use of AI for undesirable aims, damage to people's sense of being unique, loss of accountability in AI-operated systems, and revision of the amount and structure of

[56] Nilsson (2010), p. 634.

[57] Müller and Bostrom (2016), p. 568.

[58] Grace et al. (2018), JAIR, p. 731.

[59] Grace et al. (2018), JAIR, p. 731.

[60] Arkoudas and Bringsjord (2014), p. 58.

[61] McCarthy (2007), p. 5.

[62] Stone et al. (2016), p. 39.

people's leisure time.[63] Therefore, scientifically grounded predictions and opinions from researchers are essential for a general view of the field's prospective progress. Otherwise, organisations and entire systems may be caught unprepared for these challenges, as it is emphasised by Chief Justice of the US Supreme Court, John Roberts: "*The impact of technology has been across the board and we haven't yet really absorbed how it's going to change the way we do business.*"[64]

1.2.3 Definition

1.2.3.1 Etymological Investigation

A brief investigation into the etymological roots of the term 'artificial intelligence' in the relevant languages in this study may provide hints for clearer terminological definitions and a deeper understanding. The term 'artificial intelligence' consists of two words. 'Artificial' is rooted in 'art' and first used in writing in the fifteenth century to refer to a thing that is "*made, produced, or done by humans especially to seem like something natural.*"[65] In other words, the word 'artificial' refers to the systematic utilisation of techniques to model and create imitations of entities in nature. Thus, it clearly shows the connection between art and science in AI.[66] The word 'intelligence' is derived from the word '*intellegere*,' which is the composition of the prefix '*inter*' (between) and the verb '*legere*' (pick, choose). This etymological structure makes it evident that intelligence primarily involves selection.[67] Its first written usage dates to the fourteenth century, with the meaning "*the ability to learn or understand things or to deal with new or difficult situations.*"[68] Given this meaning, intelligence may be considered as the vital ability to survive in nature. Hence, it is not surprising that the surviving human species is named *homo sapiens* (wise man).

'*Yapay zekâ*' is the term formed by combining two words. It is used in Turkish to mean artificial intelligence. '*Yapay*' is rooted in the verb '*yap(mak)*' that

[63] For a detailed analysis of these challenges, see Russell and Norvig (2010), pp. 1034–1040.

[64] Liptak, A. (2017, May 1). "Sent to prison by a software program's secret algorithms", The New York Times. Available at: https://www.nytimes.com/2017/05/01/us/politics/sent-to-prison-by-a-software-programs-secret-algorithms.html. (Last accessed: 25.12.2025)

[65] Merriam-Webster Dictionary. "Artificial." Available at: https://www.merriam-webster.com/dictionary/artificial. (Last accessed: 25.12.2025)

[66] McCorduck (2004), p. 115.

[67] Iafrate (2018), p. 1.

[68] Merriam-Webster Dictionary. "Intelligence." Available at: https://www.merriam-webster.com/dictionary/intelligence. (Last accessed: 25.12.2025)

means to build or create. As a word, '*yapay*' is a late product of the language-simplification movement in Türkiye. This word was first used in a written source in 1937.[69] It is created to match the meaning of the Arabic-rooted word '*suni'* that shares the same root with '*san'at*' (art).[70] Today, the word '*yapay*' is widely used in the context of AI. '*Zekâ*' is an Arabic-rooted word that nominally means sharpness.[71] It is used in Turkish in the meaning of 'intelligence,' 'understanding,' 'cleverness,' and 'comprehension.'[72]

In German, '*künstliche Intelligenz*' is the term equivalent to artificial intelligence. '*Künstlich*' is derived from '*Kunst*' (art) [73] and means "*made by man; not natural; not real.*"[74] '*Intelligenz*' is rooted in '*inter legere*' in Latin. It means "*the quality of being intelligent.*"[75]

In light of the explanations mentioned above, it is clear that the denomination of '*yapay zekâ*' in Turkish differs from its English and German equivalents in terms of the etymological roots of the word "*yapay.*" If the word '*yapay*' could not be created and popularised under the influence of the language simplification movement, the word '*suni*' would be used for 'artificial' in Turkish. It would have its root in the word 'art', as is the case with 'artificial' and '*künstliche*' in English and German, respectively. Apart from this difference, the structure and etymological roots of the words that match artificial intelligence in the abovementioned languages are very similar. This comparative etymological inquiry demonstrates that the terminological construction for artificial intelligence across all three languages integrates two core components: artificial genesis (non-natural) and cognitive function (the capacity for deliberative selection), mirroring key attributes of human intellect.

---

[69] Nişanyan Etymological Turkish Dictionary. "Yapay." Available at: https://www.nisanyansozluk.com/?k=yapay. (Last accessed: 25.12.2025)

[70] Nişanyan Etymological Turkish Dictionary. "Suni." Available at: https://www.nisanyansozluk.com/?k=suni. (Last accessed: 25.12.2025)

[71] Nişanyan Etymological Turkish Dictionary. "Zekâ." Available at: https://www.nisanyansozluk.com/?k=zeka. (Last accessed: 25.12.2025)

[72] Parker (2008), p. 519.

[73] Wolfgang P. et al. (1993), Etymologisches Wörterbuch des Deutschen (Digitalized Version in Digitalen Wörterbuch der deutschen Sprache). "Künstlich." Available at: https://www.dwds.de/wb/etymwb/K%C3%BCnstlich. (Last accessed: 25.12.2025)

[74] Cambridge Online German-English Dictionary. "Künstlich." Available at: https://dictionary.cambridge.org/dictionary/german-english/kunstlich?q=k%C3%BCnstlich. (Last accessed: 25.12.2025)

[75] Cambridge Online German-English Dictionary. "Intelligenz." Available at: https://dictionary.cambridge.org/dictionary/german-english/intelligenz. (Last accessed: 25.12.2025)

1.2.3.2 The Research-Specific Definition

There is no consensus on the definition of AI among the researchers in the field.[76] Thus, AI is considered an umbrella term[77] with various definitions.[78] This definitional diversity may be a consequence of interdisciplinary perspectives and wavering trajectories of AI.[79] Even if a standard definition of AI is established, it cannot resist constant change in the field. All definitions of AI are based on current knowledge and are doomed to be revised by future work. However, a working definition for AI remains a necessary foundation for any scholarly research.[80]

Distinct definitions of AI can be given in different contexts and for various purposes. A working definition should be sufficiently specific to enable the researcher to work with it. In other words, a working definition should be research-specific.[81] Because the purpose of this study is to comparatively examine the use of AI in corporation management under Turkish and German law, the underlying definition of AI must be both functional across these jurisdictions and grounded in a legal perspective. The definition of an AI system provided in the EU AI Act satisfies these criteria by offering stable and normative framework. By virtue of Germany's membership in the EU, the EU AI Act is binding as a Regulation under German law. For Türkiye, although the EU AI Act is not legally binding, it serves as a guide for Turkish law, given Türkiye's status as an EU accession candidate. Moreover, given that the harmonisation of Turkish law with the EU AI Act is planned in the 2026–2028 Medium-Term Program, it is expected that the EU AI Act's definitions will soon be transposed into Turkish law and become binding. Consequently, this study adopts the EU AI Act's definition of an AI system. According to the EU AI Act, an AI system is "*a machine-based system that is designed to operate with varying levels of autonomy and that may exhibit adaptiveness after deployment, and that, for explicit or implicit objectives, infers, from the input it receives, how to generate outputs such as predictions, content, recommendations, or decisions that can influence physical or virtual environments.*"[82]

---

[76] See Lucci and Kopec (2016), p. 4 ff.; Loza de Siles (2021), Buff. L. Rev., p. 1418 ff.

[77] The Royal Society, (2019), p. 5 and 7.

[78] For a comprehensive investigation regarding definition of AI, see Samoili et al. (2021), p. 7 ff.

[79] Baruffaldi et al. (2020), p. 10; DIN e.V. & DKE (2020), p. 36.

[80] Wang (2019), JAGI, p. 1 ff.

[81] For the criteria of a good working definition, see Wang (2019), JAGI, pp. 3–6.

[82] Article 3(1) of the EU AI Act.

1.2.4 General Description of AI Systems and Prominent AI Methodologies

1.2.4.1 In General

A typical AI system is architecturally composed of three core components: algorithms for processing and learning, databases for information storage and retrieval, and a user or system interface for interaction.[83] This integrated structure provides collective capabilities in perception, understanding, action, and communication.[84] The lifecycle of a typical AI system can be divided into separate phases of design, data and model verification and validation, deployment, operation and monitoring, and retirement.[85] Problem-solving, searching, optimisation, decision-making, planning, knowledge representation and inference, machine learning, and hybrid learning methods are the main techniques used by AI systems throughout these phases.[86] Every AI system employs a specific set of strategies and methodologies tailored to achieve its designated objectives. Therefore, the inherent design specificity of each AI system must be incorporated as a foundational consideration within evaluations.

1.2.4.2 Prominent AI Methodologies

The evolution of AI is marked by distinct methodological shifts, from the logical frameworks of symbolic AI and expert systems to the data-driven approaches of modern machine learning, encompassing supervised, unsupervised, and reinforcement learning. As pioneers of AI, symbolic AI systems display intelligence by formally manipulating symbols within computers.[87] These systems are classic AI systems, also known as Good Old-Fashioned AI (GOFAI).[88] GOFAI was the prevailing approach in the AI field between the 1950s and 1980s.[89] Although GOFAI has become taken for granted and thus invisible, it is still serving as a foundation stone for various AI systems.[90]

One of the most common applications of symbolic AI is an expert system. A typical expert system is composed of four core components: a knowledge base,

---

[83] DIN e.V. & DKE (2020), p. 81.

[84] DIN e.V. & DKE (2020), pp. 45–47.

[85] OECD (2020), p. 8.

[86] Boden (2016), p. 23; Chowdhary (2020), p. 10.

[87] Franklin (2014), p. 15.

[88] Boden (2014), p. 97.

[89] Boden (2014), p. 89.

[90] Boden (2014), pp. 101–103.

which stores facts and rules, a problem-solving element (or inference engine), which applies logical reasoning, an explanatory element, which justifies its conclusions, and a knowledge acquisition and dialogue element, which facilitates interaction with human experts.[91] Expert systems differ from computer programming in their methods for knowledge representation. Computer programming follows a procedural approach that involves dividing the problem into a sequence of steps to solve it. In contrast, expert systems utilise natural application of symbolic systems that include the creation of a knowledge base,[92] with domain-specific facts, the rules and representation of relations in a symbolic form, and an inference engine that deals with the manipulation and combination of these symbols.[93] These systems hinge on knowledge engineering.[94] In this engineering process, necessary information is extracted from human experts, converted into 'If-Then rules', and installed in expert systems to provide advice.[95] 'If-Then rules' systems work as follows: after the occurrence of specific circumstances listed under 'If', the system gives certain decisions or displays pre-determined actions specified under 'Then'. Nevertheless, reducing all intelligent behaviours is not possible in these systems[96] due to the environment's uncertain and fuzzy nature. Since they work with pre-programmed 'If-Then rules' and cannot represent uncertain features of the environment, expert systems lack autonomy. Moreover, their learning ability is primitive and not a result of their self-operation.

As another type of AI (methodology), machine learning (ML) is the process of meaning distillation via exposure to training data. Since ML techniques help the AI field overcome key challenges on the path to human-level AI, it is considered the 'holy grail' of AI.[97] The ML process consists of at least two main components. One component learns from the training data and creates a model. Another component makes decisions by using this model.[98] These ML systems differ from classical computer programming and expert systems because their dynamic decision-making processes may not be specified, predicted, or even understood by their designers.[99] These ML systems derive rules from patterns in the dataset.

[91] Mainzer (2020), p. 47 ff.

[92] Mainzer (2020), pp. 47–48.

[93] Kaplan (2016), p. 23.

[94] Kaplan (2016), p. 23.

[95] Boden (2014), p. 91; Lucci and Kopec (2016), p. 15; Mainzer (2020), p. 49.

[96] Lucci and Kopec (2016), p. 208.

[97] Lucci and Kopec (2016), p. 298.

[98] Castelluccia and Le Métayer (2019), p. 4.

[99] Bathaee (2018), JOLT, p. 891.

They apply these rules to new data and generate original results. Therefore, ML systems do not rely on explicit programming but on training.[100] In the learning phase of this dynamic decision-making process, two main challenges may occur. If the environment changes, the model's reflection of reality can become inadequate. This challenge is called 'concept drift'.[101] Moreover, the model may change during operation due to its learning ability.[102] This challenge is called 'model drift'.[103] Therefore, the assessment and monitoring of ML systems should be based on their dynamic features.[104]

The most distinctive characteristic of ML systems is their ability to learn. Different ML systems may have different levels of learning ability. Some machine learning techniques, such as deep learning, exhibit a high degree of learning ability, which introduces unpredictability and autonomy. New ML methods, such as support vector machines, probabilistic graphical models, reinforcement learning, random forests, and deep learning neural networks, are operationally efficient but not transparent in terms of explainability.[105] For instance, deep learning provides the most accurate results at the expense of system opacity.[106]

According to their learning methodologies, ML systems can be categorised into supervised, unsupervised, and reinforcement learning.[107] Supervised ML refers to ML systems that learn by example. In these ML systems, the underlying classification algorithms learn to label the data using a large training dataset[108] that is already classified.[109] The ML system should be provided with training data with correct labels, a suitable ML model, and a cost function to assess performance.[110] Therefore, necessary feedback can be provided to the algorithm immediately.[111] Furthermore, in supervised learning systems based on regression

---

[100] The Royal Society (2017), p. 16; Craglia et. al. (2018), p. 20.

[101] For examples of concept drift, see Gama et. al. (2013), CSUR, pp. 7–10.

[102] DIN e.V. & DKE (2020), p. 82.

[103] For the causes of model drift, see Patchipala (2023), IJSRA, p. 1201 ff.

[104] DIN e.V. & DKE (2020), p. 82.

[105] Gunning et al. (2019), Sci. Robot., p. 1.

[106] Gunning et al. (2019), Sci. Robot., p. 1. DIN e.V. & DKE (2020), p. 83.

[107] Boden (2016), p. 47; Lucci and Kopec (2016), p. 300; Haddadin and Knobbe (2020), p. 21.

[108] Lucci and Kopec (2016), p. 299.

[109] The Royal Society (2017), p. 20; Chowdhary (2020), p. 383; Haddadin and Knobbe (2020), p. 22.

[110] Buchanan and Miller (2017), p. 6.

[111] Lucci and Kopec (2016), p. 300.

algorithms, these algorithms determine the relationships between dependent and independent variables. Thus, these systems can predict outputs for new inputs. Apart from their advantages, supervised learning systems also pose some challenges. These systems require some degree of human expertise to build the structure (like expert systems). Besides, these systems are vulnerable to human errors. These human errors may result in incorrect outputs. Moreover, the training phase can be very time-intensive.

Unlike supervised ML, algorithms can build classifications by analysing data without prior categorisation or tagging. These systems that identify clusters and their boundaries in data samples as an outcome of automatic data processing are called unsupervised ML systems.[112] These systems do not require human intervention. Instead, they are used to discover knowledge[113] by themselves. Unsupervised ML systems do not require human intervention to find hidden patterns and possible data groupings. Clustering, association, and dimensionality reduction are the main techniques in an unsupervised ML system.[114] Clustering algorithms group unclassified data by relying on similarities and differences within datasets. Association algorithms attempt to discover relations between variables, such as different products in a market basket. Dimensionality reduction is a tool used before data processing in high-dimensional data sets. This tool helps reduce the amount of input data while preserving data integrity.[115]

Generally, unsupervised learning systems handle large volumes of unstructured data, as they are well-suited for prediction and structure construction in such datasets.[116] However, a high volume of data can increase computational complexity and prolong training time. Moreover, unsupervised learning systems generally require human validation since the risk of inaccurate results is higher. Besides, it is not always easy to find clustering criteria for the system. This difficulty may cause transparency problems.[117] These systems are primarily used for

---

[112] The Royal Society (2017), p. 20; Haddadin and Knobbe (2020), p. 22.

[113] Boden (2016), p. 47.

[114] IBM (n.d.). "Unsupervised Learning." Available at: https://www.ibm.com/think/topics/unsupervised-learning. (Last accessed: 25.12.2025).

[115] IBM (n.d.). "Unsupervised Learning." Available at: https://www.ibm.com/think/topics/unsupervised-learning. (Last accessed: 25.12.2025)

[116] Buchanan and Miller (2017), p. 5 and 9.

[117] IBM (n.d.). "Unsupervised Learning." Available at: https://www.ibm.com/think/topics/unsupervised-learning. (Last accessed: 25.12.2025)

computer vision, medical imaging, anomaly detection, recommendation engines, and customer persona determination.[118]

Reinforcement ML is seen as an extension of dynamic programming, as it can handle complex problems that involve more unknowns about prospective actions. It is a goal-directed trial-and-error learning method in which algorithms aim to reach a rewarding state (and avoid punishment) by traversing a cluster of states.[119] This process consists of four components: a policy that represents the agent's actions, a reward function that connects the current state to the goal, a value mapping that measures that connection, and a model of the environment in which these actions take place.[120] Reinforcement learning is also called 'weak supervision' and can be placed between supervised and unsupervised learning methods[121] in terms of human intervention. In these systems, humans do not tell what action should be taken. The system should discover the rewarding action during an iterative process.[122] Tasks in dynamic environments, such as game playing and vehicle driving, are better suited to this approach. For instance, DeepMind's AlphaGo, which employs reinforcement learning, defeated top Go players, a game with more possible combinations than atoms in the universe.[123]

1.2.5 Essential Categorisations

1.2.5.1 Functional Categorisation

1.2.5.1.1 Weak/Narrow AI

The principal criterion for qualifying an AI system as 'weak AI' or 'narrow AI' may differ depending on the researcher's goals. Some practitioners aim to create AI systems that support human mental activities rather than duplicate them.[124] These practitioners are not concerned with whether the intelligent behaviour is similar to human behaviour or can be executed across different domains. The only criterion is the accuracy of the performance.[125] These AI systems are called

[118] IBM (n.d.). "Unsupervised Learning." Available at: https://www.ibm.com/think/topics/unsupervised-learning. (Last accessed: 25.12.2025)

[119] Boden (2016), p. 47; Haddadin and Knobbe (2020), p. 22.

[120] Chowdhary (2020), p. 398.

[121] The Royal Society (2017), p. 20.

[122] Turner (2019), p. 73.

[123] Buchanan and Miller (2017), pp. 11–12.

[124] Nilsson (2010), pp. 388–389. Cf. Kaplan (2016), p. 68.

[125] Lucci and Kopec (2016), p. 12.

weak AI systems. Exhibition of intelligent behaviour is enough for weak AI qualifications. On the other hand, AI systems are called 'narrow AI' systems if they aim to construct systems that can execute single or, in some cases, limited numbers of tasks that require intelligence.[126] Therefore, if an AI system can only perform specific actions, which is the current situation for AI systems, this system is qualified as a narrow AI system.[127]

Qualifications of weak AI and narrow AI are two sides of the same coin. An AI system is called weak AI because it can display some degree of intelligent behaviour through the simulation of intelligence. And the same AI system is called narrow AI because it can perform only a single, or very limited, number of intelligent behaviours. Routine and repetitive tasks are ideal for deploying weak/narrow AI systems.[128] Hence, personal assistants such as Siri and Alexa, recommendation systems, translation systems, facial identification, and image recognition technologies employ these systems.[129]

Most of today's AI technologies can be qualified as weak/narrow AI.[130] Therefore, it is not surprising that national AI strategies focus on these systems.[131] Deduction systems, knowledge-based systems, pattern recognition methods, robotics, self-optimisation techniques and smart multi-modal human-machine interaction techniques have been utilised by weak/narrow AI systems.[132] Currently, machine learning systems are advancing weak/narrow AI systems.[133]

1.2.5.1.2 Strong/General AI

The strong AI approach intends to imitate brain processes[134] and build persons.[135] In other words, a strong AI approach focuses on duplicating human

[126] Turner (2019), p. 6. For the argument that 'weak' and 'strong' AI categorization made according to the extent of domains where relevant AI system can exhibit intelligence is mistaken, see Kaplan (2016), p. 68.

[127] European Commission's High-Level Expert Group on Artificial Intelligence (2019), p. 5.

[128] Delipetrev et al. (2020), p. 5.

[129] Delipetrev et al. (2020), p. 5.

[130] Delipetrev et al. (2020), p. 5; Turner (2019), p. 6.

[131] The Federal Government of Germany (2018), p. 5.

[132] The Federal Government of Germany (2018), pp. 4–5.

[133] The Royal Society (2017), p. 24.

[134] Buxmann and Schmidt (2019), p. 6.

[135] Arkoudas and Bringsjord (2014), p. 35.

intelligence rather than simulating it.[136] To duplicate human intelligence, an artificial reconstruction of the human brain is necessary. It is a fact that the human brain can perform various activities across different environments due to its complex operational structure and interconnectivity. Therefore, a strong AI system that is claimed to be a duplicate of the human brain should be able to perform most human activities across distinct domains. If it happens, this AI system qualifies as a general AI or human-level intelligence.[137] It means that a strong AI system must also be a general AI system.

A general AI system is capable of succeeding unrestricted goals in various fields because an agent with general AI can learn and act in any environment by using its universal algorithm.[138] Moreover, general AI can create new goals without human intervention in the face of uncertainty and vagueness.[139] As AI technology approaches general AI, it will also approach human capabilities, because the ultimate aim of the AI field is to achieve human-level intelligence.[140]

In the initial days of AI, the researchers aimed to create general AI systems. Then, its extra difficulty became evident, and the aim shifted toward the creation of weak/narrow AI systems. In the 1990s, the construction of a complete agent with a general AI architecture became popular again following advances in AI subfields. Today, researchers study more general AI that can operate in various domains.[141] Although a general AI system does not exist today, and some sceptics think it is not possible, AI technology is getting closer to general AI every day.[142]

1.2.5.2 A Categorisation Concerning Human-AI Relations in Decision-Making

Humans and AI may play different roles in decision-making processes depending on the specific domain's conditions. The balance regarding the influence of these roles should be delicately examined since it affects the efficiency of the process and liability structure. In a decision-making process, an AI system may behave in three different ways. It may serve as an assistant to a human, collaborate with a human to augment overall intelligence, or act independently of a human.

---

[136] Kaplan (2016), p. 68; Delipetrev et al. (2020), p. 6.

[137] Boucher (2019), p. 8.

[138] Russell and Norvig (2010), p. 27.

[139] Turner (2019), p. 6.

[140] McCarthy (2007), p. 5; Nilsson (2010), p. 388.

[141] Franklin (2014), p. 16; Baruffaldi et al. (2020), p. 10.

[142] Turner (2019), pp. 6–7.

Considering the AI's abovementioned roles, the literature commonly categorises AI into three distinct evolutionary forms—assisted, augmented, and autonomous[143]—each defined by a shifting balance of decision-making authority between humans and AI systems. The spectrum begins with assisted intelligence, where AI perform specific, defined tasks, while all decision rights remain exclusively with humans. This evolves into augmented intelligence, a collaborative stage characterised by a shared allocation of decision rights and a reciprocal learning relationship between human and AI. The final stage is autonomous intelligence, in which AI assume complete control over decision-making. Autonomous intelligence may be employed either through sufficient human trust in AI judgment or out of necessity, when the overwhelming volume of data or the need for ultra-rapid decisions surpasses human cognitive capabilities.[144]

1.2.5.2.1 Assistant AI

AI systems may provide humans with information and insights in specific domains. Especially if these domains are complex and a decision needs to be made quickly, humans may prefer to utilise AI systems. In that case, an AI system is not a constant element of the decision-making process. Besides, it does not have a separate role in final decision-making. Therefore, it is called 'assistant AI'. These systems assist human decision makers only by providing information. Since these systems do not actively participate in decision-making, they cannot be considered autonomous.

Assistant AI systems have been utilised in a wide range of sectors. The use of virtual personal assistants such as Google Assistant, Apple's Siri and Amazon's Alexa has penetrated everyday life.[145] In the legal domain, recidivism prediction systems for judicial discretionary decisions can be qualified as assistant AI. For example, the 'Harm Assessment Risk Tool' is a program that assists courts in determining whether a suspect should be kept in custody or released on bail.[146]

---

[143] Möslein (2025a), p. 623.

[144] Möslein (2025a), p. 623.

[145] Haddadin and Knobbe (2020), p. 14.

[146] Matt Burgess (2018, March 1). "UK police are using AI to inform custodial decisions—but it could be discriminating against the poor." Available at: https://www.wired.co.uk/article/police-ai-uk-durham-hart-checkpoint-algorithm-edit. (Last accessed: 25.12.2025)

1.2.5.2.2 Augmented AI

An AI system that combines human intelligence and AI is called augmented AI.[147] It differs from assistant AI in two respects. Contrary to assistant AI systems, the collaboration between AI and humans is not a one-time or rare incident in augmented AI systems. Secondly, designers of augmented AI systems can determine whether humans or AI serve as the final decision-maker for specific tasks.

Augmented AI systems are provided for this collaboration by their designs because they are based on the view that augmented AI systems reach better results than their components' (AI and human) separate results for specific tasks. This advantage is displayed as $1 + 1 > 2$.[148]

1.2.5.2.3 Autonomous AI

Before the advancement of ML systems, an AI system could be considered autonomous as long as it was the final decision-maker in the decision-making process. For instance, all algorithmically determined systems were considered autonomous because they made necessary decisions independently of humans. Thus, it was accepted that these systems were displaying a high degree of autonomy. However, these systems were not different from 'automated decision systems' that are static systems, which means their outcomes are predictable in the face of specific input. Besides, these automated systems do not involve human mediation in the decision-making process. They are the final decision-makers. For example, online instant loan application systems are generally based on these automated decision systems.

With advances in ML, the meaning of autonomy has become more complex. Some ML-based AI systems, such as deep learning, are not fully predictable or explainable. As explained above,[149] these systems develop their modelling algorithms themselves based on the data sets. It can choose the means (design of algorithms) to accomplish its given goal. In other words, systems have autonomy in selecting tools, while humans determine the system's ultimate aim.[150]

In light of the abovementioned explanations, an autonomous AI system has two sides to define. When an AI system and a human are considered together,

---

[147] Ginni Rometty states, "*Some people call this artificial intelligence, but the reality is this technology will enhance us. So instead of artificial intelligence, I think we'll augment our intelligence.*" Delipetrev et al. (2020), p. 17.

[148] Pan (2016), Engineering, p. 411.

[149] See, 1.2.4.2.

[150] DIN e.V. & DKE. (2020), p. 76.

the AI system can be regarded as autonomous if the final decision-maker is the AI system. In this case, the AI system is considered autonomous because it makes decisions independently of humans. Therefore, the AI system's static structure does not affect its qualification. In another respect, an AI system can be considered autonomous if it has a dynamic structure that can generate unpredictable results. In other words, this system can have outcomes independent of its designers.

1.2.6 The Black Box Problem

A typical AI system operates through an algorithmic decision-making structure. This structure provides outputs from the processing of inputs. Early examples of AI systems were fully transparent because their data-processing structures were pre-programmed. However, emergent AI systems, especially ML systems, lack transparency. Therefore, transparency is one of the *Achilles' heels* of emergent AI systems.[151] It is often more complicated, and sometimes almost impossible, to understand how the AI system generates the outcome.

The opacity problem is also called the black-box problem. If an AI system's reasoning for a decision cannot be traced, this system is qualified as black box AI.[152] If the opacity problem can be partially overcome by techniques such as reverse engineering, the system is considered a weak black box.[153] If the decision-making process is entirely opaque to humans, it is called a strong black box. This type of system cannot be explained even with reverse engineering, because the very nature of these systems is opaque.[154] Designers of such a system may verify the accuracy of its results, but they cannot understand how and why these results are generated.

New ML techniques, such as support vector machines, probabilistic graphical models, reinforcement learning, random forests, and deep learning neural networks, are providing the most accurate results and are the most opaque techniques in the spectrum. On the contrary, the least performing techniques, such

---

151 Burgess (2018), p. 8.

152 Bathaee (2018), JOLT, p. 893 and 905; European Commission's High-Level Expert Group on Artificial Intelligence (2019), p. 6; Ebers (2020), p. 48.

153 Bathaee (2018), JOLT, p. 906.

154 For a detailed analysis of the inherent opacity, see de Laat, (2018), Philos. Technol., pp. 536–539.

as decision trees, are the most transparent ones.[155] For example, deep neural networks contain thousands of artificial neurons and countless interconnections. Therefore, the complexity of deep neural networks complicates or even precludes the determination of the system's reasoning from a human point of view.[156]

Conventional expert systems mostly employ decision tree methodology.[157] Cognitive reasoning systems are new types of expert systems that employ knowledge maps methodology. By creating knowledge maps, various concepts and relationships are connected. By considering different weights and probabilities, the system can make recommendations by starting anywhere on the map and finding the shortest routes in more complex datasets. Process traceability is the most important advantage of cognitive reasoning systems over the black-box issue in machine learning. Therefore, regulated industries that prioritise transparency may prefer cognitive reasoning systems.[158]

1.2.7 Interim Result

AI is a field with scientific and philosophical foundations dating back to ancient times, which developed in its modern sense after World War II. Following two 'AI winters,' the most substantive advances have occurred in the last thirty years. After rule-based expert systems, the development of data-driven machine learning, particularly encompassing various techniques such as supervised, unsupervised, and reinforcement learning, has made AI systems more successful and efficient in different application areas. As its success and speed increase, the 'black box' characteristic, the difficulty in understanding how AI arrives at its results, has also increased. Despite this opacity, in recent years, the use and application areas of AI systems have expanded dramatically with the development of generative AI and large language models. Furthermore, agentic AI is advancing rapidly, and the first general examples of physical AI are emerging. Although various predictions have been made regarding the advancement of AI, its actual development has consistently differed from forecasts, as it is progressing at an unpredictable pace and in unforeseen directions.

---

[155] Gunning et al. (2019), Sci. Robot., p. 1; DIN e.V. & DKE. (2020), p. 83; Ebers (2020), p. 50.

[156] Bathaee (2018), JOLT, pp. 901–903.

[157] Lucci and Kopec (2016), pp. 175 and 304–305.

[158] Burgess (2018), p. 43.

A comparative etymological inquiry demonstrates that the terminological construction for the term 'artificial intelligence' in Turkish, German, and English integrates two core components: artificial genesis (non-natural) and cognitive function (the capacity for deliberative selection), mirroring key attributes of human intellect. Notwithstanding these linguistic commonalities, there are many definitions of AI from various perspectives. These definitions are bound to change as technology advances. Nevertheless, for this study, the definition of an AI system provided by the EU AI Act has been adopted because of its legal-formal perspective, which offers a stable and normative framework under the EU AI Act's binding nature in German law and its prospective influence on Turkish law's expected harmonisation with EU law. This definition focuses on AI systems' machine-based architecture, varying levels of autonomy and subsequent adaptiveness as well as their core function of inferring outputs that influence environments in line with explicit or implicit objectives.

AI systems are classified as weak/narrow AI and strong/general AI based on the methods used to create intelligence and the breadth of their scope. Presently, as strong/general AI has not yet been achieved, deployed AI systems consist of weak/narrow AI systems that simulate human intelligence but produce results in limited domains. AI systems are also categorised as assistant, augmented, and autonomous AI systems based on the level of human-AI interaction within decision-making processes. Contemporary AI systems comprise heterogeneous systems that may exhibit characteristics across these three categories, depending on their technical capacity and the configuration choices of human operators. Today, each AI system possesses different capacities and capabilities as a result of the combined use of various methodologies, and this design singularity must be considered in legal evaluations. Therefore, while general evaluations of AI systems can be made, they need to be reviewed for each individual AI system regarding probable legal consequences.

1.3 Scope and Research Questions

In a scholarly investigation, determining the research scope and the questions within it are prerequisites for conducting the research to optimal depth and achieving the intended outcomes. This study aims to perform a comparative examination of the regulatory and practical implications of integrating AI in the boardrooms of two distinct jurisdictions: Turkish boards of directors and German management boards. The rationale for this specific scope is driven by several deliberate considerations.

While corporate digitalisation encompasses a broad spectrum of technologies,[159] AI systems were selected as the technological object for this study due to their transformative potential for decision-making structures.[160] This selection is justified by AI's distinctive impact on the corporation's core function as a "decision factory."[161] Despite their current limitations, AI introduces an unprecedented capability to generate insights and recommendations[162] beyond the scope of any previous non-human tool. Therefore, it was chosen to examine the legal aspects of AI systems' involvement in corporate decision-making processes, a domain traditionally and exclusively occupied by human actors. Given that strong/general AI remains unrealised, the scope of this study is specifically limited to weak/narrow AI.[163] Moreover, the roles that AI plays in interacting with humans in decision-making processes (assistant, augmented, and autonomous) were considered contextually during the study.

Another delimitation in determining the scope of this study is the selection of stock corporations,[164] among all company types, as the primary subject. This focus is justified on several grounds. Firstly, the complex, data-rich environments required for advanced AI deployment are most encountered in large-scale enterprises.[165] The significant financial investment needed for the development and implementation of AI systems is only feasible for large-scale enterprises, which are predominantly structured as stock corporations primarily due to their capital structure,[166] organisational characteristics that favour professional management, and specific legal obligations. Secondly, stock corporations, due to their significant size and operational fields, have a greater economic, social, and environmental impact than other types of companies. Hence, the integration of AI systems into corporation management may significantly influence these economic, social, and environmental impacts, rendering the legal scrutiny of this integration a matter of critical and growing importance. Moreover, this scholarly focus on

---

159 Such as big data, blockchain, smart contracts and AI etc. The term of "Corp-tech" is coined as an umbrella term for these technologies in the doctrine. Among others, see Enriques and Zetzsche (2020), UCLJ, p. 59.

160 Agnese et al. (2025), CG, p. 278. For key-findings of recent studies on AI and decision-making, see Agnese et al. (2025), CG, pp. 277–278.

161 For organizations in general, see Kahneman (2011), pp. 417–418.

162 Agnese et al. (2025), CG, p. 279.

163 See 1.2.5.1.

164 This study employs the terms 'corporation' and 'stock corporation' interchangeably for the '*Anonim Ortaklık*' in Turkish law and its German counterpart, the '*Aktiengesellschaft.*'

165 Möslein (2022), p. 75; Telle (2023), p. 29.

166 Möslein (2022), p. 75.

stock corporations reflects commercial practice, as they constitute the dominant segment of the corporate landscape that is actively deploying or developing AI systems. Consequently, this study focuses on stock corporations, as they represent the entities with the highest probability for AI adoption and where the economic, social, and environmental repercussions will be most profound.

While AI systems can be deployed in multiple corporate bodies, this study focuses on the board of directors in Turkish corporate law and the management board in German corporate law. As the corporation's central governing body,[167] the board oversees the corporation's operations and makes high-level strategic decisions, thereby shaping the corporation's management and destiny.[168] Therefore, this study investigates the use of AI systems at the board level, where strategic decisions and a demanding workload make such augmentation most consequential.[169]

Finally, Turkish and German law were selected as the jurisdictional frameworks for this comparative analysis. This choice was influenced by both the author's academic background and familiarity with these legal systems, as well as the interpretative richness that a comparative approach to the research topic would offer, given the similarities and differences between the two. Despite sharing a civil law tradition, their distinct approaches to corporate governance promise a rich, interpretative dialogue on the regulatory challenges posed by AI.

Within the comparative framework of Turkish and German law, this study seeks to answer the following fundamental research questions: (1) In what specific roles can AI systems be integrated into corporate management at the board level? and (2) What are the ensuing organisational obligations and legal responsibilities of the board (members) regarding the integration of AI into corporation management?

1.4 Methodology

The research methodology for this study rests upon three principal approaches. By using descriptive methodology, an attempt was made to present the current legal landscape accurately and systematically within the scope of the research

[167] In corporate governance literature, the board is often conceptualized as the corporation's "brain," responsible for its highest cognitive functions such as strategy, foresight, and conscious control. Möslein (2025a), pp. 622–623.

[168] For the principles of comprehensive management authority in stock corporation law, see Möslein (2007), pp. 23–50.

[169] For a similar reasoning, see Möslein (2022), p. 75; Möslein (2025a), pp. 622–623.

topic. For this purpose, the study entailed a systematic examination of relevant legal statutes, regulatory instruments, and judicial precedents to ensure a comprehensive analysis. Because the subject of study is an emergent phenomenon, the use of an explanatory methodology alongside the descriptive method was necessary to analyse the underlying causes and potential future trajectories. In this context, the opinions and suggestions presented in the legal doctrine on the subject of study have been critically evaluated, and our own opinions and suggestions have been expressed. Both the descriptive and explanatory analyses were conducted through a comparative lens. For this purpose, the current legal landscape and doctrinal positions were examined comparatively with respect to Turkish and German law as they pertain to the research problem. During this comparative analysis, points of legal convergence were placed in dialogue to reveal shared underlying logics, while efforts were made to provide separate, system-specific assessments of points of divergence to highlight the distinct jurisprudential values and policy choices inherent to each system.

1.5 Relevance

The scholarly examination of AI systems within the specific context of corporate boardrooms remains in its nascent stages, with a limited but growing body of literature. Existing legal frameworks lack specific regulations governing the use of AI in corporation management. Therefore, this regulatory gap necessitates rigorous academic inquiry to formulate foundational principles and guide future legal development. While academic discourse on AI in corporation management has achieved a significant level of maturity in German legal scholarship, the same cannot be said of Turkish legal doctrine. This disparity provides a robust foundation for a comparative examination with the emerging discourse in Turkish law.

Nevertheless, academic studies on this topic need to be increased and diversified in both legal doctrines. This research is expected to contribute to scholarly studies on the emergent topic of the use of AI systems in corporation management. It is believed that this research, particularly its comparative approach based on Turkish and German law, will add a new dimension and depth to academic discussions on this topic. Furthermore, this research aims to provide practical guidance for corporations and their boards navigating the use of AI in management, a field currently characterised by regulatory gaps and ongoing scholarly debate.

1.6 Structure

The first chapter of this study presents a brief historical and technical background of AI systems as well as a working definition, followed by an explanation of the scope, fundamental questions, methodology, relevance and structure of the study.

The second chapter begins with explanations regarding the board of directors in Turkish law and the management board in German law, both within the scope of the research topic. In this context, board models, the qualifications and selection of board members, and their responsibilities relevant to the research topic are explained specifically in these legal systems, followed by a contextual comparison. The contemporary discussion on legal personality and civil law liability of AI systems is then briefly addressed, followed by an examination of the possibility of AI systems becoming board members. This examination first assesses whether AI systems can, under current legal rules, serve as board members, either directly or indirectly. Subsequently, the possibility of AI systems becoming board members is considered *de lege ferenda*, and the points to be considered in this assessment are examined individually.

The third chapter examines the use of AI systems by boards as a right and/or obligation. In this context, the board's authority to make decisions regarding the use of AI in corporate management and whether it can delegate this authority are examined. It is followed by a discussion of whether the board's use of AI in corporate management constitutes a right. After this discussion, it is examined whether the board can delegate management tasks to AI systems. In this context, the delegation systems in both legal systems are first explained, particularly the tasks that may be delegated and the board's obligations towards the delegates. Then, within the scope of the current delegation system, it is discussed whether delegation can be made to AI systems in terms of the legal personality and responsibility of the delegate and the subject-matter and process of delegation. Finally, it is examined whether delegation to AI systems constitutes an obligation for the board under the duty of care and business judgment rule. This analysis is based on both the explanations of the board members' duty of care provided in the second section and the business judgment rule provided in this section for both legal systems.

The fourth chapter examines the organisational duties that boards may be subject to in both legal systems when integrating AI into corporation management, as well as the board's responsibilities with respect to these duties.

The fifth chapter presents the study's conclusions.

AI as a Board Member

2

2.1 In General

The accelerating capabilities of AI, particularly for complex data-driven business decisions,[1] are challenging the very architecture of corporate leadership, prompting a radical question: Can an AI be entrusted with a fiduciary seat at the table? Granting an AI system the formal authority of a board member represents a fundamental reimagining of corporate governance. This technological shift introduces a regulatory challenge,[2] since the integration of AI systems as decision-makers into corporate governance fundamentally challenges the foundational strategies of corporate law, which were designed for human decision-makers.[3] Under this chapter, the abovementioned radical question will be addressed *de lege lata* and *de lege ferenda.*

To examine AI's integration into corporation management at the board level and to systematically analyse the behavioural and organisational duties of boards, it is essential to understand the conventional framework of corporation management and the relevant duties of board members under stock corporation law.[4] Therefore, the following subsection will provide the necessary information, limited to the scope of the thesis's investigation, in this regard.

---

[1] Möslein (2022), p. 74; Agnese et al. (2025), CG, p. 279.

[2] Möslein (2022), p. 74.

[3] Eroğlu and Karatepe Kaya (2022), EBOR, p. 557; Möslein (2025b), ERA Forum, pp. 629–630.

[4] For a similar approach see, Li (2022), p. 69.

S. T. İnce, *Artificial Intelligence and Corporation Management*,
Juridicum – Schriftenreihe zum Wirtschafts-, Unternehmens- und Bankrecht / Series on Business, Corporate and Banking Law,
https://doi.org/10.1007/978-3-658-52672-6_2

2.1.1 The Board of Directors in Turkish Law and the Management Board in German Law

2.1.1.1 The Board Model

The formal structure of corporate management at the board level varies across different jurisdictions. There are two main models for the organisation of boards in modern corporations' law: the monist and the dualist model. The monist model, which is the most common board model,[5] is adopted in Sweden, Switzerland, Spain, Belgium, and Türkiye (*yönetim kurulu*), as well as in the Anglo-Saxon jurisdictions (board of directors).[6] In this board system, the board exercises legal authorities of management and supervision together.[7] In contrast, jurisdictions following the dualist model legally mandate a separation of governance functions between distinct management and supervisory boards. Within this dualist structure, a non-executive supervisory board is authorised to exercise oversight and to appoint a separate management board, comprising senior executives responsible for strategic and operational leadership.[8] Such a dualist structure is mandatory in German and Austrian law.[9] French, Italian, and EU company law (i.e. European Company[10]) provide for an optional board structure, allowing corporations to select their preferred governance model.[11] Neither the monist nor the dualist model can be definitively labelled the best or most functional, as each has distinct advantages and disadvantages.[12]

Turkish Commercial Code (TCC) mandates a monist board model, concentrating both executive and supervisory functions in the board of directors.[13] As

---

[5] Hopt (2011), AJCL, p. 21.

[6] Hopt (2011), AJCL, p. 21; Davies and Hopt (2013), AJCL, p. 310; Kraakman et al. (2017), p. 50; Büyükatak (2019), p. 49 ff.; Pulaşlı (2022), § 35, para. 19, p. 1179; Kalender (2024), p. 25.

[7] Davies and Hopt (2013), AJCL, p. 311; Kraakman et al. (2017), p. 50.

[8] Kraakman et al. (2017), p. 50.

[9] Hopt (2011), AJCL, p. 21; Davies and Hopt (2013), AJCL, p. 310; Kırca in Kırca et al. (2013), p. 529; Akdağ Güney (2016), p. 70; Büyükatak (2019), p. 44 ff. and 53; Kalender (2024), p. 27.

[10] Pulaşlı (2002), BATİDER, p. 15; Hopt (2011), AJCL, p. 23. For a detailed analysis of European Company's optional board structure, see Küçükgüngör (2018), p. 290 ff.

[11] Davies and Hopt (2013), AJCL, p. 315; Kraakman et al. (2017), p. 50; Kalender (2024), p. 28.

[12] Hopt (2011), AJCL, p. 22; Kayıhan (2011), pp. 36–37 and 53; Kırca in Kırca et al. (2013), p. 529; Küçükgüngör (2018), pp. 254–255; Özatlan (2023), p. 72; Kalender (2024), p. 29.

[13] Tekinalp (2020), p. 230.

indicated in the preamble to Article 367 of the TCC, the delegation of some management and representation authorities, as permitted under Article 367(1) and Article 370(2) of the TCC, may converge the monist structure of the board of directors in Turkish law to a dual structure.[14] However, this view is criticised by the authors,[15] since alteration of the board structure is not possible under the strict language of Article 340(1) of the TCC.[16] Moreover, since the board of directors' non-transferable responsibilities are explicitly regulated by law, it is not possible to completely switch to a dualist board system.[17] Consequently, while the delegation of tasks may introduce quasi-dualist features,[18] the foundational governance structure for Turkish corporations remains unequivocally monist in its legal design.[19]

The dualist model is a mandatory legal requirement for corporations in German law. The supervisory board and the management board are two mandatory components of the corporation's management.[20] In principle, the supervisory board, whose members are appointed by the general assembly,[21] appoints and monitors the members of the management board.[22] Hence, these two boards constitute the corporation's dualistic management structure.[23] Creating a single board structure by drafting the articles of association to merge the supervisory board and the management board is not legally possible under German law,[24] as the strict language of Section 23(5) of the German Stock Corporation Act (*Aktiengesetz*, AktG)[25] precludes such a merger.

---

14 Gürpınar (2013), MÜHF-HAD, pp. 1103–1104; Kendigelen (2016), pp. 258–259; Kalender (2024), p. 26.

15 Pulaşlı (2022), § 35, paras. 23–24, p. 1181–1182; Kalender (2024), p. 29.

16 Art. 340 sentence 1 of the TCC: "*The articles of association may deviate from the provisions of this Code relating to corporations if only permitted explicitly by this Code...*".

17 Küçükgüngör (2018), p. 312; Eryiğit (2023), pp. 29–30.

18 Kırca in Kırca et al. (2013), pp. 529–530.

19 Kırca in Kırca et al. (2013), p. 530; Kaya (2014), DEÜHFD, pp. 3273–3274.

20 Wirth et al. (2017), p. 95.

21 AktG § 101.

22 AktG § 84.

23 Link in Wachter (2022), AktG, § 76, para. 2.

24 Seibt in Schmidt and Lutter (2020), AktG, § 76, para. 1; Link in Wachter (2022), AktG, § 76, para. 2. However, some scholars propose that board structure should be optional for German stock corporation as well. See references in Seibt in Schmidt and Lutter (2020), AktG, § 76, para. 1, fn. 1.

25 AktG § 23(5): "*The articles of association may deviate from the provisions of the present Act only where this has been expressly permitted. Supplementing the articles of association*

2.1.1.2 Appointment of Board Members

2.1.1.2.1 In Turkish Law

Juridical persons, such as corporations,[26] exercise their capacity for rights and legal transactions through their organs.[27] The general assembly and the board of directors are mandatory organs of a corporation.[28] As the body responsible for management and representation,[29] the board of directors is the permanently functioning organ of a corporation.[30]

The TCC requires every corporation to have a board of directors composed of one or more members, appointed at incorporation by the articles of association or later elected by a general assembly resolution.[31] The business field and size, the number of shareholders and the amount of capital are factors to be considered when determining the optimum number of board members in the articles of association.[32] It is a new opportunity granted by the TCC that allows the board of directors to consist of one member.[33] However, there are different minimum numbers of board members for certain corporations, such as banks,[34]

---

by additional determinations is permissible unless the present Act provides conclusively for the matter."

[26] Art. 125 and Art. 355 of the TCC.

[27] Art. 50 of the Turkish Civil Code. Also, see Dural and Öğüz (2020), p. 256; Oğuzman et al. (2021), pp. 316–317.

[28] Art. 359 and Art. 407 of the TCC. Also, see Tekinalp (2020), p. 220.

[29] Art. 365 of the TCC.

[30] İmregün (2001), p. 325; Tekinalp (2011), p. 165; Akdağ Güney (2016), p. 3; Koç (2018), p. 56; Çamoğlu in Poroy et al. (2025), para. 520b, p. 355.

[31] Art. 359(1) of the TCC. Although there is no explicit provision in the TCC, appointment of substitute members for the board of directors is accepted by the doctrine and the precedents. İmregün (1989), pp. 194–195; Kırca in Kırca et al. (2013), p. 401; Üçışık and Çelik (2013), p. 379 ff.; Akdağ Güney (2016), p. 7; Kayar (2018), p. 438 ff.; Pulaşlı (2022), § 35, para. 327, p. 1303; Çamoğlu in Poroy et al. (2025), para. 548, p. 392; İlbasmış Hızlısoy and Ağırbaş (2025), TFM, p. 279; Şener (2026), p. 288. 11th Civil Chamber of Supreme Court of Appeals, Decision Date: 08.02.1990, Case No: 1989/5478, Decision No: 1990/708.

[32] Akdağ Güney (2016), p. 27.

[33] According to Preamble to Article 359(1) of the TCC, allowing one-member board of directors is a result of the efforts for harmonization with the EU law and simplification of the management in small corporations.

[34] Art. 23(1) of the Banking Code numbered 5411, Official Gazette dated 1/11/2005 and numbered 25983-Duplicate-.

cooperatives,[35] insurance corporations,[36] leasing and factoring corporations,[37] and publicly traded corporations.[38]

The names and other relevant information of the board members must be registered with the trade registry and announced in the Türkiye Trade Registry Gazette.[39] The said registration has a declaratory effect, as the board membership status commences with the election or appointment of the person as a board member and the acceptance of this role.[40] If the board of directors is not properly staffed, the initial registration of the corporation is rejected by the trade registry according to Articles 339 and 354 of the TCC.[41] However, a subsequent loss of all board members of the corporation (due to death, resignation, dismissal, etc.) does not automatically affect the corporation's existence.[42]

The board members and natural-person representatives, who will be registered in the name of the legal entity, must have full legal capacity.[43] Minors, wards and natural persons who are not of sound mind cannot be elected as a board member.[44] Juridical persons can be appointed as board members.[45] In that case, a natural person shall be designated by that juridical person to act on its behalf and be registered and announced along with the juridical person.[46] Moreover, being a

---

[35] Art. 55 of the Cooperatives Code numbered 1163, Official Gazette dated 10/05/1969 and numbered 13195.

[36] Art. 4(1) of the Insurance Code numbered 5684, Official Gazette dated 14/06/2007 and numbered 26552.

[37] Art. 13(2) of the Financial Leasing, Factoring and Financing Companies Code numbered 6361, Official Gazette dated 13/12/2012 and numbered 28496.

[38] Art. 17 of the Capital Markets Law numbered 6362, Official Gazette dated 30/12/2012 and numbered 28513. Principle 4.3.1. of the Corporate Governance Communique-(II-17.1), Official Gazette dated 03/01/2014 and numbered 28871.

[39] Art. 31(1), Art. 35(3) and Art. 354(1) of the TCC.

[40] Kırca in Kırca et al. (2013), p. 452.

[41] Akdağ Güney (2016), p. 26.

[42] In this case the lack of mandatory organ situation occurs. Hence, the relevant court may appoint temporary board members to convene general assembly for the appointment of new board members.

[43] Art. 359(3) of the TCC. Also, see Kırca in Kırca et al. (2013), p. 410; Develi (2016), p. 84; Pulaşlı (2022), § 35, para. 161, p. 1232; Çamoğlu in Poroy et al. (2025), para. 548b, p. 392.

[44] Kırca in Kırca et al. (2013), p. 410.

[45] Art. 359 of the TCC. Also, see Kırca in Kırca et al. (2013), p. 401; Tekinalp (2020), p. 233; Pulaşlı (2022), § 35, para. 160, p. 1232; Çamoğlu in Poroy et al. (2025), para. 548 g, p. 399.

[46] Art. 359(2) of the TCC.

shareholder is not a prerequisite to being appointed a board member.[47] The TCC does not explicitly list any other eligibility criteria or qualifications for serving as a board member. However, circumstances that would lead to termination of board membership also constitute an obstacle to election.[48]

Additional facultative criteria for appointment as a board member can be stipulated in the articles of association.[49] For instance, being under or above a certain age, or having a master's degree or other professional qualifications, can be set as criteria for serving as a board member in the articles of association.[50] As it is clearly explained in its preamble, Article 340 of the TCC does not prevent the determination of such criteria.[51]

If a person who does not meet the requirements to be elected as a board member is elected, the appointment resolution is null and void. Such an election should not be registered in the trade registry because it contravenes the mandatory provisions of the law. If the registration has been made in any way, all interested parties may request that the court declare this resolution invalid.[52]

Board members can be appointed in different ways. As a practical exception, board members are appointed by the articles of association in the incorporation phase.[53] However, as a rule, board members are appointed by the general assembly since the appointment of the board members is one of the un-transferable

[47] Tekinalp (2020), p. 228; Pulaşlı (2022), § 35, para. 173, p. 1237. The absence of a shareholding requirement for board membership enables the appointment of expert individuals. It demonstrates the TCC's alignment with the corporate governance principle of professional management. Kırca in Kırca et al. (2013), p. 413; Eminoğlu (2014), p. 181; Akdağ Güney (2016), p. 39; Kayar (2018), p. 452; Küçükgüngör (2018), p. 313; Tekinalp (2020), p. 231; Bahtiyar (2024), p. 202; Çamoğlu in Poroy et al. (2025), para. 548ba, p. 393.

[48] Art. 359(4) of the TCC.

[49] Kırca in Kırca et al. (2013), p. 413; Akdağ Güney (2016), p. 30; Develi (2016), p. 47; Pulaşlı (2022), § 35, para. 158, p. 1228; Çamoğlu in Poroy et al. (2025), para. 548c, p. 396.

[50] Kırca in Kırca et al. (2013), p. 414; Akdağ Güney (2016), pp. 30–31; Metin (2021), p. 109; Pulaşlı (2022), § 35, para. 158, p. 1228. For examples of additional facultative criteria regarding juridical person board members, see Develi (2016), pp. 48–50.

[51] See Preamble to Art. 340 of the TCC, para. 4: "*Even if it is not explicitly understood from any provision of this Code, Article 340 does not preclude the establishment, through the articles of association, of age, additional professional qualifications, and personal requirements for managers including especially members of the board of directors, auditors, transaction auditors,... This is because every stock corporation has the right to require qualifications in addition to those stipulated in the Code for its managers,...*"

[52] Çamoğlu in Poroy et al. (2025), para. 548d, p. 396.

[53] Art. 339(3) of the TCC.

duties of the general assembly.[54] In the event of any vacancy on the board for any reason, the existing board members may temporarily appoint a person who meets the legal requirements (*co-optation*)[55] and seek the approval of the general assembly at the subsequent meeting. A member so appointed holds office until the first general assembly at which such membership is submitted for approval. If this cooptative appointment is approved, the newly appointed person will complete the predecessor's term of office.[56] The term of office for board members is determined in the articles of association. Board members are elected for a maximum period of three years.[57] Unless otherwise provided in the articles of association, reappointment is possible with an express resolution of the general assembly.[58]

2.1.1.2.2 In German Law

A corporation is a juridical person[59] that has the management board,[60] alongside the supervisory board and the general assembly, as its mandatory organs. The management board serves as the core decision-making and action hub within the corporation.[61] The articles of association must clearly specify the number of members who will comprise the management board, or the criteria for determining that number.[62] It may set a minimum or maximum limit, or grant the supervisory board the authority to make that decision entirely.[63] The AktG does not impose a maximum limit on the number of management board members.[64] Factors to consider in determining the optimal number of board members include the corporation's size, industry, operational complexity, regional presence, and

---

[54] Art. 408(2-b) of the TCC.

[55] This co-optation authority can be taken from the board of directors via the articles of association. Kırca in Kırca et al. (2013), p. 424; Üçışık and Çelik (2013), p. 382; Pulaşlı (2022), § 35, para. 248, p. 1270; Çamoğlu in Poroy et al. (2025), para. 547, p. 390.

[56] Art. 363(1) of the TCC.

[57] Art. 362 of the TCC.

[58] Art. 362 of the TCC.

[59] AktG § 1 para. 1.

[60] AktG § 23 and § 30.

[61] Seibt in Schmidt and Lutter (2020), AktG, § 76, para. 2.

[62] AktG § 23 para. 3 subpara. 6.

[63] Kort in Großkomm-AktG (2015), AktG, § 76, para. 194; Fleischer in Spindler and Stilz (2019), AktG, § 76, para. 111; Spindler in MünchKomm-AktG (2019), AktG, §76, para. 116; Seibt in Schmidt and Lutter (2020), AktG, § 76, para. 54; Link in Wachter (2022), AktG, § 76, para. 62.

[64] Link in Wachter (2022), AktG, §76, para. 62.

stakeholder diversity, among others.[65] If the management board is not properly staffed, the initial registration of the corporation is rejected according to Section 38 para. 1, sentence 2 and Section 39 of the AktG. A subsequent loss of all members of the management board (due to death, resignation, dismissal, etc.) does not directly affect the corporation's existence.[66]

Only natural persons with full legal capacity can serve as board members.[67] Hence, neither corporations nor partnerships qualify for these positions.[68] A member of the management board is not required to hold shares in the corporation.[69] Persons who are under guardianship and who, in managing their financial affairs, are fully or partially subject to a reservation of consent may not serve as board members.[70] The articles of association may set out supplementary eligibility criteria, including age restrictions or specific professional qualifications. However, the supervisory board's authority in the selection of candidates must not be constrained to such an extent that it eliminates any potential for discretion,[71] since the supervisory board exercises its own entrepreneurial discretion in making its decisions.[72]

A breach of the eligibility requirements outlined in Section 76 para. 3 sentence 1 of the AktG results in the appointment being deemed invalid under Section 134 of the German Civil Code (*Bürgerliches Gesetzbuch*, BGB).[73] If a board member subsequently becomes incapacitated to serve, their position will end automatically

---

[65] Kort in Großkomm-AktG (2015), AktG, § 76, para. 197; Spindler in MünchKomm-AktG (2019), AktG, § 76, para. 116; Seibt in Schmidt and Lutter (2020), AktG, § 76, para. 54.

[66] Spindler in MünchKomm-AktG (2019), AktG, § 76, para. 7; Grigoleit (2020), AktG, § 76, para. 6; Seibt in Schmidt and Lutter (2020), AktG, § 76, para. 3 and 57; Link in Wachter (2022), AktG, § 76, para. 3.

[67] AktG § 76 para. 3.

[68] Fleischer in Spindler and Stilz (2019), AktG, § 76, para. 120; Spindler in MünchKomm-AktG (2019), AktG, § 76, para. 124; Seibt in Schmidt and Lutter (2020), AktG, § 76, para. 60.

[69] Seibt in Schmidt and Lutter (2020), AktG, § 76, para. 60; Link in Wachter (2022), AktG, § 76, para. 66.

[70] AktG § 76 para. 3 subpara. 1.

[71] Kort in Großkomm-AktG (2015), AktG, § 76, para. 266; Wirth et al. (2017), p. 101; Spindler in MünchKomm-AktG (2019), AktG, § 76, para. 129; Seibt in Schmidt and Lutter (2020), AktG, § 76, para. 61; Link in Wachter (2022), AktG, § 76, para. 67.

[72] Seibt in Schmidt and Lutter (2020), AktG, § 84, para. 10; Link in Wachter (2022), AktG, § 84, para. 8.

[73] Link in Wachter (2022), AktG, § 76, para. 68; Weber in Hölters and Weber (2022), AktG, § 76, para. 79.

without the need for a formal dismissal.[74] The removal of the incapacitated board member's name from the commercial register will also take place automatically.[75]

The supervisory board holds exclusive authority over personnel decisions regarding the management board.[76] This power cannot be altered by any conflicting provisions in the articles of association pursuant to Section 23 para. 5 of the AktG.[77] The key elements for appointment include the appointment resolution from the supervisory board under Section 108 AktG, the formal notification of the new management board members' appointment,[78] and their acceptance of the role, which is communicated back to the supervisory board.[79] The management board members can be appointed for a maximum of five years. Reappointment by the supervisory board through an express resolution is permissible.[80]

Since Section 107 para. 3 of the AktG explicitly prohibits delegation to a committee[81] or to the chairperson,[82] the supervisory board must make decisions regarding the appointment of the management board members collectively.[83] This authority is non-negotiable; neither the articles of association nor the general assembly can allow for any exceptions.[84] However, it is still acceptable for a supervisory board committee to conduct preparatory work for the appointment.[85]

---

[74] Link in Wachter (2022), AktG § 76, para. 68.

[75] Link in Wachter (2022), AktG § 76, para. 68.

[76] AktG § 84 para. 1. Spindler in MünchKomm-AktG (2019), AktG, § 84, para. 12 ff.; Seibt in Schmidt and Lutter (2020), AktG, § 84, para. 8.

[77] Seibt in Schmidt and Lutter (2020), AktG, § 84, para. 1; Link in Wachter (2022), AktG, § 84, para. 1.

[78] Spindler in MünchKomm-AktG (2019), AktG, § 84, para. 8 and 21; Seibt in Schmidt and Lutter (2020), AktG, § 84, para. 6; Koch in Hüffer and Koch (2021), AktG, § 84, para. 3.

[79] Spindler in MünchKomm-AktG (2019), AktG, § 84, para. 8 and 24; Seibt in Schmidt and Lutter (2020), AktG, § 84, para. 6; Koch in Hüffer and Koch (2021), AktG, § 84, para. 3; Link in Wachter (2022), AktG, § 84, para. 3.

[80] AktG § 84 para. 1. Also, see Spindler in MünchKomm-AktG (2019), AktG, § 84, para. 49; Seibt in Schmidt and Lutter (2020), AktG, § 84, para. 17.

[81] Fleischer in Spindler and Stilz (2019), AktG, § 84, para. 9; Seibt in Schmidt and Lutter (2020), AktG, § 84, para. 8.

[82] Seibt in Schmidt and Lutter (2020), AktG, § 84, para. 8.

[83] Fleischer in Spindler and Stilz (2019), AktG, § 84, para. 9; Seibt in Schmidt and Lutter (2020), AktG, § 84, para. 8; Koch in Hüffer and Koch (2021), AktG, § 84, para. 5; Link in Wachter (2022), AktG, § 84, para. 6.

[84] Spindler in MünchKomm-AktG (2019), AktG, § 84, para. 12; Link in Wachter (2022), AktG, § 84, para. 6.

[85] Seibt in Schmidt and Lutter (2020), AktG, § 84, para. 8; Link in Wachter (2022), AktG, § 84, para. 6.

2.1.1.3 Duties of the Board Members

The duties of the board members typically stem from legal requirements tied to their roles within the corporation.[86] These duties can be derived from the individual provisions of fundamental statutory sources, i.e. the TCC and the AktG, and further elaborated and clarified through legal doctrine to ensure effective practical implementation and judicial application.

2.1.1.3.1 In Turkish Law

2.1.1.3.1.1 Duty of Care

Instead of defining care, the TCC articulates the standard of care for board members through two fundamental criteria that collectively outline the requisite diligence expected of the board of directors and its individual members.[87] The first criterion, as stipulated in Article 369 of the TCC, obliges board members and managing third parties to exercise the care of a "*tedbirli bir yönetici*, (prudent manager)" in the performance of their duties. Secondly, they are obliged to safeguard the corporation's interests in accordance with the principle of honesty. According to these two statutory criteria, board members must exercise care in every decision and action during their tenure.

TCC does not define the "prudent manager" standard in its Article 369 or elsewhere. Instead, this key criterion for assessing director conduct is only expressed in the preamble to Article 369.[88] The Article 369's preamble clarifies that the "prudent manager" standard differs from the stricter "prudent/reasonable businessperson" criterion. According to this rationale, the legislature opted for the "prudent manager" standard since the Supreme Court of Appeals has interpreted the "prudent/reasonable businessperson" standard with rigorous, sometimes excessive expectations, which, if applied to board members, could lead to unfair outcomes.[89] This choice and its underlying rationale reveal the lawmaker's more flexible view of the board members' duty of care standard, balancing prior precedents and business realities.[90]

---

[86] Weber in Hölters and Weber (2022), AktG, § 84, para. 53; Link in Wachter (2022), AktG, § 84, para. 41.

[87] Art. 369 of the TCC.

[88] Seçer (2025), p. 36.

[89] Preamble to Art. 369 of the TCC.

[90] Çamoğlu in Poroy et al. (2025), para. 582, p. 426.

In accordance with the balancing approach, the principle of 'diligence more than in one's own affairs (*diligentia quam in suis*)' is not taken into consideration for the standard care expected from board members.[91] The standard of care is objectified as the care expected of a prudent manager.[92] This concept of 'objectivity' is further defined in the rationale as encompassing the competence to perform a task, the ability to evaluate pertinent information, and the possession of the essential skills and education required to monitor and supervise both implementation and subsequent developments.[93] Personal excuses, such as lack of knowledge[94] and time scarcity, cannot be used to decrease the expected standard of care.[95] However, it is not fixed but varies depending on contextual factors.[96] With the increase in a corporation's size, available resources and operational complexity, the board's decisions carry greater financial and operational consequences, thereby requiring a higher degree of care from members.[97]

Board members cannot claim 'prudence' unless their decisions and actions satisfy all applicable laws.[98] Moreover, determining whether the board members acted as prudent managers requires examining the degree of care shown in establishing the corporate management organisation, the performance of overall monitoring and their decision-making processes.[99]

Establishing an efficient, expedient and inclusive organisation, and monitoring its overall performance, are part of the board's duty of care. In this regard, setting up committees in accordance with Article 366(2) of the TCC and appointing qualified people to these committees are part of the duty of care.[100] Moreover, this duty obliged the board to exercise care in the selection, instruction and monitoring of the persons entrusted with the management of the business.[101]

While board members are making business decisions, they are obliged to be impartial and adequately informed, and to act with good intentions and in the best

---

[91] Preamble to Art. 369 of the TCC. Kırca in Kırca et al. (2013), p. 657; Pulaşlı (2022), § 37, para. 144, p. 1562.

[92] Kırca in Kırca et al. (2013), p. 657; Akdağ Güney (2016), p. 187; Tekinalp (2020), p. 287.

[93] Kalender (2024), p. 268.

[94] Çamurcu (2015), pp. 73–74; Akdağ Güney (2016), pp. 193–194.

[95] Kırca in Kırca et al. (2013), p. 662; Bozkurt Yaşar (2015), p. 169.

[96] Hacımahmutoğlu (2014), BATİDER, p. 137; Çamurcu (2015), pp. 73–74.

[97] Akdağ Güney (2016), p. 316.

[98] Yaşar (2018), p. 252.

[99] Bozkurt Yaşar (2015), p. 169.

[100] Bozkurt Yaşar (2015), p. 144; Pulaşlı (2022), § 37, para. 145, p. 1563.

[101] Pulaşlı (2022), § 37, para. 153, p. 1566.

interests of the corporation. This principle is called the business judgment rule (BJR). The BJR can be considered a special manifestation of the duty of care and the standard of conduct in business decision-making. Failing this, board members become liable for the damage they cause to the corporation, its shareholders, and its creditors.[102] There is a debate in Turkish legal doctrine over its applicability, as it is not explicitly codified in the TCC. Nevertheless, this rule will be explained, and its relationship with AI use in corporate management will be discussed under separate titles in the following chapters.[103]

2.1.1.3.1.2 Duty of Overall Management and Organisational Design

The board of directors' overall management duty in stock corporations represents the core of its governance powers.[104] As a core governance function, this duty involves setting the corporation's general business policy, developing actionable plans for its execution, and determining whether the policy goals have been achieved or will be achieved.[105] In this context, strategic decisions encompass fundamental decisions and practices for developing and monitoring the means to achieve corporation's strategic goals,[106] which are essential for a corporation's future success and continued existence.[107] The board is under a duty to monitor and review the management structure and make interventions and changes whenever necessary to align with the corporation's evolving needs.[108]

The board's duty to determine the corporation's management organisation is stipulated separately in Article 375(1-b) of the TCC as a non-transferable and indispensable duty.[109] This duty can also be deemed an integral part of the overall management duty,[110] since the establishment of the corporation's organisational structure is closely linked to strategic management. This duty

[102] Pulaşlı (2022), § 37, para. 155d, p. 1568.

[103] See 3.5.3.

[104] Doğan (2012), MÜHF-HAD, p. 612; Kalender (2024), p. 107.

[105] Preamble to Art. 375(1-a) of the TCC. Doğan (2012), MÜHF-HAD, p. 613; Kırca in Kırca et al. (2013), p. 541; Akdağ Güney (2016), p. 148; Koç (2018), p. 94; Ayhan et al. (2022), p. 266; Pulaşlı (2022), § 36, para. 9, p. 1320; Özatlan (2023), p. 62.

[106] Özatlan (2023), p. 62.

[107] Gözübüyük (2022), HBV-HFD, p. 148.

[108] Yanlı (1997), İHFM, p. 266 (based on the Swiss corporate law); Altay (2011), p. 109; Pulaşlı (2022), § 36, para. 12, p. 1321.

[109] Kırca in Kırca et al. (2013), pp. 544–545; Bozkurt Yaşar (2015), p. 143; Ayan (2021), p. 73.

[110] Cf. Koç (2018), p. 95.

involves the board establishing the internal management structure, through executive members/directors and committees,[111] to exercise its duties effectively while maintaining ultimate oversight and control. This task is also referred to as the corporation's architectural design task ("*architektonische Gestaltungsaufgabe*")[112] since the board is expected to demonstrate creativity in the corporation's operations.[113] Under this duty, the board is expected to design the architecture of the corporation's management, enabling coherence and efficiency in decision-making, execution, and control processes, while promptly providing the necessary instructions.

2.1.1.3.1.3 Duty of Overall Monitoring and Legality

The source of the board of directors' overall monitoring duty is Articles 375, 369(1), and 553(1) of the TCC.[114] In light of these provisions, overall monitoring consists of two dimensions. One dimension is normative monitoring (also called the 'duty of legality'), which ensures compliance with the law, articles of association, internal directives, and the board's instructions.[115] The other dimension is business monitoring, which requires evaluating whether senior management's actions, operations, and decisions align with the corporation's objectives and are suitable for achieving them.[116]

The duty of overall monitoring prioritises normative monitoring, since board members cannot claim 'prudence' unless their decisions and actions first comply with all applicable laws.[117] However, this duty extends beyond merely verifying the legality of actions to include assessing their appropriateness and soundness ('business monitoring').[118] As it is also known as prospective monitoring, this duty focuses on evaluating the decision-making process[119] and assessing potential future risks.[120]

---

[111] Ayhan et al. (2022), pp. 266–267.

[112] Krneta, para. 1219 as cited in Özatlan (2023), p. 258, fn. 682.

[113] Özatlan (2023), p. 258.

[114] Kalender (2024), p. 314.

[115] Kırca in Kırca et al. (2013), p. 562; Kaya (2014), DEÜHFD, p. 3275; Tekinalp (2020), p. 252; Çamoğlu in Poroy et al. (2025), para. 564, p. 415.

[116] Kırca in Kırca et al. (2013), pp. 563; Kaya (2014), DEÜHFD, p. 3275; Koç (2018), p. 99; Özatlan (2023), p. 44; Yıldırım Soysal (2023), AÜHFD, p. 1823.

[117] Yaşar (2018), p. 252.

[118] Hacımahmutoğlu (2015), BATİDER p. 48; Kalender (2024), pp. 290–291.

[119] Özatlan (2023), p. 226 and 333.

[120] Özatlan (2023), p. 226.

Given the continuous nature of the overall monitoring duty, establishing a permanent, systematic monitoring framework is essential.[121] The legislative mandate for overall monitoring is considered fulfilled when the board of directors institutes the requisite systems and controls to ensure the duty is carried out effectively.[122] Hence, the board does not need to exercise this oversight authority directly.[123] Monitoring management activities and providing necessary instructions[124] are adequate to perform this duty since it does not involve micromanaging the corporation's routine operations.[125] In the same vein, preamble to Article 375(1-e) of the TCC also clarifies that the board's overall monitoring duty refers to establishing an organisational monitoring system, not conducting direct, hands-on oversight.[126] To fulfil this duty effectively, the board may exercise its right to information and inspection[127] to have complete and accurate information about the corporation's operations, risks, and performance. Thus, a critical function of the board is to design and maintain a robust information flow system under the organisational monitoring system.[128]

Contemporary legal literature presents divergent views on whether there is a separate compliance duty apart from the overall monitoring duty.[129] Neither capital markets legislation nor the TCC explicitly mentions the concept of compliance duty.[130] Therefore, an independent 'compliance duty' for the board of directors or its members does not exist from a technical legal perspective. Nevertheless, it must be acknowledged that establishing a compliance organisation within corporations is necessary to fulfil the overall monitoring duty,[131] given the volume and complexity of operations that may obstruct efficient monitoring directly by

---

[121] Doğan (2011), p. 197; Hacımahmutoğlu (2015), BATİDER, pp. 47–48.

[122] Doğan (2012), MÜHF-HAD, pp. 620–621.

[123] Doğan (2011), p. 197; Ay Kaplan (2017), p. 133; Salman (2024), p. 138.

[124] Altay (2011), p. 118; Akdağ Güney (2016), p. 165.

[125] Kayıhan (2011), p. 129; Hacımahmutoğlu (2015), BATİDER, pp. 49–50; Akdağ Güney (2016), p. 165; Koç (2018), p. 99.

[126] Kırca in Kırca et al. (2013), p. 561; Yaşar (2018), p. 278.

[127] Koç (2018), p. 100; Pulaşlı (2022), § 37, para. 126, p. 1556.

[128] Kırca in Kırca et al. (2013), p. 560; Kaya (2014), DEÜHFD, p. 3275; Hacımahmutoğlu (2015), BATİDER, pp. 47–48; Akdağ Güney (2016), pp. 166–167; Yıldırım Soysal (2023), AÜHFD, p. 1823.

[129] Yaşar (2018), p. 245 ff.; Pulaşlı (2019), BATİDER, p. 46 ff.

[130] Pulaşlı (2019), BATİDER, p. 46 ff.

[131] Özatlan (2023), p. 337. For the argument that the emerging duty of compliance represents not a new obligation but a reformulation of the board's traditional fiduciary duties, see Çamoğlu in Poroy et al. (2025), para. 586 g, pp. 433–434.

board members. The legal basis for establishing a compliance system can be derived from the overall monitoring mandate.[132] Notwithstanding the doctrinal debate over its status as an entirely independent duty, the board's compliance responsibilities, derived from the duty of overall monitoring, encompass defining the corporate risk profile, developing a corresponding compliance program and organisational structure, and ensuring its correct implementation throughout the corporation.[133]

Moreover, even if management of the corporation is delegated, all board members remain obliged to monitor the delegate's actions and transactions under their overall monitoring duty.[134] The TCC grants the board certain powers directly tied to its overall monitoring duty. Hence, the board of directors must regularly request and review reports on the conduct of business from those with management authority.[135] Furthermore, the board must ask questions and request the necessary information on matters it considers critical.[136] To systematically utilise these instruments in fulfilling the board's overall monitoring responsibilities,[137] provisions regarding the organisation of the compliance system can and should be included in an internal directive issued by the board of directors.[138]

The board retains ultimate responsibility for overall management and monitoring as these core duties are legally indivisible and non-transferable, ensuring the board remains the supreme governing body for strategic monitoring.[139] A cyclical relationship exists between overall management and monitoring. The board's instructions to management (as part of its overall management duty) are based on data from its monitoring function, while oversight of how management implements those instructions, in turn, falls within the scope of overall monitoring. This interdependence creates a continuous interaction between the two duties.[140]

---

[132] Kırca in Kırca et al. (2013), p. 562; Pulaşlı (2019), BATİDER, p. 53.

[133] Yaşar (2018), pp. 312–314.

[134] See Preamble to Art. 553(2): "*There is no doubt that in "delegation" the duty of monitoring lies with the one who delegates the task.*" Also, see Çamoğlu (2010), p. 197; Kırca in Kırca et al. (2013), pp. 560–563; Paslı (2013), İÜHFM, pp. 332–333; Hacımahmutoğlu (2015), BATİDER, pp. 47–48; Kalender (2024), p. 284 and 301; Çamoğlu in Poroy et al. (2025), para. 564, p. 415.

[135] Pulaşlı (2022), § 37, para. 149, p. 1564.

[136] Küçüktuncay (2023), p. 50.

[137] Özatlan (2023), pp. 178–179.

[138] Özatlan (2023), p. 341.

[139] Metin (2021), p. 90.

[140] Özatlan (2023), p. 322.

2.1.1.3.1.4 Duty of Loyalty

The board members are supposed to be loyal to the corporation.[141] The base of this duty in Turkish corporate law is good faith. In the preamble to Article 369 of the TCC, the duty of loyalty is defined as prioritising the interests of the corporation over the interests of the board members and third parties.[142] The board members' duty not to enter into transactions with the corporation and become indebted to it, the duty not to compete with the corporation, and the duty not to involve themselves in discussions are special manifestations of the duty of loyalty.[143] Furthermore, the protection of the corporation's trade secrets is a part of the duty of loyalty.[144]

2.1.1.3.1.5 Right to Information and Inspection

The right to information and inspection is one of the most essential rights of board members, as they can perform their duties most effectively if they have information about the corporation's business.[145] Furthermore, their responsibility extends not only to what they actually know but also to information they reasonably should have known.[146] Hence, this right, which may not be restricted or withdrawn but may be expanded.[147] Its timely and proper exercise also constitutes an integral part of duty of care and overall monitoring duty.[148] In other words, board members may be found liable for damages arising from their decisions if they cannot prove they actively exercise their right to information and inspection to provide an appropriate informational basis for their decision.

If it is not peculiarly stipulated (as facilitating the use of this right) by a board decision or in the articles of association, this right can be exercised as indicated in

---

141 Art. 369 of the TCC. Also, see Bozkurt Yaşar (2015), p. 136; Akdağ Güney (2016), p. 203; Pulaşlı (2022), § 37, para. 333, p. 1676.

142 Preamble to Art. 369 of the TCC.

143 Ansay (1975), pp. 129–132; Çamoğlu (2010), p. 76; Kırca in Kırca et al. (2013), p. 663; Bozkurt Yaşar (2015), p. 137; Akdağ Güney (2016), p. 207; Çamoğlu in Poroy et al. (2025), para. 585, p. 430.

144 Çamoğlu (2010), p. 76; Kırca in Kırca et al. (2013), p. 664; Bozkurt Yaşar (2015), p. 137; Pulaşlı (2022), § 37, para. 339, p. 1678; Çamoğlu in Poroy et al. (2025), para. 586, p. 430.

145 Kortunay (2015), p. 310; Akdağ Güney (2016), p. 170; Karslıoğlu (2021), AkdHFD, p. 380; Pulaşlı (2022), § 37, para. 9, p. 1497; Çamoğlu in Poroy et al. (2025), para. 558a, p. 411.

146 Akdağ Güney (2016), p. 170.

147 Art. 392(6) of the TCC. Also, see Akdağ Güney (2016), p. 171; Ayhan et al. (2022), p. 277.

148 Kırca in Kırca et al. (2013), p. 703.

Article 392 of the TCC. Under this article, the right to information and inspection is reserved for individual board members in their personal capacity.[149] It is not a right granted to the board of directors as a collective entity.[150] Accordingly, any board member has the right to request information, ask questions, and conduct inspections of the corporation's businesses and transactions.[151] Board members may receive support from an expert to inspect documents if the chairperson allows such a support request.[152]

The procedure for exercising the right of information and inspection differs in the TCC depending on whether it is exercised during or outside board meetings. During board meetings, persons authorised to manage the corporation shall be obliged to provide information to every board member.[153] If this request is denied or questions are left unanswered, the relevant board member may apply to the court for a decision to use the right to information and inspection.[154]

Outside board meetings, any board member may, with the permission of the chairperson,[155] obtain information from those authorised to manage the corporation.[156] Moreover, the board member may request the chairperson to make the corporation's books and files available for inspection.[157] If the chairperson rejects such a request to obtain information, ask questions, or conduct an inspection, the board shall decide on this request within two days. If the board fails to convene or rejects such a request, the requesting member may apply to the relevant court.[158] The chairperson must request approval of the board to obtain information or inspect the corporation's books and files outside board meetings.[159] If the board rejects such a request, the chairperson may apply to the court.[160]

---

[149] Gürpınar (2013), MÜHF-HAD, pp. 1104–1105; Kırca in Kırca et al. (2013), p. 704; Akdağ Güney (2016), p. 171; Pulaşlı (2022), § 37, para. 11, p. 1497.

[150] Preamble to Art. 392(1) of the TCC.

[151] Art. 392 of the TCC.

[152] Akdağ Güney (2016), p. 173; Çamoğlu in Poroy et al. (2025), para. 558c, p. 412; Özatlan (2023), pp. 305–306.

[153] Art. 392(2) of the TCC. Also, see Özatlan (2023), p. 307.

[154] Kırca in Kırca et al. (2013), p. 714; Bozkurt Yaşar (2015), p. 171; Akdağ Güney (2016), p. 175; Tekinalp (2020), pp. 280–281; Ayhan et al. (2022), p. 278; Çamoğlu in Poroy et al. (2025), para. 558b, p. 412.

[155] Özatlan (2023), pp. 310–311.

[156] Art. 392(3) of the TCC.

[157] Art. 392(3) of the TCC.

[158] Art. 392(4) of the TCC.

[159] Tekinalp (2020), p. 280.

[160] Art. 392(5) of the TCC.

2.1.1.3.2 In German Law

2.1.1.3.2.1 Duty of Care

The German corporate law obligates the management board members to act with the diligence of a prudent and conscientious manager (*Sorgfalt eines ordentlichen und gewissenhaften Geschäftsleiters*) in their roles.[161] This duty of care for corporate boards encompasses four core functional areas of management diligence: planning and control, organisational responsibility, financial responsibility and information responsibility.[162] Hence, this duty requires the management board to implement an effective, legally compliant organisational structure that aligns with the corporation's articles of association.[163]

The board's duty of care is a normative standard. A board member's actual incompetence or negligence typical in other corporations, does not relieve the board of its responsibility.[164] Nevertheless, in assessing the management board's due diligence, reference must be made to a specific type of corporation, so that the economic situation, the nature of the activity and the size of the corporation must be taken into account.[165] Moreover, this duty involves establishing a robust organisational structure that clearly defines responsibilities, accountabilities, reporting lines, and monitoring mechanisms. This structure is essential for effectively pursuing the corporation's objectives as outlined in its mission.[166]

This organisational structure should aim to ensure informed decision-making.[167] In this respect, the situation at the time of the board's decision should be considered when assessing the board's diligence.[168] If the board has carefully decided on a particular course of action, it is not liable if this decision later turns

---

[161] AktG §93 para. 1. Also, see Link in Wachter (2022), AktG, § 84, para. 42.

[162] Fleischer in Spindler and Stilz (2019), AktG, § 76, para. 18; Grigoleit and Tomasic in Grigoleit (2020), AktG, § 93, para. 37.

[163] Fleischer in Spindler and Stilz (2019), AktG, § 93, para. 56; Hoffmann-Becking in Hoffmann-Becking (2020), § 25, para. 6.

[164] Hopt and Roth in Großkomm-AktG (2015), AktG, § 93, para. 59; Spindler in MünchKomm-AktG (2019), AktG, § 93, para. 25; Link in Wachter (2022), AktG, § 93, para. 10.

[165] Sailer-Coceani in Schmidt and Lutter (2020), AktG, § 93, para. 6; Koch in Hüffer and Koch (2021), AktG, § 93, para. 4; Link in Wachter (2022), AktG, § 93, para. 8.

[166] Hopt and Roth in Großkomm-AktG (2015), AktG, § 93, para. 151; Seyfarth (2016), § 8, para. 114; Link in Wachter (2022), AktG, § 93, para. 13.

[167] Fleischer in Spindler and Stilz (2019), AktG, § 93, para. 58.

[168] Spindler in MünchKomm-AktG (2019), AktG, § 93, para. 25; Sailer-Coceani in Schmidt and Lutter (2020), AktG, § 93, para. 6; Link in Wachter (2022), AktG, § 93, para. 11.

out to be wrong.[169] Hence, the management board is authorised to exercise its managerial discretion in line with the BJR.[170]

In German legal doctrine, it is accepted that the general duty of care comprises three core obligations: the duty of management, the duty of monitoring and the duty of legality.[171] Because of their significance for this thesis, these specialised appearances of duty of care will be investigated under their own titles below.

2.1.1.3.2.2 Duty of Management

As the core hub for decision-making and action within the corporation,[172] the management board is granted the exclusive and primary duty of managing the corporation under Section 76 of the AktG. This duty of independent management confers upon the board comprehensive and autonomous authority to undertake all actions, not expressly reserved by law for other organs, that are necessary to direct the corporation's operations and achieve its objectives.

While the content of the corporation management differs according to the size, structure and complexity of the corporation,[173] the scope of corporate management typically encompasses several critical areas: strategic planning (including strategy and business plan development), risk oversight (involving the early identification of opportunities and risks, as well as crisis management), human capital management (the search for and development of executives), and stakeholder relations.[174] Under the management duty, as a special appearance of duty to care,[175] the board must display diligence in establishing the corporation's organisation, planning and control processes.[176] In this direction, the board is expected to implement an effective, legally compliant organisational structure that aligns with

---

[169] Seyfarth (2016), § 23, para. 19; Spindler in MünchKomm-AktG (2019), AktG, § 93, para. 26; Link in Wachter (2022), AktG, § 93, para. 11.

[170] Kort in Großkomm AktG (2015), AktG, § 91, para. 66; Hopt and Roth in Großkomm AktG (2015), AktG, § 93, para. 153; Spindler in MünchKomm-AktG (2019), AktG, § 93, para. 115; Link in Wachter (2022), AktG, § 93, para. 13. See 3.5.3. for the BJR in details.

[171] Fleischer in Fleischer (2006), § 7, para. 1; Fleischer in Spindler and Stilz (2019), AktG, § 93, para. 12.

[172] Seibt in Schmidt and Lutter, AktG, § 76, para. 2.

[173] Ihrig and Schäfer (2020), § 16, para. 421; Seibt in Schmidt and Lutter (2020), AktG, § 76, para. 12; Link in Wachter (2022), AktG, § 76, para. 8.

[174] Seibt in Schmidt and Lutter, AktG, § 76 paras. 16–21.

[175] Fleischer in Spindler and Stilz (2019), AktG, § 93, para. 12.

[176] Fleischer in Spindler and Stilz (2019), AktG, § 76, para. 18; Grigoleit and Tomasic in Grigoleit (2020), AktG, § 93, para. 37.

the corporation's articles of association.[177] Since effective management depends on accurate, timely, and actionable information, the board is also expected to establish and maintain an efficient internal information organisation to fulfil this duty.[178]

2.1.1.3.2.3 Duty of Monitoring and Legality

An essential part of the management board's mandate for independent management under Section 76 AktG is its monitoring duty. The management board itself must create and maintain an efficient internal monitoring system to regulate the corporation's operations,[179] since a well-functioning corporate organisation necessitates an internal monitoring system that enables effective planning and management, a robust reporting framework, and competent control mechanisms.[180] Moreover, the management board must maintain a clear understanding of the corporation's financial position at all times to fulfil its responsibilities effectively.[181] Depending on the corporation's size and operational complexity, the management board's duty of care and monitoring may require establishing internal monitoring systems or at least specific key components.[182]

Fulfilment of the legality duty is another crucial reason to establish an internal monitoring system. The management board is always obliged to comply with applicable law in corporation management.[183] This duty also involves compliance with the articles of association, the rules of procedure,[184] and resolutions of the general assembly.[185] Members of the board are tasked with overseeing

[177] Fleischer in Spindler and Stilz (2019), AktG, § 93, para. 56; Hoffmann-Becking in Hoffmann-Becking (2020), § 25, para. 6.

[178] Fleischer in Spindler and Stilz (2019), AktG, § 93, para. 58.

[179] The supervisory board has the primary statutory responsibility for supervising the management board under Section 111 of the AktG.

[180] Sailer-Coceani in Schmidt and Lutter (2020), AktG, § 93, para. 9; Link in Wachter (2022), AktG, § 93, para. 14.

[181] Hopt and Roth in Großkomm-AktG (2015), AktG, § 93, para. 153; Link in Wachter (2022), AktG, § 93, para. 14.

[182] Link in Wachter (2022), AktG, § 93, para. 14.

[183] Spindler in MünchKomm-AktG (2019), AktG, § 93, para. 63; Sailer-Coceani in Schmidt and Lutter (2020), AktG, § 93, para. 7; Koch in Hüffer and Koch (2021), AktG, § 93, para. 6; Link in Wachter (2022), AktG, § 93, para. 12.

[184] Seyfarth (2016), § 23, para. 13; Sailer-Coceani in Schmidt and Lutter (2020), AktG, § 93, para. 7; Link in Wachter (2022), AktG, § 93, para. 12.

[185] Hopt and Roth in Großkomm-AktG (2015), AktG, § 93, para. 74; Link in Wachter (2022), AktG, § 93, para. 12.

the corporation's adherence to legal standards[186] and ensuring corporate compliance.[187] Whether corporations are required to establish a systematic compliance organisation for this purpose is a significant question that warrants doctrinal debate.[188] The necessity of establishing such a systematic structure is evaluated based on various case-specific factors, such as the corporation's size and risk exposure, making it a largely situational obligation rather than a universal one.[189] It is convincingly argued that when compliance cannot be ensured through other means, members of the management board are obliged to establish a systematic compliance system that includes prevention, detection, and response mechanisms.[190]

Implementing an internal monitoring system to identify potential risks that could threaten the corporation's viability aligns with the management board's obligation to proactively recognise any possible threats to the corporation's ongoing viability and implement the necessary actions outlined in Section 91(2).[191] The management board is expected to consider these developments comprehensively and maintain a holistic overview, enabling them to assess the likelihood of various scenarios unfolding.[192] Information derived from such systemic monitoring dramatically enhances this holistic assessment process.

While determining the necessary and appropriate measures to prevent any breach of law by the corporation the management board must act according to the prudent and conscientious manager standard.[193] In practice, typical core elements of a compliance organisation have already emerged.[194] The management board members fulfil their monitoring and legality duties if they choose a compliance model that is highly regarded both theoretically and practically, and they have

---

186 Wirth et al. (2017), p. 106.

187 Fleischer in Spindler and Stilz (2019), § 91, AktG, para. 50; Seibt in Schmidt and Lutter (2020), AktG, § 76, para. 22.

188 Wirth et al. (2017), p. 108; Seibt in Schmidt and Lutter (2020), AktG, § 76, para. 24; Link in Wachter (2022), AktG, § 93, para. 21.

189 Seibt in Schmidt and Lutter (2020), AktG, § 76 para. 24.

190 Seibt in Schmidt and Lutter (2020), AktG, § 76, para. 24.

191 Seyfarth (2016), § 8, para. 115; Spindler in MünchKomm-AktG (2019), AktG, § 93, para. 114; Link in Wachter (2022), AktG, § 91, para. 5 and § 93, para. 14.

192 Sailer-Coceani in Schmidt and Lutter (2020), AktG, § 91, para. 9; Link in Wachter (2022), AktG, § 91, para. 8.

193 Seyfarth (2016), § 8, para. 39; Link in Wachter (2022), AktG, § 93, para. 20.

194 Sailer-Coceani in Schmidt and Lutter (2020), AktG, § 93, para. 8.

confirmed that it is pertinent to the particular characteristics and circumstances of their own corporation.[195]

2.1.1.3.2.4 Duty of Loyalty

Board members have a duty of loyalty to the corporation,[196] which entails acting in the best interests of the corporation, ensuring they protect and promote the corporation's welfare, rather than pursuing personal interests.[197] To uphold this duty diligently, management board members need to avoid any potential conflicts of interest.[198] Hence, they must base their decisions on the principles of economic efficiency and expediency from the corporation's perspective.[199] In this context, the non-competition clause (*Wettbewerbsverbot*)[200] in AktG Section 88(1) is one of the special appearances of this duty. Furthermore, the overarching duty of loyalty encompasses a duty of confidentiality (*Verschwiegenheitspflicht*).[201] As explicitly stated in AktG § 93(1), sentence 3, board members are bound to keep any confidential information and trade secrets they encounter during their tenure strictly confidential.

2.1.1.3.2.5 Duty of Reporting

The management board bears a formal reporting obligation to the supervisory board.[202] This duty enables the supervisory board to monitor the management board. The purpose is to exercise preventive control over decisions that could

---

[195] Link in Wachter (2022), AktG, § 93, para. 16.

[196] Wirth et al. (2017), p. 106; Spindler in MünchKomm-AktG (2019), AktG, § 76, para. 13 and § 93, para. 125; Sailer-Coceani in Schmidt and Lutter (2020), AktG, § 93, para. 21; Koch in Hüffer and Koch (2021), AktG, § 93, para. 28; Link in Wachter (2022), AktG, § 84, para. 42 and § 93, para. 51.

[197] Hopt and Roth in Großkomm-AktG (2015), AktG, § 93, para. 145; Sailer-Coceani in Schmidt and Lutter (2020), AktG, § 93, para. 21; Link in Wachter (2022), AktG, § 84, para. 42 and § 93, para. 51 and § 93, para. 7.

[198] Spindler in MünchKomm-AktG (2019), AktG, § 93, para. 125; Link in Wachter (2022), AktG, § 93, para. 51.

[199] Sailer-Coceani in Schmidt and Lutter (2020), AktG, § 93, para. 10; Link in Wachter (2022), AktG, § 93, para. 7.

[200] Spindler in MünchKomm-AktG (2019), AktG, § 93, para. 125; Link in Wachter (2022), AktG, § 93, para. 51.

[201] Hoffmann-Becking in Hoffmann-Becking (2020), § 25, para. 38; Grigoleit and Tomasic in Grigoleit (2020), AktG, § 93, para. 73 ff.; Link in Wachter (2022), AktG, § 93, para. 51.

[202] AktG § 90.

lead to long-term obligations for the corporation.[203] The management board must act according to the prudent and conscientious manager standard while performing the reporting duty.[204] Therefore, reports of the management board must be conscientious and faithful.[205]

The duty of reporting framework is organised into four distinct categories in Section 90 of the AktG. The first category requires at least an annual report on the corporation's plans (financial, investment, personnel[206]) with the details tailored to the corporation's specific circumstances.[207] The second category mandates a detailed report on profitability metrics, submitted alongside the annual financial statements.[208] The third category requires a quarterly operational report that provides a comparative snapshot of performance[209] (e.g., sales, liquidity) against past data and forecasts.[210] The fourth category is an *ad hoc*, immediate report for any transaction that could significantly impact profitability or liquidity, submitted in advance to allow for supervisory board feedback.[211] Beyond these categories, the management board must immediately report to the chairperson any 'other important' adverse events,[212] such as major operational disruptions or liquidity crises.[213] Furthermore, the supervisory board, including individual members, can demand reports at any time on the corporation's affairs and on matters of affiliated enterprises that could significantly influence the corporation.[214]

---

[203] Link in Wachter (2022), AktG, § 90, para. 1.

[204] Sailer-Coceani in Schmidt and Lutter (2020), AktG, § 90, para. 52; Link in Wachter (2022), AktG, § 90, para. 28.

[205] AktG § 90 para. 4 sentence 1.

[206] AktG § 90 para. 1, sentence 1, no. 1.

[207] Spindler in MünchKomm-AktG (2019), AktG, § 90, para. 18; Sailer-Coceani in Schmidt and Lutter (2020), AktG, § 90, para. 8; Link in Wachter (2022), AktG, § 90, para. 6.

[208] Sailer-Coceani in Schmidt and Lutter (2020), AktG, § 90, para. 17; Koch in Hüffer and Koch (2021), AktG, § 90, para. 5; Link in Wachter (2022), AktG, § 90, para. 10.

[209] Kort in Großkomm AktG (2015), AktG § 90, para. 58; Koch in Hüffer and Koch (2021), AktG, § 90, para. 6; Link in Wachter (2022), AktG, § 90, para. 12.

[210] Sailer-Coceani in Schmidt and Lutter (2020), AktG, § 90, para. 21; Link in Wachter (2022), AktG, § 90, para. 13.

[211] Spindler in MünchKomm-AktG (2019), AktG, § 90, para. 29; Koch in Hüffer and Koch (2021), AktG, § 90, para. 7; Link in Wachter (2022), AktG, § 90, para. 16.

[212] AktG § 90 para. 1, sentence 3.

[213] Fleischer in Spindler and Stilz (2019), § 90, AktG, para. 31; Spindler in MünchKomm-AktG (2019), AktG, § 90, para. 31; Sailer-Coceani in Schmidt and Lutter (2020), AktG, § 90, para. 33; Koch in Hüffer and Koch (2021), AktG, § 90, para. 8; Link in Wachter (2022), AktG, § 90, para. 20.

[214] AktG § 90 para. 3.

Section 90 of the AktG establishes a mandatory minimum reporting standard that cannot be waived due to its public-interest role.[215] The supervisory board has the authority to expand upon these minimum requirements by establishing more extensive and specific reporting obligations. It is typically done through the management board's rules of procedure or a separate information policy,[216] which can mandate more frequent reports, additional reporting triggers, and specific submission deadlines.[217] While such internal policies can tighten reporting standards, they must avoid excessive restrictions that would hinder efficient corporate operations.[218]

2.1.1.4 Supervisory Board

The supervisory board (*Aufsichtsrat*) is a mandatory, non-eliminable monitoring body in German corporations.[219] The supervisory board members are appointed by the general assembly, subject to certain exceptions.[220] The maximum term for individual board members is generally about five years.[221] The supervisory board must comprise at least three members.[222] Section 100(1) of the AktG provides that legal entities may not serve as members of the supervisory board.[223] Only natural persons who possess full legal capacity and do not require a guardian's consent are eligible to become supervisory board members.[224] Supervisory board members do not need to hold shares.[225] Although Section 100(1) of the AktG does not establish any additional personal qualifications,[226] Article 11 of the German Corporate Governance Codex (*Der deutsche Corporate Governance Kodex*, DCGK) specifies that the supervisory board should be structured so that its

[215] Spindler in MünchKomm-AktG (2019), AktG, § 90, para. 8; Link in Wachter (2022), AktG, § 90, para. 2.

[216] Link in Wachter (2022), AktG, § 90, para. 2.

[217] Sailer-Coceani in Schmidt and Lutter (2020), AktG, § 90, para. 73.

[218] Sailer-Coceani in Schmidt and Lutter (2020), AktG, § 90, para. 73.

[219] Wirth et al. (2017), p. 95; Schick in Wachter (2022), § 95, AktG, paras. 1–3.

[220] Schick in Wachter (2022), § 101, AktG, para. 3.

[221] Hoffmann-Becking in Hoffmann-Becking (2020), § 30, para. 80; Schick in Wachter (2022), AktG, § 102, para. 2.

[222] AktG § 95. Also, see Schick in Wachter (2022), AktG, § 95, para. 1.

[223] Schick in Wachter (2022), AktG, § 100, para. 2.

[224] Schick in Wachter (2022), AktG, § 100, para. 2.

[225] Hoffmann-Becking in Hoffmann-Becking (2020), § 30, para. 3; Schick in Wachter (2022), AktG, § 100, para. 2.

[226] Hoffmann-Becking in Hoffmann-Becking (2020), § 30, para. 4; Schick in Wachter (2022), AktG, § 100, para. 2.

members collectively possess the requisite knowledge, skills, and professional experience.[227] Likewise, each member is expected to "*possess or acquire the minimum knowledge and skills necessary to understand and adequately evaluate all typically occurring business transactions, even without external assistance,*"[228] according to the Federal Court of Justice (*Bundesgerichtshof*, BGH).

The supervisory board's core function is the comprehensive monitoring of the management board, as mandated by Section 111 of the AktG.[229] This supervisory mandate extends beyond mere legal compliance to include the expediency and economic efficiency of management decisions,[230] with the intensity of scrutiny proportionally increasing during corporate crises or for high-risk transactions.[231] The supervisory board's powers are substantial and include the right of inspection and examination (AktG § 111(2)), adopting and amending the rules of procedure for the management board (AktG § 77(2) sentence 1) or the allocation of responsibilities,[232] the authority to appoint and dismiss management board members (AktG § 84), auditing and asserting claims for compensation against management board members[233] and the critical tool of imposing specific approval reservations for fundamental transactions.[234] However, the supervisory board's preventive control must not encroach upon the management board's independent operational leadership *(Geschäftsführungsverbot*[235]*)*.

The supervisory board's monitoring duties also cover the oversight of the compliance system established by the management board, as well as the compliance measures implemented by the management board.[236] The supervisory

---

[227] Schick in Wachter (2022), AktG, § 100, para. 5.

[228] BGH, Judgment of 15.11.1982—II ZR 27/82 (Hertie), BGHZ 85, p. 295 ff.

[229] Wirth et al. (2017), p. 119; Hopt and Roth (2019), § 111, para. 102; Lutter et al. (2020), § 3, para. 61; Schick in Wachter (2022), AktG, § 111, para. 3.

[230] Wirth et al. (2017), p. 119; Hoffmann-Becking in Hoffmann-Becking (2020), § 29, para. 33 and para. 37; Lutter et al. (2020), § 3, para. 73; Schick in Wachter (2022), AktG, § 111, para. 6 and § 116 para. 7.

[231] Hoffmann-Becking in Hoffmann-Becking (2020), § 29, para. 36; Lutter et al. (2020), § 3, para. 95 ff.; Schick in Wachter (2022), AktG, § 111, para. 6

[232] Lutter et al. (2020), § 3, para. 109 und § 7 para. 463 ff.; Schick in Wachter (2022), AktG, § 111, para. 8.

[233] Schick in Wachter (2022), AktG, § 111, para. 8.

[234] Schick in Wachter (2022), AktG, § 111, para. 20.

[235] Habersack in MünchKomm-AktG (2019), AktG, § 111 para. 110; Koch in Hüffer and Koch (2021), AktG, § 111 para. 51; Schick in Wachter (2022), AktG, § 111, para. 19.

[236] Schick in Wachter (2022), AktG, § 111, para. 11.

board must ensure that the management board fulfils its compliance responsibilities.[237] The supervisory board's responsibilities are dynamically evolving, now explicitly encompassing the monitoring of compliance and risk management systems, with recent legislative developments, such as the Supply Chain Due Diligence Act[238] and the EU's Corporate Sustainability Due Diligence Directive,[239] formally integrating sustainability oversight into its core monitoring duties.[240]

The delegation of these responsibilities to a committee or individual board members is generally not allowed.[241] Therefore, the supervisory board must supervise management activities as a body.[242] Nevertheless, the supervisory board may utilise a committee or individual members to assist with specific monitoring aspects. However, such assistance does not diminish the supervisory board's overall responsibility for monitoring.[243]

Section 93 AktG also applies to the supervisory board (with the reference in AktG § 116). Hence, the basis for the liability of a supervisory board members is a breach of their duty resulting from the disregard of the care of a prudent and conscientious manager[244].[245] The BJR (codified in AktG § 93) applies to supervisory board members when the supervisory board makes a business decision.[246]

---

[237] Lutter et al. (2020), § 3, para. 75; Schick in Wachter (2022), AktG, § 111, para. 11.

[238] *Gesetz über die unternehmerischen Sorgfaltspflichten zur Vermeidung von Menschenrechtsverletzungen in Lieferketten (LkSG)* v. 16.7.2021, BGBl. I 2021, 2959.

[239] Directive (EU) 2024/1760 of the European Parliament and of the Council of 13 June 2024 on corporate sustainability due diligence and amending Directive (EU) 2019/1937 and Regulation (EU) 2023/2859.

[240] Schick in Wachter (2022), AktG, § 111, para. 2

[241] Habersack in MünchKomm-AktG (2019), AktG, § 111, para. 60; Koch in Hüffer and Koch (2021), AktG, § 111, para. 32; Schick in Wachter (2022), AktG, § 111, para. 10.

[242] Schick in Wachter (2022), AktG, § 111, para. 10.

[243] Habersack in MünchKomm-AktG (2019), AktG, § 111, para. 60; Koch in Hüffer and Koch (2021), AktG, § 111, para. 32; Schick in Wachter (2022), AktG, § 111, para. 10.

[244] Since supervisory board members are not actually managers, it should be understood that they must perform their duties with the care expected of a prudent and conscientious 'supervisory board member'. Wirth et al. (2017), p. 128; Schick in Wachter (2022), AktG, § 116, para. 7.

[245] Hopt and Roth (2019), § 116, para. 11; Hoffmann-Becking in Hoffmann-Becking (2020), § 33, para. 74; Schick in Wachter (2022), AktG, § 116, para. 7.

[246] Habersack in MünchKomm-AktG (2019), AktG, § 116, para. 39 ff; Hoffmann-Becking in Hoffmann-Becking (2020), § 33, para. 87; Koch in Hüffer and Koch (2021), AktG, § 116, para. 5; Schick in Wachter (2022), AktG, § 116, para. 20.

2.1.1.5 Contextual Comparison

A contextual comparative examination of the frameworks governing the boards of directors in Turkish stock corporations and the management boards in German stock corporations reveals significant parallels in core fiduciary duties, alongside notable divergences in board structure, supervisory mechanisms, and their respective roles within the corporate hierarchy.

The major difference between these two legal systems is that Turkish law adopts a monist board model, while German law adopts a dualist board model. While the prevailing opinion in Turkish legal doctrine is that completely changing the board's monist structure is impossible, it appears possible to approximate a dualist structure through methods such as delegation. For instance, a functional distinction between executive and non-executive roles can emerge even within a monistic board structure. This practical distinction is typically achieved through the delegation, enabling non-executive members to assume a supervisory role. However, due to the board of directors' clearly enumerated non-delegable powers and duties under Turkish law, non-executive board members cannot serve as a full oversight body. Moreover, the German supervisory board's monitoring role entails extensive duties and, when required, the authority for executive action. It contrasts with the monist board structure of the Turkish corporations, where oversight is an internal function focused on senior managers rather than a separate entity. Therefore, although the German model shares a general concept of overall monitoring with Turkish systems, its specific function is not entirely equivalent, as it incorporates responsibilities that extend past mere supervision.[247]

The conditions for board membership are similar in both legal systems. In both legal systems, fully qualified natural persons can become board members. The most fundamental difference is that, under Turkish law, legal entities may serve as board members, whereas this is not yet possible under German law.

Another point of convergence lies in the treatment of the articles of association, which, under both Turkish and German law, are not merely contractual documents but are subject to a mandatory and comprehensive statutory framework designed to ensure legal certainty and protect stakeholders. According to Article 340 of the TCC and Section 23(5) of the AktG,[248] deviations from the articles of association regulations stipulated in these laws can only be made if

---

[247] Özatlan (2023), p. 20.

[248] According to Preamble to Art. 340 of the TCC, this article is modelled on § 23 (5) of the AktG. For an analysis of the historical development and key features of this provision within both Turkish and German law, see Veziroğlu (2021), p. 343 ff.

expressly permitted by the relevant laws. This rigid approach, on the one hand, ensures the preservation of the legislator's prescribed order and balance of interests. On the other hand, it prevents the articles of association from being shaped according to constantly changing business requirements.

Moreover, neither Turkish nor German law provides an exhaustive, itemised catalogue of board duties; instead, their precise content and scope are developed through statutory interpretation and jurisprudence. They are derived directly or indirectly from individual articles of the TCC and AktG by doctrine and judicial authorities. Within the scope of this thesis, in both legal systems, the fundamental duties of boards are highlighted as care, management, monitoring, legality, and loyalty. However, their legal or commercial justifications are not always the same.

While the terms 'prudent manager' in Turkish law and 'prudent and conscientious manager' in German law are not the same, they do imply similar levels of diligence. As a special appearance of the duty of care, the BJR is directly regulated in Section 93 of the AktG. However, in the TCC, the BJR is mentioned in the preamble to Article 369 rather than being regulated in a separate legal article. Nevertheless, Turkish legal doctrine considers the BJR generally applicable.[249] In both legal systems, the monitoring obligation is understood to encompass both legality and compliance with the corporation's objectives. Establishing a compliance system or department for this purpose is not considered a general obligation in either system and should be evaluated on a case-by-case basis. In both systems, a duty of loyalty is recognised, requiring board members to prioritise the corporation's interests over their own.

Due to the monist structure of Turkish law, the board's reporting obligations are not explicitly regulated, and those directed to the general assembly can be derived from the relevant articles. In German law, however, due to the dualist board structure, the board's reporting obligation to the supervisory board is regulated in detail. The right to information and inspection granted to board members under Turkish law also constitutes an obligation as a prudent management measure.[250] Hence, this right, even within a monist board structure, can also create a *de facto* reporting obligation for delegates towards board members.

---

[249] See 3.5.3.1.

[250] Karslıoğlu (2021), AkdHFD, p. 380; Bahtiyar (2024), p. 208.

Considering the scope of this thesis, the above contextual comparison of board membership requirements and board member duties across both legal systems will shed light on subsequent comparative analyses of AI use by boards.

2.1.1.6 Interim Result

While Turkish corporate law adopts a monist board structure and German corporate law a dualist one, the strict approach to articles of association, core fiduciary duties, and their pragmatic implementation are common for both legal systems. One of the most fundamental differences between these legal systems is the personal eligibility criteria for board membership. Under Turkish corporate law, legal entities may serve as board members, whereas this is not yet possible under German corporate law.

The fundamental duties of the board members in both legal systems, primarily care (of prudent manager), management, monitoring, legality, and loyalty, bring these systems closer together and enable management that prioritises the balance of power, transparency, and accountability in accordance with modern corporate management principles. Furthermore, the explicit reporting obligations in German corporate law and the right to information and inspection in Turkish corporate law demonstrate the similar importance placed on the flow of information within and between bodies in both legal systems. These distinct yet parallel architectures of the Turkish and German corporation management systems serve as a natural test-bed. Hence, the comparative analysis of these management structures, highlighting both common principles and distinct models, provides a critical framework for predicting the legal challenges and opportunities of integrating AI into corporate boards.

2.1.2 Comparative Analysis of AI's Board Membership

2.1.2.1 In General

The announcement of an AI system's, i.e. VITAL (Validating Investment Tool for Advancing Life Sciences), appointment to the board of Deep Knowledge Ventures[251] sparked significant discourse on the legal feasibility of AI board

[251] BBC (2014, May 16). "Algorithm appointed board director." Available at https://www.bbc.com/news/technology-27426942. (Last accessed: 25.12.2025).

members in both Turkish[252] and German[253] legal doctrine. Later, it is understood that VITAL served not as a formal director with voting rights, but in an advisory, observer capacity.[254] Despite their informal character,[255] this initial case and subsequent parallel disclosures by other corporations[256] collectively illustrate a

---

[252] Dönmez Canseven (2021), p. 75 ff.; Eryiğit (2021), p. 105 ff.; Gözübüyük (2021), HHFD, p. 1194 ff.; Güçlütürk (2021), p. 453 ff.; Karatepe Kaya (2021), HBV-HFD, p. 75 ff.; Metin (2021), p. 519 ff.; Akın (2022), TAÜHFD, p. 18 ff.; Bora Çınar (2022), p. 128 ff.; Gözübüyük (2022), HBV-HFD, p. 148 ff.; Altaş (2023), SÜHFD, p. 1371 ff.; Karadeniz (2023), TAAD, p. 265 ff.; Yıldırım Soysal (2023), AÜHFD, p. 1825 ff.; Kaya (2024), p. 77 ff.; Keskin (2024), p. 45 ff.; Uğurerkan (2024), p. 55 ff.; Karatepe Kaya et al. (2025), p. 1 ff.; Özer and Tomrukçu (2025), BATİDER, p. 240 ff.; Seçer (2025), p. 81 ff.; Töre (2025), SÜHFD, p. 888 ff.; Varlı (2025), p. 236 ff.

[253] Fleischer (2018), AR, p. 121; Möslein (2018), ZIP, p. 206 ff.; Strohn (2018), ZHR, p. 371 ff.; Weber et al. (2018), NZG, p. 1131 ff.; Armour and Eidenmüller (2019), ZHR, p. 169 ff.; Hoch (2019), AcP, p. 646 ff.; Lücke (2019), BB, p. 1986 ff.; Zetzsche (2019), AG, p. 9 ff.; Möslein (2020b), p. 509 ff.; Noack (2021), p. 947 ff.; Li (2022), p. 13 ff; Lieder (2022), p. 333 ff.; Nowak (2022), p. 171 ff.; Calabro (2023), p. 42 ff.; Möslein (2023a); p. 177 ff.; Telle (2023), p. 45 ff.; Ahern (2024), p. 418 ff.; Frey (2024), p. 48 ff.; Langenbucher (2024), EuZW, p. 854 ff.; Casper and Möslein (2025), ZGR, p. 870 ff.; Möslein (2025a), p. 614 ff.; Rolsing (2025), p. 31 ff.; Windorf (2025), p. 372 ff.

[254] Nicky Burridge (2017, May 10). "Artificial intelligence gets a seat in the boardroom." Nikkei Asian Review. Available at https://asia.nikkei.com/business/artificial-intelligence-gets-a-seat-in-the-boardroom. (Last accessed: 25.12.2025).

[255] While reports indicated that an AI system with 'voting rights' was appointed to the board of directors of Kazakhstan's Samruk-Kazyna state fund, the legal infrastructure enabling such a grant of rights remained undocumented and unclear. See, Vagit Ismailov (2025, October 7). "Artificial Intelligence Joins Board of Directors at Samruk-Kazyna." The Times of Central Asia. Available at https://timesca.com/artificial-intelligence-joins-board-of-directors-at-samruk-kazyna/. (Last accessed: 25.12.2025).

[256] Finextra (2016, October 18). "Tieto appoints bot to leadership team." Available at https://www.finextra.com/newsarticle/29606/tieto-appoints-bot-to-leadership-team. (Last accessed: 25.12.2025); David Meyer (2018, January 2025). "An AI Bot Named Einstein Critiques Salesforce Execs Every Week." Fortune News Tech Section. Available at https://fortune.com/2018/01/25/salesforce-benioff-einstein-davos-ai. (Last accessed: 25.12.2025); Abu Dhabi Media Office (2024, February 27). "Artificial Intelligence board observer appointed by International Holding Board of Directors." Available at https://www.mediaoffice.abudhabi/en/economy/artificial-intelligence-board-observer-appointed-by-international-holding-board-of-directors/. (Last accessed: 25.12.2025); Reinsw (2024, May 30). "REINSW appoints Australia's first AI Board Advisor." Available at https://www.reinsw.com.au/Web/Web/News/Media_Releases/2024/05-May/ai-board-advisor.aspx. (Last accessed: 25.12.2025); Aliando (2025, August 26). "ALIANDO Elects World's First AI Board Member at London Meeting." Available at https://aliando.com/news/aliando-elects-worlds-first-ai-board-member-at-london-meeting. (Last accessed: 25.12.2025). Aside from specially developed AI systems, generative AI tools are also beginning to be positioned in various roles within

growing trend toward the practical integration of AI into corporation management frameworks.

As Yuval Harari notes, the VITAL case exemplifies the rise of 'algorithmic authority,'[257] where AI systems increasingly shape critical corporate decisions, even in the absence of formal power, as human board members defer to their recommendations. This trend prompts a pressing legal question: Can AI systems legally serve as board members in stock corporations? Although the inquiry is still in its nascent stages, it is attracting increasing scholarly attention.

Current corporate legal frameworks are largely unprepared for 'robo-directors.'[258] Presently, no jurisdiction has enacted specific legislation governing the board membership of AI systems. Moreover, there is a fundamental divergence across jurisdictions in the current eligibility criteria for board membership. Some systems, e.g., German law, explicitly require directors to be natural persons, while others, e.g., Turkish law, permit legal entities to serve as board members.[259] The absence of a universal legal status for AI leaves its present (*de lege lata*) and prospective (*de lege ferenda*) eligibility for directorship in debate, necessitating reliance on legal analogy and speculative doctrinal innovation.

Apart from its novel benefits,[260] the integration of AI into boards presents several profound challenges,[261] including concerns over its decision-making legitimacy, the risk of uncritical human deference to its outputs, which may stifle

---

senior management of corporations. For example, ChatGPT serves as CEO of an organization called CS India in India. For more information, see Bharat Sharma (2023, February 9). "Youth organisation appoints ChatGPT AI bot as its CEO, calls it 'groundbreaking'." India Times. Available at: https://www.indiatimes.com/technology/news/organisation-appoints-chatgpt-bot-as-its-ceo-592620.html. (Last accessed: 25.12.2025). For another example of ChatGPT being appointed as CEO, see TPN/Lusa (2023, April 28). "Portuguese entrepreneur creates viral company." The Portugal News. Available at: https://www.theportugalnews.com/news/2023-04-28/portuguese-entrepreneur-creates-viral-company/77089. (Last accessed: 25.12.2025).

[257] Harari (2017), Chapter 9, p. 260.

[258] Karatepe Kaya (2021), HBV-HFD, p. 92.

[259] Möslein (2025a), p. 630. For the information on history of natural person requirement for board membership in the early corporations and recent discussions on the eligibility of legal persons for board membership, see Daeenabi (2025), UCLJ, p. 1276 ff.

[260] Gramitto Ricci (2020), Cornell L. Rev., p. 901. For a comprehensive investigation of AI board members' benefits, see Daeenabi (2025), UCLJ, pp. 1287–1289.

[261] Gramitto Ricci (2020), Cornell L. Rev., p. 901 ff.

independent judgment, and, most critically, a lack of precise accountability mechanisms due to the AI's lack of legal personality.[262] Thus, traditional civil liability frameworks struggle to address the harms caused by algorithmic decisions, creating a significant governance gap. AI's lack of a widely accepted legal status and liability regime is a key problematic focus of the legal debate over AI board membership.[263] Therefore, before delving deeper into these corporate law-specific challenges and analysing the legal feasibility of AI board members, the following sections will provide a brief review of the legal debate surrounding AI's legal personality and liability.

2.1.2.2 Preliminary Issue of AI's Legal Personality and Liability

2.1.2.2.1 A Brief Review

With the integration of AI into risky domains, scholarly debate on AI's legal status and the corresponding liability has begun, as AI's autonomous nature, which makes it difficult to attribute responsibility for damages to any actor,[264] creates a novel liability gap. This challenge forces a re-examination of current legal categories and requires the development of new regulatory approaches to adequately address the unique characteristics of AI systems.

Under both Turkish and German law, AI systems lack legal personality. The foundational question is whether AI should be granted legal personality, a status that would recognise AI as a direct subject of rights and obligations.[265] Currently, several analogies are being explored, though each presents significant shortcomings. The simplest approach treats AI as property, which fits comfortably within existing legal frameworks but fails to account for AI's autonomy, self-learning capabilities, and potential for unpredictable decision-making.[266] More ambitious

[262] Kaya (2024), p. 85.

[263] Zhao (2022), Cath. U. L. Rev., p. 680 ff.

[264] Parties who can be considered responsible for damages caused by AI systems can be categorized under two general groups. The manufacturer group involves all the parties that develop, design and produce the end product as considered together with hardware and software components. Parties who have interaction with the product after its circulation in the market constitute the second group. This group includes owners, operators and users of the AI systems. Wagner (2019), p. 32.

[265] Solaiman (2017), Artif Intell Law, p. 158. Also, see Gordon (2021), AI & Soc, p. 457 ff.

[266] Üner (2020), pp. 238–239.

comparisons to animal law[267] or even to ancient slave status have been discussed[268] but are widely rejected as ethically problematic and legally inadequate for a transformative technology.[269]

In response to the limitations of analogical approaches, scholars have investigated granting AI full legal personality analogous to that of corporations.[270] Some scholars argue that in granting legal personality to AI, society's response,[271] its effect on current legal rules, and its necessity should be considered holistically in every case. Since there is no single type of AI, the decision to grant legal personality to different AI systems should be made on a case-by-case basis.[272] A more moderate suggestion advocates for creating a new category of 'limited personality' that would grant AI-specific, tailored rights and obligations[273] without conferring the full spectrum of rights.[274] On the other hand, some scholars focus on the argument that AI fundamentally lacks the necessary traits, such as moral agency, consciousness, and intentionality, for genuine legal personality.[275] Moreover, it is also claimed that granting legal personality to AI may be troublesome and that such a legal fiction could ultimately allow human actors to evade responsibility.[276]

---

[267] Bak (2018), TAAD, p. 223; Yünlü (2019), YÜHFD, p. 197, Sarı (2020), TBBD, pp. 271–273.

[268] Solum (1992), N.C. L. Rev., p. 1279; Chesterman (2020), ICLQ, p. 833; Sarı (2020), TBBD, p. 266, fn. 58; Dönmez (2025), AD, pp. 955–956.

[269] Bak (2018), TAAD, pp. 218–219; Akkurt (2019), UMD, p. 45; Üner (2020), p. 239; Dönmez Canseven (2021), p. 32.

[270] Laukyte (2019), p. 209 ff.; Karatepe Kaya (2021), HBV-HFD, pp. 85–87; Bora Çınar (2022), p. 135.

[271] The attribution of legal personality is ultimately a social artifact. Consequently, a lack of social recognition forms a primary obstacle to granting such status to AI. The legal personality accorded to various rivers and idols illustrates that the law has formally ratified a personality already constructed and demanded by society. Dremliuga et al. (2019), JPL, pp. 109–110.

[272] Dremliuga et al. (2019), JPL, p. 112.

[273] As it is, legal entities do not currently possess all the rights that natural persons have. For example, legal entities cannot marry, adopt children, or draw up wills. Dural and Öğüz (2020), pp. 248–254; Oğuzman et al. (2021), pp. 307–316.

[274] See references cited in Windorf (2025), p. 379, fn. 46. For a novel proposal of integrated personality for AI, see Ekici (2025), BHD, p. 338 ff. For information on proposal of 'limited legal capacity' for AI systems in Turkish law, see Çekin (2021), p. 54 ff.

[275] Solaiman (2017), Artif Intell Law, p. 157 and 175 ff.; Pagallo (2018), Information, p. 7 ff.

[276] Bryson et al. (2017), Artif Intell Law, p. 285 ff.

Simultaneously with the debate over legal personality, legal systems are striving to establish effective liability regimes for AI-caused damage. At both the international and national levels, civil liability for AI systems' acts and omissions is not yet adequately regulated. There is a gap in German law regarding the liability of AI systems.[277] Similarly, there is no specific liability regime in Turkish law governing the civil liability of AI systems.[278] At the European level,[279] the proposed EU AI Liability Directive[280] would have provided guidance.[281] However, the European Commission has abandoned it due to the "*No foreseeable agreement*," as cited in the Commission's 2025 work program.

The strict liability model, especially for high-risk AI systems, offers a compelling approach by imposing responsibility without requiring proof of fault.[282] This model may also prevent actors in the AI ecosystem from exploiting AI's black-box nature.[283] It also appears particularly suitable for high-risk AI applications where the technology's autonomy makes traditional fault-based analysis impractical.[284] A more established path relies on product liability frameworks, holding manufacturers responsible for damages caused by 'defective' AI systems,[285] as the expanded definition of 'product' in the updated Product Liability Directive[286] (PLD) places software,[287] such as AI systems, within the scope

---

277 Borges (2019), p. 149.

278 Güner (2020), UMD, p. 235. For a comprehensive examination of non-contractual civil liability of autonomous systems in Turkish law, see Polat (2022), p. 41 ff.

279 For a brief history of technology regulation in European level, see Bertolini (2025), pp. 16–25.

280 Proposal for a Directive of the European Parliament and of the Council on adapting non-contractual civil liability rules to artificial intelligence (AI Liability Directive), COM(2022) 496 final.

281 The European Parliament has proposed a distinctive operator liability model that explicitly rejects AI legal personality while imposing joint responsibility on both 'front-end operators' who deploy AI for specific purposes and 'back-end operators,' who provide technical support. For this proposal, see European Parliament resolution of 20 October 2020 with recommendations to the Commission on a civil liability regime for artificial intelligence (2020/2014(INL)).

282 Bertolini (2025), pp. 11–12.

283 Cowger (2023), JOLTI, p. 197.

284 Spindler (2019a), p. 135; Cowger (2023), JOLTI, p. 197.

285 Cf. Cowger (2023), JOLTI, p. 196.

286 The Directive (EU) 2024/2853 of the European Parliament and of the Council of 23 October 2024 on liability for defective products and repealing Council Directive 85/374/EEC (Text with EEA relevance).

287 Article 4(1) of the PLD.

of the product liability regime.[288] Moreover, the PLD marks a pivotal doctrinal departure by stipulating that the inherent unpredictability of certain products, including AI systems, cannot be claimed by manufacturers as a valid defence.[289]

Additional proposals include risk-management approaches that allocate liability to the party best positioned to manage particular risks, and hybrid, multilayered regimes[290] that combine elements of strict and fault-based liability tailored to different AI applications across various sectors. The present analysis under this heading is now concluded, as further exploration would extend beyond the parameters of this study.

2.1.2.2.2 Interim Result

Legal debates concerning the attribution of legal personality to AI and the establishment of a special civil liability regime for AI are expected to continue for a long time in Turkish and German law. Regulations regarding disruptive technologies such as AI should be enacted after lengthy doctrinal discussions. In this way, the right choices can be made in the law-making process. However, rapid progress and the spread of AI systems increase the risk of liability gaps. Therefore, transitional regulatory frameworks regarding AI systems must be implemented immediately to mitigate such risk. In the legislative process, lawmakers should balance the theoretical frameworks of the doctrine with practical realities. In this context, attribution of legal personality to AI constitutes a secondary problem. The real issue is determining a civil liability framework for the damages caused by AI systems, which are becoming more autonomous and unpredictable by the day. Consequently, the civil liability of actors in the AI ecosystem must be determined promptly to ensure legal certainty and predictability.

2.1.2.3 Comparative Analysis

2.1.2.3.1 De Lege Lata

2.1.2.3.1.1 Direct Membership

It is undisputed in Turkish legal doctrine that AI systems cannot serve as board members under Turkish corporate law, as they lack legal personality.[291] The appointment of an AI system as a member of the board of directors would be

---

[288] Bertolini (2025), p. 61.

[289] "*Consequently, a manufacturer that designs a product with the ability to develop unexpected behaviour should remain liable for behaviour that causes harm.*" Recital 32 of the PLD.

[290] Lohsse et al. (2019), p. 23.

[291] Dönmez Canseven (2021), p. 106; Eryiğit (2021), p. 106; Güçlütürk (2021), p. 459; Karatepe Kaya (2021), HBV-HFD, pp. 82–83; Metin (2021), p. 523; Karadeniz (2023),

contrary to Article 359 of the TCC, which explicitly restricts board membership to natural and legal persons,[292] categorically excluding AI systems from serving as directors.[293] Furthermore, in accordance with Article 340 of the TCC, which allows deviations from the provisions of the TCC regarding stock corporations only if the TCC expressly permits this, the inclusion of a clause in the articles of association stipulating that an AI system can be elected as a board member or the inclusion of an AI system on the board members' list at the corporation's incorporation or appointment of an AI system at a general assembly meeting will be invalid and will not be registered by the trade registry.[294]

In German stock corporation law, Section 76(3) of the AktG unequivocally mandates that only a "*natural person with unlimited legal capacity*" may serve as a member of the management board.[295] As AI systems lack personality, i.e. natural personality, and the requisite capacity to act, current German corporate law categorically prohibits the appointment of AI systems to the management board.[296] Any attempt to appoint an AI system as a board member would be void under Section 134 of the BGB[297] and Section 76(3) sentence 1 in conjunction with Section 23(5) of the AktG[298] for violating mandatory corporate law rules.

As the preceding analysis demonstrates, neither Turkish nor German corporate law currently possesses the requisite legal framework to permit the formal election of an AI system as a board member. However, under Turkish law, legal entities can serve as board members. Hence, having a legal personality

---

TAAD, p. 266; Kaya (2024), p. 89; Keskin (2024), p. 48; Seçer (2025), p. 101; Töre (2025), SÜHFD, p. 888; Varlı (2025), p. 244.

[292] See 2.1.1.2.1.

[293] Kaya (2024), p. 89.

[294] According to Art. 354 (1-g) of the TCC, corporation registration must include "*the names, surnames, business names, residences, and citizenships of the members of the board of directors and those authorized to represent the corporation.*" It is not possible for AI systems to provide such information.

[295] Möslein (2018), ZIP, pp. 207–208; Möslein (2025a), p. 630; Möslein (2025b), ERA Forum, p. 631. See 2.1.1.2.2.

[296] Fleischer (2018), AR, p. 121; Möslein (2018), ZIP, pp. 207–208; Strohn (2018), ZHR, p. 371; Weber et al. (2018), NZG, p. 1136; Lücke (2019), BB, p. 1988; Schubert (2019), p. 27; Zetzsche (2019), AG, p. 10; Noack (2021), p. 957; Hoerdemann-Napp and Pauli (2021), p. 127 ff; Linke (2021), p. 53; Dany (2022), BB, p. 2057; Lieder (2022), p. 333; Nowak (2022), p. 171; Calabro (2023), p. 42; Telle (2023), p. 45; Frey (2024), p. 49; Koch (2024), AktG, § 76, para. 141; Roth (2025), SSRN, p. 21. For a similar view regarding AI's inclusion to the board as a decision-maker, see Rolsing (2025), p. 334.

[297] Telle (2023), p. 45. Also see 2.1.1.2.2.

[298] Strohn (2018), ZHR, p. 371.

is sufficient for AI to become a board member under Turkish law, though this presents practical challenges.[299] Within the German corporate law framework, there are two principal pathways to AI board membership. The first requires concurrent legal reform[300] of permitting legal entities to serve as board members and granting AI a form of legal personality. The alternative pathway is the legislative creation of a novel, *sui generis* category of board membership, specifically designed for qualified AI systems, which would operate without requiring traditional legal personality. Nevertheless, even if these steps are taken in both legal systems, AI board members without adapted rights and obligations would not deliver the expected benefits and would pose accountability risks. In fact, such a status without an adapted legal structure may threaten the core principles of corporate management tailored for human board members.

As a legally creative alternative, it is proposed that AI systems with specific characteristics be granted organ capacity as a form of legal capacity.[301] Granting this legal capacity would enable AI systems to exercise the rights and assume the obligations necessary to become board members. For this purpose, when granting such capacity, the lawmaker should also determine the rights and obligations suited for this capacity. Just as not every legal entity is subject to all the rights and obligations intended for humans,[302] AI systems granted organ capacity could also be granted the rights and obligations deemed necessary for them.[303] Within the framework of this proposal, it could initially be attempted to grant AI systems organ capacity for corporations with narrow and well-defined operational scopes,[304] such as algorithmic trading corporations.[305] However, it should be noted that granting organ capacity to AI systems may be incompatible with the traditional enforcement and accountability framework designed for human board

[299] Dönmez Canseven (2021), p. 107; Eryiğit (2021), p. 106; Karatepe Kaya (2021), HBV-HFD, p. 82; Bora Çınar (2022), p. 185; Altaş (2023), SÜHFD, p. 1376; Keskin (2024), p. 46; Uğurerkan (2024), p. 74; Varlı (2025), p. 238 ff.

[300] Lieder (2022), p. 333.

[301] Windorf (2025), p. 388.

[302] Dural and Öğüz (2020), pp. 248–254; Oğuzman et al. (2021), pp. 307–316; Windorf (2025), p. 394.

[303] Windorf (2025), p. 394.

[304] Armour and Eidenmüller (2019), ZHR, p. 182; Linardatos (2022), ZIP, p. 156; Windorf (2025), p. 395. Cf. Calabro (2023), p. 80.

[305] Windorf (2025), p. 395. Cf. Zetzsche (2019), AG, p. 10.

members.[306] Therefore, even if AI is granted organ capacity, it would be appropriate to comprehensively update traditional frameworks to realise the expected benefits of AI and to mitigate the anticipated risks.

2.1.2.3.1.2 Indirect Membership via 'AI Housing' Legal Entity

Some authors in the doctrine posit that, in jurisdictions that allow legal persons to serve as board members, an AI system may theoretically become a board member if it were legally 'housed' within an eligible entity structure.[307] Corporations, e.g. board service provider corporations[308] that professionally provide such services, can also be appointed as board members to function as legal vessels for AI systems.[309] This proposal is a valid option under Turkish corporate law, as legal entities may serve as board members in stock corporations. A (AI-housing) legal entity, such as a stock corporation or limited liability company, can be established to 'house' the AI system and can be appointed as a board member.

Under TCC Article 359(2)'s model for legal entity board members, a designated human representative can be registered to execute board member duties by carrying out directives of the 'housed' AI system. There are two main concerns regarding the indirect appointment of AI systems to board seats. It may be questioned whether the natural person representing the legal entity on the board may avoid such a role, which requires acting on AI's instructions, due to concerns about personal liability. However, while the legal entity board member exercises its will (AI system's outputs in this context) through this natural person representative, liability for any damages resulting from the natural person representative's actions or omissions under TCC Articles 553 and subsequent provisions rests with the legal entity board member[310] (AI housing legal entity in this context), not the designated natural person representative.[311] Therefore, there will be no increase in the liability of the natural person representing the 'AI-housing' legal entity due to AI's integration. If the 'AI-housing' legal entity stands behind its

---

[306] Windorf (2025), p. 395.

[307] Bayern et al. (2017), UCLSTJ, p. 135 ff.; Kremer and Langenbucher (2024), p. 77, 3.13; Möslein (2025a), p. 631.

[308] For a detailed information about board service providers, see Bainbridge and Henderson (2018), p. 90 ff.

[309] Fatih Buğra Erdem in Karatepe Kaya et al. (2025), p. 84; Möslein (2025a), p. 631.

[310] Preamble to Art. 359(2) of the TCC. Akdağ Güney (2016), p. 45; Tekinalp (2020), pp. 235–236; Pulaşlı (2022), § 35, para. 179, p. 1241. Cf. Develi (2016), p. 149 ff.

[311] Nevertheless, the legal entity may seek recourse against the natural person in internal relations. Kırca et al. (2013), p. 407.

AI's decisions, it becomes directly accountable for any breaches.[312] Therefore, this proposed framework enables AI's indirect board membership from formal and liability-related perspectives in Turkish law.

A further concern arises from the potential for AI to be indirectly appointed to a board via a corporate board service provider. Given the significant technical and financial barriers to developing in-house AI governance systems, a specialised market for third-party AI board member services would likely emerge.[313] Appointing AI board service providers as corporate board members poses significant risks, as it would grant a handful of dominant AI service providers concentrated power. With access to sensitive information across multiple industries and influence over critical decisions, these firms could create systemic conflicts of interest.[314] To avoid such problems, specific statutory and contractual precautions, similar to behavioural or structural competition law commitments, can be taken.

This indirect model of appointing an AI through a 'housing' legal entity is incompatible with the German corporate law framework, as Section 76(3) of the AktG explicitly restricts membership of the management board to natural persons with full legal capacity, thereby excluding legal entities.[315] This exclusion of legal entities from board membership may constitute an infringement of their fundamental right to exercise a trade or profession freely. The constitutionality of such exclusion has been challenged on the grounds that it may violate fundamental rights. The German Constitutional Court (*Bundesverfassungsgericht*) will decide whether legal persons must also be permitted to act as board members.[316] Such a permission, via court decision or subsequent legal change, may allow indirect AI board membership via AI-housing legal entities under German corporate law, too.

2.1.2.3.2 De Lege Ferenda

2.1.2.3.2.1 In General

Apart from its *de lege lata* impossibility of (direct) AI board membership, as explained above, legal opinions regarding the *de lege ferenda* possibility of AI

[312] Fatih Buğra Erdem in Karatepe Kaya et al. (2025), p. 84.

[313] Dönmez Canseven (2021), p. 112.

[314] For a similar concern, see Çonkar in Karatepe Kaya et al. (2025), pp. 84–85. For information on the analogous concern regarding the 'monopolisation of intelligence,' see Hilb (2020), J Manag Gov, p. 860.

[315] See 2.1.1.2.2.

[316] Möslein (2025a), p. 630.

board membership in Turkish and German legal doctrine can be classified into different categories. Most scholars explain their views by conditioning their (opinions') validity on the current state of corporate law and AI systems, and make reservations regarding future legal adaptations and anticipated advancements in AI capabilities. A group of scholars who argue against the possibility of AI board membership contend that integrating AI members into corporate boards poses several challenges. These challenges can be categorised into two distinct types: those rooted in the fundamental doctrines of existing corporate law, which would necessitate significant legal reform and those stemming from inherent limitations in contemporary AI capabilities (technological realism).

From the corporate law's doctrinal perspective, scholars emphasise that corporate law rules are designed exclusively for human board members and their compatibility with AI's integration into corporate boards is questionable.[317] The growing use of algorithmic decision-making in corporate management requires updating corporate law provisions to address these new challenges.[318] For instance, granting management authority to AI requires resolving key legal debates on AI's legal personality and establishing formal board membership status for AI systems.[319] Instead of dealing with these debates, significant improvements in board structure could largely be realised through the strategic design and implementation of appropriate internal rules governing the use of AI systems. According to this view, reforming corporate law to allow legal entities, or digital legal entities, to become members of the management board of a stock corporation is not advisable since it is currently indeterminable whether a board model including AI board members would yield any comparative advantages over governance led by natural persons.[320]

Even if these reforms regarding AI's legal personality or board membership criteria are realised, questions persist regarding the legal authority and decision-making legitimacy of AI board members.[321] Moreover, it is argued that human board members may unconsciously defer to AI recommendations, potentially suppressing their independent judgment and expectations for internal discussion during board meetings.[322] Furthermore, the lack of precise accountability mechanisms for AI board members' decisions creates substantial governance risks, as

---

[317] Töre (2025), SÜHFD, p. 880.

[318] Varlı (2025), p. 240.

[319] Akın (2022), TAÜHFD, p. 21.

[320] Kremer and Langenbucher (2024), p. 77, 3.13.

[321] Kaya (2024), p. 85.

[322] Gramitto Ricci (2020), Cornell L. Rev., pp. 907–908.

traditional liability frameworks cannot easily sanction or remedy harmful algorithmic outcomes.[323] Hence, the inclusion of an AI as a board member alongside human members could create a liability loophole, as human directors might shift responsibility onto the AI board members.[324] In the light of these arguments, some authors consider AI's board membership undesirable,[325] even as a future legal consideration.[326]

From a technological realism perspective, scholars argue that AI systems should serve as board advisors rather than formal directors at their current stage of development.[327] The purely analytical, emotionless nature of AI may lead to blind spots in decision-making by neglecting human, social, and organisational nuances critical to effective corporation management.[328] Therefore, it is also argued that the need for AI board members should be considered only once AI achieves full autonomy, though even then, the complete replacement of human board members remains doubtful.[329]

A significant proportion of those in favour of the *de lege ferenda* possibility of AI board membership propose models or conditions for AI board members. The moderate view in Turkish legal doctrine argues that the most effective governance model combines human board members and AI on corporate boards,[330] and that such an interim hybrid boardroom model, requiring at least one human board member, may serve a critical transitional purpose of building institutional trust in AI decision-making through human oversight.[331] Moreover, hybrid boardrooms, where AI and human directors collaborate, can mitigate risks of biased or erroneous AI decisions by maintaining human oversight.[332] From a trust-building perspective, it is also proposed that AI board membership be phased in gradually,

---

[323] Kaya (2024), p. 85.

[324] İpekel Kayalı in Karatepe Kaya et al. (2025), p. 76.

[325] Gramitto Ricci (2020), Cornell L. Rev., pp. 907–908.

[326] Hoerdemann-Napp and Pauli (2021), p. 131 ff.; Thiel and Nazari-Khanachayi (2021), RDi, p. 142; Dany (2022), BB, 2056–2057.

[327] Metin (2021), p. 525; Akın (2022), TAÜHFD, pp. 19–20; Altaş (2023), SÜHFD, p. 1376.

[328] Altaş (2023), SÜHFD, p. 1374. AI lacks the capacity to access the full suite of human tools, such as intuition, that are integral to human judgment. Özer and Tomrukçu (2025), BATİDER, p. 265.

[329] Gözübüyük (2022), HBV-HFD, p. 152.

[330] Eryiğit (2021), p. 117.

[331] Dönmez Canseven (2021), p. 110.

[332] Keskin (2024), p. 51.

beginning with partial delegation of managerial authority to build trust before full board membership is granted.[333]

Some scholars from both legal systems are of the opinion that while current AI lacks the capability to fully replace human board members, the concepts of an 'AI-governed boardroom' represent, if not immediately,[334] future developments that may yet emerge in the field of corporate governance.[335] Meanwhile, even as technology assumes operational control, corporate structures will likely maintain human-centric legal frameworks and ceremonial boards to preserve the illusion of human oversight.[336]

A distinctive feature of the German doctrinal debate is its detailed conceptual exploration of AI board membership from a *de lege ferenda* perspective, analysing the essential concerns for such a development. The following sections provide a comparative analysis of these essential concerns by examining detailed discussions within German legal doctrine, complemented by Turkish scholarly perspectives. Each subsection addresses a specific argument under its respective heading. Discussions on these essential concerns provide solid guidance regarding the holistic examination of the *de lege ferenda* appointment of AI board members.

2.1.2.3.2.2 Examination of the Essential Concerns Regarding AI's Board Membership

2.1.2.3.2.2.1 The Need for Structural Reconfiguration of Corporate Structures for Enforcing Fiduciary Duties and Ensuring Accountability

Corporate law includes structural and behavioural measures to ensure compliance with board members' fiduciary duties. However, these measures were designed with human board members in mind. There are significant behavioural differences between human and prospective AI board members. The diligence and legal compliance that human board members will demonstrate in fulfilling their duties cannot be predicted or determined beforehand. Therefore, *ex post* measures, such as personal liability regimes or liability lawsuits, are stipulated for human board members. Because AI systems are algorithmically determinable in the creation stage, *ex ante* measures for AI board members would be more beneficial and effective. Hence, the appointment of AI board members may force a strategic realignment in corporate law by placing *ex ante* (pre-emptive) regulatory

[333] Dönmez Canseven (2021), p. 108.

[334] Calabro (2023), p. 21; Kaya (2024), p. 87.

[335] Karatepe Kaya (2021), HBV-HFD, p. 77; Özer and Tomrukçu (2025), BATİDER, p. 267.

[336] Bora Çınar (2022), pp. 220–221.

strategies,[337] such as the review of underlying algorithms before and during their deployment, the codification of legal rules governing director behaviour[338] and the adaptation of incentive systems.[339]

Even if all necessary measures were taken, a liability gap[340] would remain because AI lacks a personality and cannot be held accountable. Thus, it is argued that AI board membership's incompatibility with corporate law's foundational accountability principles[341] necessitates fundamental legislative reform. However, it is also argued that alternative accountability mechanisms, such as mandatory insurance,[342] shareholder-approved opt-in models,[343] contractual liability for outsourced AI systems, and the requirement of at least one human board member to maintain liability, for AI board members, can be established to substitute for traditional personal liability.[344] According to this enabling perspective, if appropriate safeguards are implemented, the potential use of AI in management boards does not fundamentally conflict with conventional corporate structures of compensation principles or behavioural control requirements.[345]

2.1.2.3.2.2.2 Risks Regarding the Principle of Independent Personal Judgment in Collegial Governance

According to corporate law principles, particularly in terms of fulfilling the duty of care, decision-making processes on boards must involve discussion and negotiation[346] among members of equal standing, and each member must vote independently without being subject to any instructions. Non-compliance with these duties not only establishes liability for flawed decision-making procedures but also fundamentally impairs the doctrinal basis for holding members personally accountable for the resulting substantive decisions. If an AI system becomes

---

337 Möslein (2025a), p. 633.

338 Möslein (2025a), p. 633.

339 Lieder (2022), pp. 334–335.

340 Telle (2023), p. 47.

341 Kaya (2024), p. 85.

342 Dönmez Canseven (2021), p. 115; Karatepe Kaya (2021), HBV-HFD, p. 83; Karadeniz (2023), TAAD, p. 280; Bora Çınar (2022), p. 204; Keskin (2024), p. 48; Seçer (2025), p. 114.

343 Amour and Eidenmüller (2019), ZHR, p. 185; Becker and Pordzik (2020), ZfPW, p. 355; Calabro (2023), p. 45.

344 Calabro (2023), p. 46.

345 Becker and Pordzik (2020), ZfPW, p. 354; Calabro (2023), p. 50.

346 For an analysis of the potential benefits and risks within the board's collective decision-making framework, see Petrin (2019), Colum. Bus. L. Rev., p. 999 ff.

a board member, problems may arise regarding the principle of independent personal judgment in collegial governance.

Firstly, the independence of an AI board member's decisions is questionable[347] due to a lack of will.[348] Hence, their decisions may be subject to interference from third parties who program, train, and correct the AI, or from human board members who determine the goals the AI board member should pursue.[349] This situation will not only prevent the AI board member from making independent decisions and bearing the responsibility that arises from them, but will also create inequality between human and AI board members within the board.[350] Conversely, the integration of AI directors could also pressure human board members to automatically adopt AI's outputs, making it challenging for them to exercise independent judgment within their legal duties.[351]

Furthermore, it is questionable how AI board members will participate in the discussions and negotiations that should occur when making board decisions. If AI board members cannot communicate with human board members, the collaboration, discussions, or negotiations required by corporate law to make decisions that best serve the corporation's interests will not occur,[352] and the duty of care in this regard will be violated. While doctrinal criticisms on this matter[353] generally remain significant, with the proliferation of AI systems capable of written or verbal communication with humans (such as ChatGPT), it is beginning to lose its status as a barrier to AI board membership.

2.1.2.3.2.2.3 Sector-Specific Concerns

When evaluating AI board membership, corporations' business areas should also be assessed for the contextual suitability of AI board members. For example, the appointment of an AI board member to a single-member board of a corporation operating solely in a specialised, individual field may meet with less doctrinal resistance. Furthermore, for financial firms operating in big data and

---

347 For the premise that current AI systems are not suitable for making independent corporate decisions, see, among others, Lieder (2022), p. 335.

348 Calabro (2023), p. 57.

349 Calabro (2023), pp. 56–57.

350 Calabro (2023), pp. 58–59.

351 Gramitto Ricci (2020), Cornell L. Rev., pp. 901–902 and 907–908; Eryiğit (2021), pp. 117–118; Kaya (2024), p. 85; Seçer (2025), p. 101.

352 Calabro (2023), pp. 64–65; Telle (2023), p. 49. On the importance of human and AI board member interaction for balancing each other's contributions in corporate decision-making processes, see Ahern (2024), p. 428.

353 Telle (2023), p. 49.

prediction-based sectors, such as algorithmic trading and fund management, AI board members could be considered more functionally viable and, therefore, a more conceivable governance option.[354] However, corporations engaged in activities that require human judgment and creativity, and that do not conduct data-intensive work, will have less need for AI board members. However, it should be noted that, with the digitalisation of markets, the growing functionality of big data, and the advancement of AI systems, data-driven work is increasing across almost every corporation, loosening the selective criteria for AI board membership regarding data insensitivity.

2.1.2.3.2.2.4 Concerns Regarding Entrepreneurial Leadership and Managerial Prerogative

Board members, considering the level of diligence expected of them, must possess management and leadership competencies that enable them to effectively and ethically identify and achieve short- and medium-term interim goals to achieve the long-term core objectives of the corporations they manage. It is possible for AI board members to effectively and ethically pursue the traditional board objectives, even if their approach differs methodologically from that of human board members.[355] However, doctrine identifies a difference between human board members and AI board members in terms of entrepreneurial management and leadership. According to this view, while AI board members can currently ensure the effective management of the corporation, their limited holistic and creative reasoning abilities, along with their lack of creativity and strategic intuition,[356] prevent them from fulfilling the entrepreneurial management and leadership roles required of corporation management.[357] However, it can be argued that this obstacle to AI board membership will be eliminated in the future as AI systems acquire the skills currently lacking.[358]

2.1.2.3.2.2.5 Concerns Regarding Operational Continuity and Uninterrupted Governance

The potential for disruptions in the functionality or accessibility of an AI system raises critical questions about corporate operational stability and the uninterrupted

[354] Möslein (2025a), p. 629.

[355] Calabro (2023), p. 62.

[356] Amour and Eidenmüller (2019), ZHR, p. 181; Calabro (2023), p. 63; Özer and Tomrukçu (2025), BATİDER, p. 265.

[357] Calabro (2023), p. 65.

[358] Karadeniz (2023), TAAD, p. 271.

fulfilment of directorial duties. In this context, when an AI system requires reprogramming or retraining, or when a technical malfunction occurs, these processes may interrupt the AI board member's performance.[359] Furthermore, concerns are expressed that knowledge and experience transfer during the handover process may create problems due to the potential black-box problem.[360] For these reasons, AI board membership may potentially paralyse the corporation's management body and, consequently, the corporation.[361]

In corporate law, the board is considered a permanent body that operates continuously,[362] without being limited to meetings. Therefore, the aforementioned concern about creating a management vacuum or paralysing the corporation should be carefully evaluated. However, the situation of human board members in this regard should also be considered. Given that human board members may temporarily be unable to attend board meetings due to illness or other reasons or permanently leave their positions, it becomes clear that this concern is not unique to prospective AI board members. Similarly, the transfer of knowledge and experience between appointed and departing human board members typically occurs through written documents, such as previous decisions or minutes. Therefore, technological solutions could be developed to allow AI board members to share knowledge and experience with prior or future board members. In practice, the potential problems in these regards are no greater than those that might arise among human board members.

2.1.2.3.2.2.6 Concerns Regarding Trust Relationships

In corporate law, as with other organs and stakeholders, board members must trust each other. At the heart of good corporate governance lies the strength of these interlocking trust relationships. Therefore, an AI board member must also be a part of these trust relationships. A general trust problem with AI systems already exists, particularly those that exhibit autonomous characteristics and low predictability. Initiatives, such as the EU's Trustworthy AI,[363] establish specific principles to address this issue[364] and may provide guidance for assessing

---

[359] Calabro (2023), p. 52.

[360] Calabro (2023), p. 53.

[361] Calabro (2023), pp. 51–53.

[362] İmregün (2001), p. 325; Tekinalp (2011), p. 165; Üçışık and Çelik (2013), p. 375; Kayar (2018), p. 438; Çamoğlu in Poroy et al. (2025), para. 520b, p. 355.

[363] Communication from the Commission to the European Parliament, the Council, the European Economic and Social Committee and the Committee of the Regions: Building trust in human-centric artificial intelligence (COM/2019/168 final).

[364] European Commission (2019), p. 4 ff.

and building trust in AI board members, since no initiative directly addressing this issue within the context of corporate law has yet emerged. Hence, it has been discussed that AI board membership can be problematic for trust in AI.[365] However, a compelling counterargument reframes this issue by distinguishing between interpersonal trust and systemic trust. Trust in an AI system is not grounded in personal character or relationships, but rather in the transparency, predictability, and verifiable reliability of its underlying algorithmic architecture and governance protocols. Therefore, other corporate bodies, stakeholders, and human board members can, through their own means, establish this trust in AI.[366]

2.1.2.3.2.2.7 Concerns Regarding the Mandatory Disclosure of Director Information in Public Registers

Under corporate law, information about board members, such as their names, surnames, dates of birth, places of residence, and citizenship, must be disclosed during registration[367] to enable third parties to assess risks and opportunities related to the corporation and its management.[368] However, this mandatory framework is not suitable for AI board members since such information does not exist for AI systems. As an alternative, some features of the AI board member, such as assigned responsibilities and predicted risks,[369] or, if an external service is purchased, information about its provider, may be disclosed to the public through reasonable means, such as the corporation's website. Furthermore, if an AI system is appointed as a board member, this status may be stated in the registration and in the corporation's title. It will ensure that third parties who have or will have relationships with a corporation that has an AI board member are informed, achieving the same goal as sharing information about human board members. Hence, the purpose of the relevant legal regulations is met, and such formalities should not constitute an obstacle to AI board membership.[370] However, it is important to note that while any third party can draw conclusions about the corporation and its management through a brief investigation of the information provided about human board members, the information provided about AI board members should also be sufficient to draw these conclusions.

---

[365] Calabro (2023), p. 67; Ahern (2024), p. 428.

[366] For a detailed information on trust relations between AI board member and other corporate bodies, see Calabro (2023), pp. 69–74.

[367] Art. 354 (1-g) of the TCC; §§ 39(1) and 81(1) of the AktG.

[368] Calabro (2023), p. 74.

[369] Calabro (2023), p. 76.

[370] Calabro (2023), p. 76.

2.1.2.3.2.3 Alternative Roles for AI in the Board

An AI system's appointment as an independent or observer board member is proposed in the doctrine.[371] According to these proposals, AI systems free of human limitations could create a new type of independent board membership, free of human weaknesses and external influence.[372] Establishing an independent AI board member requires overcoming the same legal hurdles as establishing an ordinary AI board membership. Hence, there is a need for strong arguments regarding the specific benefits of establishing independent AI board membership. In the same vein, establishing observer AI board member status also requires strong arguments for its particular benefits that differentiate it from AI use as an aid, since corporations' management is always free to use AI systems as assistants to provide advises.[373] In fact, granting a formal observer board member role to AI systems may complicate boards' work and liability structures without providing a substantive benefit.

Like independent board membership, another option discussed in the legal doctrine to utilise AI in the board decision-making process is employing AI as an independent tiebreaker in boardroom disputes when human board members reach deadlocks.[374] However, current TCC provisions do not allow such an option. Even the chairperson's vote cannot be designated as a privileged vote.[375] In the event of a tie in voting, the issue will be postponed until the next meeting. Should a second tie occur at the subsequent meeting, the proposal will be considered rejected.[376] Hence, the utilisation of AI systems as a tiebreaker in board decisions is not legally possible. Even though it was not explicitly stipulated in the TCC, a tie in the voting means that half of the board members are not in favour of the resolution. If these board members are not convinced in the second meeting in favour of the resolution, the resolution needs to wait until the necessary number of board members are in favour. The board member's duty of care requires that a board member vote for a resolution if s/he believes that this resolution is beneficial for the corporation. This duty of care also requires discussion at board meetings. Ultimately, providing an AI system with a tie-breaking vote

---

[371] Bora Çınar (2022), p. 187 and 235; Uğurerkan (2024), p. 105.

[372] Bora Çınar (2022), p. 187.

[373] Telle (2023), pp. 51–52; Casper and Möslein (2025), ZGR, p. 889. For the use of AI as a right, see 3.2.2.

[374] Noack (2019a), ZHR, p. 136; Noack (2021), p. 957; Telle (2023), p. 81; Windorf (2025), p. 400.

[375] Art. 340 of the TCC prevents such a designation in the articles of association. Pulaşlı (2022), § 35, para. 280, p. 1283; Çamoğlu in Poroy et al. (2025), para. 533, p. 374.

[376] Art. 390 (3) of the TCC.

would be against the *de lege ferenda* corporate governance structure by creating a privileged class of board membership and undermining the efficient deliberations among board members to reach reconciliation.

The potential role of AI as a tiebreaker is also rejected in German legal doctrine because it would violate the natural-person requirement for board members, the management board's non-delegable management responsibility and the prohibition on binding delegation of decision-making authority to external systems.[377] Moreover, such a tie-breaking role for AI systems may create a significant risk of blind reliance on algorithmic recommendations.[378] As a consequence, AI systems cannot have a position to unilaterally determine a final board decision by superseding the voting authority of board members, even in deadlock situations.

2.1.2.4 Interim Result

Under the current statutory frameworks of both Turkish and German corporate law, the direct appointment of an AI system as a corporate board member is legally impermissible because AI systems lack legal personality. If AI systems gain legal personality, this would pave the way for AI systems to become board members under Turkish law, which permits legal entities to serve as board members. However, under German law, only natural persons can become board members; therefore, granting AI systems legal personality would not be sufficient for these systems to become board members. Hence, to ensure AI systems become board members under German law, not only must AI systems be granted legal personality, but legal amendments must also be enacted to allow legal persons to become board members.

An 'AI housing' legal entity can be operationalised to realise indirect board membership of an AI system. In this context, a legal entity eligible for board membership may be appointed to the board while an AI system is integrated into it. This formal board member legal entity may act on the directives of the 'housed AI'. However, such an indirect approach is only possible in jurisdictions that allow legal entities to serve as board members. Therefore, this alternative approach may be functional in Turkish corporate law, but it would not be viable in German corporate law.

Given AI's rapid development and widespread use across various domains, it is likely that regulations to realise AI's board membership will be enacted in the near future. In such a legislative process, concerns discussed in the legal doctrine, such as independent personal judgment, collegial and uninterrupted

[377] Noack (2021), p. 957; Telle (2023), p. 82; Windorf (2025), p. 400.

[378] Noack (2021), p. 957; Windorf (2025), p. 401.

governance, operational continuity, sector-specific suitability, internal and external trust relations, and mandatory disclosure requirements must be addressed. Mere permission of AI's appointment as a board member would not be enough to achieve the expected benefits of AI. Therefore, the current corporate frameworks designed for human board members must be comprehensively reformed to involve prospective AI board members and account for their characteristics. Otherwise, systematic incompatibilities may create risks, especially regarding liability structures. After the necessary comprehensive reform is implemented, a gradual process for appointing AI board members should be phased in through pilot applications, primarily in data-driven corporations, and an initial allowance for hybrid boards in which human and AI board members work together. Thus, unpredictable application risks may be addressed before they turn into actual aggravated damages.

AI as a Strategic Asset: The Board's Right to Use, Authority to Delegate, and Potential Duty to Integrate

3

3.1 In General

Since AI systems support strategic decision-making across key corporate areas, including investment analysis, personnel selection, procurement optimisation, production planning, pricing strategies, sales forecasting, and marketing campaigns,[1] AI-powered boards gain a competitive advantage through accelerated strategic decision-making.[2] Therefore, AI is increasingly being integrated into board operations to enhance efficiency[3] without directly making the final decisions.[4] Real-world implementations, such as OnBoard AI,[5] Board Intelligence,[6] Diligent Boards,[7] and

[1] Kaya (2024), p. 83; Uğurerkan (2024), p. 50; Möslein (2025b), ERA Forum, p. 630.

[2] Eroğlu and Karatepe Kaya (2022), EBOR, p. 543; Gözübüyük (2022), HBV-HFD, p. 143; Nowak (2022), p. 67; Telle (2023), p. 34; Erdem Aladağ (2024), Denetişim, p. 19; Ustahaliloğlu (2025), CLGR, p. 124.

[3] Möslein (2022), p. 74.

[4] Dönmez Canseven (2021), p. 97.

[5] OnBoard. Available at https://www.onboardmeetings.com/onboard-ai/. (Last accessed: 25.12.2025).

[6] Board Intelligence. Available at https://www.boardintelligence.com/ai. (Last accessed: 25.12.2025).

[7] Diligent Boards. Available at https://www.diligent.com/products/boards. (Last accessed: 25.12.2025).

S. T. İnce, *Artificial Intelligence and Corporation Management*, Juridicum – Schriftenreihe zum Wirtschafts-, Unternehmens- und Bankrecht / Series on Business, Corporate and Banking Law, https://doi.org/10.1007/978-3-658-52672-6_3

Loomion,[8] demonstrate AI's capacity to enhance decision-making while preserving human oversight.[9]

While the adoption of AI systems offers corporations a significant competitive edge through enhanced entrepreneurial advantages and operational efficiency, this technological shift simultaneously introduces regulatory challenges.[10] As part of these challenges, this chapter will examine whether AI integration into corporate management can be considered a right or an obligation in Turkish and German corporate law comparatively.

3.2 From Personal Tool to Structural Component: A Typology of AI Use by Boards

Boards can leverage AI systems across three main application categories. The first form of utilisation entails board members' private use of AI systems to gather information, conduct analyses, and otherwise inform their personal stance on matters before the board meetings. For example, regarding an investment decision to be discussed and voted on at the upcoming board meeting, each board member can use AI systems individually to obtain information and analyses to inform their decision-making. This type of use is no different from a board member's personal use of any technological tool. Therefore, such AI use will not be evident within the corporation structure but will be considered an individual board member's own way of obtaining information. There are no obstacles preventing board members from using AI systems in this way.[11]

Another way to use AI on the board is to take a board decision to integrate advisory AI systems into the board structure, either continuously or *ad hoc*. For example, by purchasing an AI system, the board could enable board members to access information and documents related to decisions before or during board meetings, and to generate analyses and insights based on this information and documentation. Although this type of AI use is considered advisory, it falls within the scope of corporate law, unlike individual board members' use of AI, as it relies on a board decision and results in integration into the board structure.

[8] Loomion. Available at https://loomion.ch/en/. (Last accessed: 25.12.2025).

[9] Dönmez Canseven (2021), pp. 97–100.

[10] Möslein (2022), p. 74.

[11] Directors must exercise caution to avoid breaching confidentiality when using external AI. Corporations can enforce policies that prohibit the sharing of privileged documents with any third party, including AI systems.

Therefore, the legal qualification of such a decision regarding the use of AI within corporate law must be determined. A comparative legal analysis of this matter is provided below.[12]

A more advanced integration occurs when the board vests an AI system with delegated authority, empowering it to execute certain complex tasks and make subsidiary decisions within a pre-defined mandate. This use of AI is further examined legally within the separate structure of the delegation system.[13]

3.3 Board's Right to Use AI

3.3.1 Determination of the Competent Organ for the Decision to Use AI

When integrating advisory AI into boards, the first question is which body of the corporation has decision-making power.[14] Since the decision to integrate AI into management decision-making processes is itself a strategic governance choice that may alter organisational management dynamics,[15] the competent organ must be determined.

3.3.1.1 Board as the Competent Organ

In Turkish law, the board of directors holds expansive authority over all corporate transactions and operations not legally reserved for the general assembly, encompassing all necessary business activities under TCC Article 374(1). This provision establishes a 'presumption of board authority' in stock corporations.[16] Since the establishment of management organisation as one of the inalienable and non-delegable duties reserved for a corporation's board of directors, the general assembly should not intervene in the decisions regarding AI integration into the management. However, the doctrine also argues that decisions regarding the deployment of transformative AI systems should be incorporated into the articles of association, similar to the adaptation of communication technologies for

[12] See 3.3.

[13] See 3.4.

[14] Windorf (2025), p. 123.

[15] Telle (2023), p. 53.

[16] Ayhan et al. (2022), p. 265; Gözübüyük (2022), HBV-HFD, p. 146.

meetings or decisions,[17] which requires amendments to the articles of association in Turkish corporate law.[18] As another option, the doctrine advises that, until legal clarity emerges, submitting critical AI-related decisions to the general assembly,[19] although not legally mandated, reflects sound practice.[20]

In German law, it is generally accepted that decision-making power regarding AI integration into corporation management belongs to the management board (in principle), as the management of the corporation is the board's responsibility and the decision to integrate AI into management decision-making processes is itself a strategic governance choice that fundamentally alters organisational management dynamics.[21] German jurisprudence requires shareholder approval only when management actions substantially affect shareholders' membership rights and their financial interests embodied in their share ownership. Since AI integration does not meaningfully impair shareholder interests, such technological adoption falls within the board's autonomous competence.[22] While the management board is not legally required to seek shareholder approval for AI adoption, it may voluntarily submit such measures to a general assembly resolution under Section 119(2) of the AktG.[23] Moreover, under Section 111(4) sentence 2 of the AktG, the supervisory board retains significant oversight authority over management decisions involving AI adoption, including the power to impose consent requirements, either through standing rules of procedure or via *ad hoc* resolutions.[24] However, such interventions must be reasonable and must not undermine the management board's core operational autonomy.

[17] For a comprehensive legal analysis regarding the technical and procedural requirements for adapting communication technologies in the context of corporate board meetings under the TCC, see Gürpınar (2013), MÜHF-HAD, p. 1111 ff.

[18] Bora Çınar (2022), p. 129.

[19] The board of directors may submit certain matters within its jurisdiction to a non-binding, consultative vote at the general assembly. This vote, as a rule, does not relieve the board of its liabilities. Kırca et al. (2013), p. 536; Akdağ Güney (2016), p. 449; Kaşak (2019), p. 341; Çamlı (2024), p. 66–67. For a general information regarding the legal effect of a consultative vote by the general assembly on subsequent directorial liability claims arising from the adopted decision, see Kaşak (2019), pp. 351–359.

[20] Bora Çınar (2022), p. 131.

[21] Lieder (2022), p. 335; Telle (2023), p. 53; Rolsing (2025), p. 494.

[22] Telle (2023), p. 55.

[23] Telle (2023), p. 55; Rolsing (2025), pp. 501–502.

[24] Telle (2023), p. 57; Rolsing (2025), pp. 503–505.

3.3.1.2 Possibility of Delegation

Article 375(1-b) of the TCC explicitly recognises the establishment of a management organisation as one of the inalienable and non-delegable duties reserved for a corporation's board.[25] Determining AI's role and implementation scope within a corporation is a fundamental management prerogative that cannot be fully delegated, as it directly affects strategic direction and fiduciary responsibilities.[26] However, the preparatory work or execution phase can be delegated to third parties, provided that the board acts diligently in selecting, instructing, and monitoring these delegates.[27]

In German law, first, whether a specific task on the integration of AI systems constitutes a core management task or an executive management task must be assessed,[28] since the result of this assessment will determine its delegability to subordinate levels.[29] This determination is inherently contextual and risk-proportional. While not every operational use requires board approval, in specific cases, particularly those of high significance and elevated risk, the choice to implement AI may rise to the level of a core management task.[30]

The classification of AI deployment decisions within corporate governance structures can be guided by existing frameworks for information technology and digital infrastructure, which increasingly fall under the core management tasks of the management board due to their strategic importance.[31] The deployment of AI systems introduces unique and amplified risks that distinguish them from conventional information technology infrastructure.[32] Hence, the prevailing position in the German legal doctrine views that AI adoption constitutes a core management task, given its strategic implications for corporate governance.[33] The management board breaches its duties if it improperly delegates AI adoption-related decision-making that significantly impacts corporate strategy or data protection.[34]

---

[25] Kaya (2024), p. 63.

[26] Varlı (2025), pp. 261–262.

[27] See 3.4.2.2. and 3.4.2.3.

[28] Langenbucher (2023a), ZHR, 725 ff.; Rolsing (2025), pp. 506; Windorf (2025), pp. 127–130.

[29] Windorf (2025), p. 127. Also, see 3.4.2.2.

[30] Casper and Möslein (2025), ZGR, p. 878.

[31] Spindler (2019b), ECFR, pp. 132–133. For different doctrinal views, see references in Windorf (2025), p. 127, fn. 26.

[32] Windorf (2025), p. 131.

[33] Li (2022), p. 88; Lieder (2022), p. 337; Telle (2023), p. 53; Windorf (2025), p. 135. Cf. Rolsing (2025), p. 318 and 506–508.

[34] Li (2022), p. 88.

In contrast, preparatory work, implementation, and technical specifications may be delegated to streamline operations, provided the management board retains ultimate authority.[35]

3.3.2 Comparative Analysis of the Board's Right to Use AI

There are no explicit restrictions in either Turkish or German corporate law that prevent boards from employing advisory AI systems in corporate management.[36] Hence, boards in both legal systems are legally permitted to utilise AI for a range of duties, from basic administrative functions like generating reports and compiling statistics to more complex applications, such as strategic planning, financial analysis, and determining corporate objectives, provided the board retains ultimate authority as the master of the decision-making process since suggestions and recommendations from the AI systems are not legally binding.[37] In other words, the board may employ algorithmic outputs as advisory inputs while preserving its decision-making prerogative.[38] When AI contributes only a subordinate, informative element to the board's deliberative process, as one data point among many, the fundamental nature of the board's decision remains unchanged[39] since AI's such utilisation leaves the board's evaluative and decisional autonomy intact.[40] Consequently, utilising AI outputs as an informational resource in corporate decision-making does not inherently constitute an abdication of the board's fiduciary authority.[41] The internal directive issued pursuant to Article 367 of the TCC can explicitly address the use of AI[42] by the board itself and by its committees. Likewise, the management board in German law

---

[35] Li (2022), p. 88 and 130–131; Lieder (2022), p. 337; Rolsing (2025), p. 318 and 512–513; Windorf (2025), p. 136. Also, see 3.4.2.2.

[36] Lieder (2022), p. 335; Frey (2024), p. 45; Kaya (2024), p. 89; Langenbucher (2025), SSRN, p. 9.

[37] Zetzsche (2019), AG, p. 7; Dönmez Canseven (2021), p. 99; Akın (2022), TAÜHFD, pp. 19–20; Gözübüyük (2022), HBV-HFD, p. 154; Altaş (2023), SÜHFD, p. 1376; Telle (2023), p. 42; Kaya (2024), p. 89; Fleischer in BeckOGK (2025), AktG, § 76, para. 77 and 78; Özer and Tomrukçu (2025), BATİDER, p. 241.

[38] Varlı (2025), p. 250.

[39] Langenbucher (2023a), ZHR, p. 727.

[40] Calabro (2023), pp. 89–90.

[41] Langenbucher (2025), SSRN, p. 11.

[42] Varlı (2025), p. 268.

may adopt an internal information directive[43] mandating AI integration for specific decision-making processes, exercising its self-organisational authority under Section 76(1) of the AktG.[44]

Nevertheless, the unique features of AI systems and human board members' attitudes toward AI may threaten the fundamental nature of the board's decision-making process, as the board may rely uncritically on AI outputs. The board members should consider AI outputs in an advisory nature and make decisions based on their own knowledge and experience to fulfil their duty of care. Otherwise, while board members may theoretically use AI systems as an advisory service and make their own decisions, they will, in reality, merely approve AI outputs. This rubber-stamping would thereby violate the governance structure prescribed by corporate law and the duty of care imposed upon them. Therefore, it is argued that when boards utilise AI, their adherence to AI's guidance must be carefully assessed against their fundamental duty of care.[45]

Apart from the board's direct use of AI, committees can be established and instructed to utilise AI systems. Committees serve as specialised advisory bodies to the boards, enhancing their professional functioning[46] without assuming management authority.[47] Their primary functions are to facilitate corporation management and improve its efficiency by ensuring optimal board performance.[48] Committees enhance board governance by providing expert-backed recommendations that discourage arbitrary decisions,[49] while fostering accountability through structured deliberation. Recognising that board members cannot be experts in all facets of a corporation's operations, committees serve as critical tools to bridge knowledge gaps by providing targeted insights and technical expertise.[50] Since AI systems are reshaping approaches to risk management and regulatory compliance,[51] they can support specific committees in their assigned missions, such as

---

[43] Telle (2023), p. 79.

[44] Telle (2023), p. 79.

[45] Özer and Tomrukçu (2025), BATİDER, p. 241.

[46] Metin (2021), p. 199.

[47] Arslanlı (1960), p. 118; Kırca in Kırca et al. (2013), p. 479; Demir (2016), p. 85; Kayar (2018), p. 451; Kalender (2024), p. 62; Çamoğlu in Poroy et al. (2025), para. 535, p. 379.

[48] Kayar (2018), p. 451.

[49] Tekinalp (2003), p. 235.

[50] Metin (2021), p. 202.

[51] Özer and Tomrukçu (2025), BATİDER, p. 240.

financial oversight, anomaly detection and predictive risk analysis.[52] Hence, it is proposed to supplement DCGK with a recommendation regarding the use of AI in risk management and internal control.[53]

While the use of AI as an auxiliary tool is legally recognised as a right in both legal doctrines, some authors argue that using AI systems lacking explainable features, due to the black-box problem, incompatible with the board's duty of care.[54] Such a restrictive approach is unconvincing in several respects.[55] First, the boards must be free to determine the corporation's management structure and choose appropriate information sources for decision-making.[56] Furthermore, the black-box nature primarily concerns the training phase of AI systems, and it has been observed that these systems generally produce understandable and stable results during deployment.[57] Additionally, boards seeking expert opinions are not required to know the technical details that led to the expert opinion, nor should they be expected to understand the technical causalities associated with AI outputs. Instead, it would be more appropriate for boards to evaluate AI outputs based on their own knowledge and experience, and for technical experts to conduct reviews to address any potential issues with AI systems.[58] Finally, it has been observed that AI systems like ChatGPT have recently reached a stage where they can communicate with their users and explain the reasons for their outputs.[59] For all these reasons, categorically prohibiting boards from using alleged non-explainable AI systems would, without a sound reason, deprive them of the benefits these systems provide.[60] Hence, a ban on the use of unexplainable AI is not recommended in the doctrine.[61] A case-by-case assessment, rather than broad prohibitions regarding the use of AI as an auxiliary by the boards, is necessary.[62] As a compromise, if the AI systems used by boards are deemed

[52] Kaya (2024), p. 89; Kremer and Langenbucher (2024), pp. 88–89; İpekel Kayalı in Karatepe Kaya et al. (2025), p. 71; Sopacı Öztuna in Karatepe Kaya et al. (2025), p. 73.

[53] Kremer and Langenbucher (2024), p. 88, 3.31.

[54] Dubovitskaya and Buchholz (2023), ECFR, p. 808 ff. Although not in favour of prohibition, recommendation for a cautious use and implementation of explainability methods, see Özer and Tomrukçu (2025), BATİDER, p. 266 ff.

[55] Langenbucher (2023a), ZHR, p. 724 and 734; Casper and Möslein (2025), ZGR, p. 881.

[56] Telle (2023), p. 42 and 56.

[57] Windorf (2025), p. 160.

[58] Casper and Möslein (2025), ZGR, p. 882.

[59] Casper and Möslein (2025), ZGR, p. 881.

[60] Telle (2023), p. 42.

[61] Kremer and Langenbucher (2024), p. 79, 3.20.

[62] Kremer and Langenbucher (2024), pp. 79–81, 3.20–3.22.

insufficiently explainable, integrating already developed explainability methods[63] into AI systems could be provided at the board's discretion.

3.3.3 Interim Result

Despite the absence of specific statutory provisions, the board of directors under Turkish law and the management board under German law retain the inherent managerial competence to decide on the integration of AI into corporation management. While Turkish law provides the board of directors with statutory protection over its competencies, the German dual-board model allows the supervisory board to intervene in the management board's decisions regarding the integration of AI into corporation management in a reasonable manner through rules of procedure or *ad hoc* decisions, without undermining the management board's right to autonomous management.

The integration of AI into corporation management may constitute a core management task when it carries strategic implications for the corporation's direction and the board's fiduciary responsibilities. In such cases, the substantive decision-making authority regarding AI's integration into corporation management is non-delegable under Turkish and German corporate law. However, tasks related to the execution of preparatory and operational processes for AI's integration into corporate management can be delegated under both legal frameworks, provided the board retains ultimate authority.

Neither Turkish nor German corporate law contains an explicit statutory prohibition on the integration of advisory AI systems into corporation management. Doctrinal arguments for categorical exclusion of specific AI systems due to their black-box problem are diminishing in relevance, given the gradual decline in the explainability problem in AI systems. Moreover, boards' inherent discretionary authority over managerial structures and information-gathering methodologies renders such a categorical exclusion untenable. Consequently, boards in Turkish and German corporations may integrate AI systems into management, either directly or through committees established and instructed by internal regulations, provided boards conduct case-specific evaluations and implement necessary safeguards to fulfil their fiduciary duties.

---

[63] For more information regarding explainability methods, see 4.1.7.2.2.3.

3.4 Board's Authority to Delegate Management to AI[64]

3.4.1 Terminological Statement

Management is one of the duties and powers of the board of directors in Turkish law[65] and the management board in German law.[66] These boards fulfil their management duties by making decisions with sufficient knowledge and ensuring their implementation. Delegation of management refers to the assignment of tasks within the scope of management duties and powers. What distinguishes 'delegation' from 'assistance' is that the tasks that require delegation are not low-importance tasks that do not involve any discretion, but are complex enough tasks that involve making discretionary decisions at certain points,[67] and this residual decision-making in delegation gives rise to the primary responsibility of the delegate. For example, while using a calculator does not require delegation, performing a competition law analysis or operational efficiency analysis may require delegation. In this context, when a task is delegated, it also refers to the delegation of power to make the subsidiary decisions needed to perform the task.

It is essential to recognise that a board decision initiates a decision-making continuum. The preparatory and implementational stages represent points along this continuum where delegates make congruent, lower-order choices that give effect to the principal decision.[68] For example, before the board makes a takeover decision, it may be necessary to determine whether the takeover would violate competition law regulations. In such a case, the performance of a competition law analysis, which will significantly impact the final takeover decision, can be delegated. While the delegation decision includes some specifications regarding the delegated competition law analysis, board members, who are not expected to be experts in every field, cannot be expected to make all the determinations regarding what will be considered in the competition law analysis. The delegate who will conduct the competition law analysis as part of the preparation process

---

[64] The following discussion pertains to the delegation of management tasks to AI. The delegation of the strategic decision to integrate AI into corporation management is treated separately in Sect. 3.3.1.2.

[65] See 2.1.1.3.1.2.

[66] See 2.1.1.3.2.2.

[67] For a similar view, see Kırca in Kırca et al. (2013), p. 593.

[68] Even the mere execution of a task necessitates a decision among alternative courses of action. Rolsing (2025), p. 114.

for the takeover decision must make subsidiary decisions, such as determining the relevant product or geographic market. As another example, board members who will assess their corporation's operational efficiency and make appropriate decisions, such as downsizing or expansion, may delegate the factual assessment to the human resources director as a preparatory step for a board decision. While it is a preparatory process, the decisions regarding the methodology to be used and its implementation will be made by the delegated human resources director.[69] The method chosen by the human resources director for this evaluation, along with the results obtained from its application, will also significantly influence the board's decision.

The abovementioned examples demonstrate that delegation triggers a chain of subordinate decision-making. The delegate performing the task must make a series of preparatory determinations to construct the factual, analytical, or procedural foundation on which the final board decision will rest. Therefore, in the legal examination to be conducted below, when delegation of management is discussed, it also refers to the board's delegation of residual decision-making authority to delegates, except for those related to core management issues.[70] Therefore, for this study, the terms 'delegation of management duties,' 'delegation of management tasks,' and 'delegation of management' shall be construed as conceptually synonymous and shall encompass the conceptual framework outlined in the preceding analysis.

3.4.2 Current Management Delegation Systems in Turkish and German Corporate Law

3.4.2.1 In General

For corporations, management encompasses the complete range of decision-making activities. These activities include decisions concerning relations between shareholders and with the corporation itself, as well as production, marketing, investment, consumer and employee relations and accounting transactions.[71] As

[69] For a similar example, see Rolsing (2025), p. 114.

[70] For the categorisation of executive and core management tasks, see 3.4.2.2.

[71] Özatlan (2023), p. 56.

corporations expand their operations, delegating management tasks may transition from a permissible option to a rational necessity[72] that allows the board to focus its attention on strategic, high-value governance functions.[73] Hence, the prudent allocation of management tasks among qualified delegates constitutes an affirmative component of the board's duty of care.[74] As part of this fundamental duty, several criteria, such as the nature of the decision, its importance, the complexity of the interests at stake, confidentiality concerns, available time, existing resources, and potential conflicts of interest, should be considered when determining the scope and level of the delegation.[75]

Under Turkish corporate law, delegation of management can be made to existing board members or to third persons[76] who do not need to be shareholders or employees of the corporation. Delegates are expected to possess independence, impartiality, and expertise in the delegated area of corporation management.[77] Given that legal entities may serve as members of the board of directors, it follows that delegating management authority to such entities must also be lawful.[78] However, if a delegation is made to a legal entity, the task must be carried out by the specific natural persons designated by that legal entity.[79]

In German corporate law, delegation of management can be made across three dimensions.[80] Horizontal delegation within the board, vertical delegation to employees, and external delegation to third parties are possible dimensions

[72] Möslein (2007), p. 38; Çamurcu (2015), pp. 33–34; Akdağ Güney (2016), p. 83; Koç (2018), p. 66; Möslein (2018), ZIP, p. 208; Möslein (2020b), p. 511; Bora Çınar (2022), p. 188; Möslein (2022), p. 76; Telle (2023), p. 34; Windorf (2025), p. 229.

[73] Lücke (2019), BB, p. 1992; Telle (2023), p. 34; Windorf (2025), p. 229.

[74] Doğan (2011), p. 113; Kalender (2024), p. 84; Rolsing (2025), p. 116.

[75] Seibt in Schmidt and Lutter (2020), AktG, § 76, para. 14.

[76] Art. 367 of the TCC: "*(1) Pursuant to an internal directive to be issued within the scope of a specific provision referred to in the articles of association, the board may be authorized to delegate the management, partially or fully, to one or more board members or third persons... (2) Unless the management is delegated, it is incumbent upon all the board members to manage the corporation.*"

[77] Demirel (2017), HHFD, p. 239; Kalender (2024), p. 133.

[78] Altay (2011), p. 84; Kırca in Kırca et al. (2013), p. 596; Akdağ Güney (2016), p. 89; Koç (2018), p. 74 and 77; Tekinalp (2020), p. 261; Eryiğit (2023), p. 49; Küçüktuncay (2023), p. 19; Çamlı (2024), p. 253; Kalender (2024), p. 133.

[79] Kalender (2024), pp. 133–134.

[80] Seibt in Schmidt and Lutter (2020), AktG, § 76, para. 14; Li (2022), p. 61 ff.; Nowak (2022), p. 134; Rolsing (2025), p. 116 ff.

of delegation to manage complex business demands.[81] The delegation of management tasks requires a clear distinction among these dimensions.[82] When the board consists of multiple persons, all members hold joint management authority.[83] However, the AktG[84] implicitly permits the horizontal delegation of tasks among board members by allowing contrary provisions in the articles of association or rules of procedure.[85] Despite lacking an explicit statutory basis in the AktG, vertical delegation, as the transfer of management tasks to subordinate organisational levels, is recognised by German corporate law.[86] Moreover, the outsourcing of certain management tasks to external third parties is implicitly permitted by the AktG,[87] as affirmed by the precedent.[88]

The delegation of management must comply with some legal requirements in both legal systems. Under Turkish corporate law, any transfer of management tasks requires explicit authorisation in the corporation's articles of association.[89] General assembly resolutions or internal regulations alone are insufficient.[90] Once there is explicit authorisation for management delegation in the articles of association, the following prerequisite is the issuance of an internal directive. The

---

[81] Spindler in MünchKomm-AktG (2019), AktG, § 76, para. 14; Ihrig and Schäfer (2020), § 1, para. 20 ff.; Seibt in Schmidt and Lutter (2020), AktG, § 76, para. 14.

[82] Li (2022), p. 61.

[83] § 77(1) of the AktG.

[84] § 77(1) of the AktG: "*(1)Where the management board consists of several persons, any and all members of the management board have authority to manage the affairs of the corporation only jointly. The articles of association or the rules of procedure of the management board may make determinations in derogation herefrom...*".

[85] Fleischer in BeckOGK (2025), AktG, § 76, para. 72 and § 77, para. 54.

[86] Fleischer in Spindler and Stilz (2019), AktG, § 76, para. 65; Li (2022), p. 64; Fleischer in BeckOGK (2025), AktG, § 76, para. 74; Rolsing (2025), p. 117.

[87] Fleischer in BeckOGK (2025), AktG, § 76, para. 75. For this interpretation, an analogy to § 292(1) subsection 3 of the AktG is also suitable.

[88] LG Darmstadt, ZIP 1986, 1389 as cited in Li (2022), p. 65, fn. 246. Fleischer in Spindler and Stilz (2019), AktG, § 76 para. 66.

[89] Art. 367(1) of the TCC. Kırca in Kırca et al. (2013), p. 599; Kendigelen (2016), p. 258; Tekinalp (2020), p. 255; Oran (2021), pp. 111–113; Pulaşlı (2022), § 35, para. 89, p. 1203; Çamoğlu in Poroy et al. (2025), para. 536, p. 379; Şener (2026), p. 302. The current delegation regime under Art. 367(1) of the TCC modelled on the pre-reform Swiss Code of Obligations (Article 716b/1). However, the revised Swiss Code, effective January 2023, introduced a fundamentally more permissive 'opt-out' framework where the board of directors may delegate management powers via its internal regulations, unless explicitly restricted by the articles of association. Kalender (2024), p. 94.

[90] Tekinalp (2020), p. 255; Kalender (2024), p. 91.

issuance of an internal directive is mandatory for the transfer of management.[91] Based on the principle that the internal directive serves as an abstract, general framework, the specific titles and scope of authority to be delegated can be defined within it, while the names of individuals can be excluded.[92] Hence, issuance of internal directives for every change can be prevented. Furthermore, a subsequent resolution from the board of directors is required to appoint the specific persons to these designated roles.[93] Hence, this subsequent board resolution must specify the names of the persons to whom the powers have been delegated, by reference to the internal directive.[94] At the substantive level, the law imposes a critical limitation that only tasks other than the non-delegable tasks may be delegated, while the board must retain all core governance functions specified under Article 375 of the TCC and other individual provisions.[95]

Unlike the Turkish framework, German corporate law permits the delegation of management authority through two exclusive, alternative channels: either the rules of procedure or the articles of association.[96] However, its stipulation in the articles of association is rare in practice, as even minor changes would require a formal amendment, making the more flexible rules of procedure the generally used method.[97] The management board may establish its own rules of procedure.[98] To adopt, amend, or repeal any content of the rules of procedure, a

[91] Kırca in Kırca et al. (2013), p. 599; Akdağ Güney (2016), p. 85; Kendigelen (2016), p. 258; Koç (2018), p. 58; Tekinalp (2020), p. 256; Oran (2021), pp. 113–114; Ayhan et al. (2022), p. 275; Pulaşlı (2022), § 35, para. 92, p. 1204; Bahtiyar (2024), p. 196; Kalender (2024), p. 97; Çamoğlu in Poroy et al. (2025), para. 536, p. 379; Şener (2026), p. 303.

[92] Kırca in Kırca et al. (2013), p. 606; Ceylan (2015), TNBHD, p. 27; Demirel (2017), HHFD, p. 229; Küçüktuncay (2023), pp. 34–35.

[93] Akdağ Güney (2016), p. 87; Demirel (2017), HHFD, p. 235; Tekinalp (2020), p. 258; Oran (2021), pp. 115–116. This two-phased procedure allows for the removal of a person from a delegated position through only a separate board resolution, making an amendment to the internal directive itself unnecessary. Kırca in Kırca et al. (2013), p. 606.

[94] Küçüktuncay (2023), p. 39.

[95] Doğan (2012), MÜHF-HAD, p. 631; Üçışık and Çelik (2013), p. 397; Akdağ Güney (2016), p. 85; Kayar (2018), p. 466; Büyükatak (2019), p. 124 ff.; Tekinalp (2020), p. 440; Oran (2021), pp. 109–110; Ayhan et al. (2022), p. 275; Pulaşlı (2022), § 35, para. 93, p. 1204; Kalender (2024), p. 90; Çamoğlu in Poroy et al. (2025), para. 536, p. 379; Şener (2026), p. 304.

[96] § 77(1) of the AktG.

[97] Spindler in MünchKomm-AktG, § 77, para. 39; Weber in Hölters and Weber (2022), AktG, § 77, para. 27.

[98] Link in Wachter (2022), AktG, § 77, para. 19.

unanimous resolution of the management board is required.[99] If the supervisory board has utilised its power to create rules of procedure for the management board,[100] or if the articles of association grant such authority to the supervisory board, then the rules of procedure issued by the management board are considered subordinate,[101] specifically in areas where their applicability overlaps.[102] The rules of procedure typically covers the management board's internal organisation and distribution of responsibilities.[103] The supervisory board often regulates the delegation of management tasks in the rules of procedure it issues for the management board, as ensuring the management board's proper organisation is a key duty of the supervisory board.[104] However, as is the case with Turkish law, the core management tasks of the management board remain strictly non-delegable under German law.[105]

In light of the above, it can be seen that the delegation system in Turkish law is directly based on the wording of specific provisions in the TCC, while in German law, it is shaped partly by the legal provisions themselves and partly by principles derived from the interpretation of legal provisions by legal doctrine, taking into account the needs of the corporations. The requirement that delegation be explicitly permitted in the articles of association under Turkish law creates both a formal difficulty and partially contradicts the board of directors' managerial autonomy. In German law, however, the ability to regulate delegation solely through procedural rules provides practicality, while the supervisory board's superior position over the management board in determining procedural rules, including those governing delegation, appears to conflict with the management board's autonomy in determining the corporation's management structure. Despite all this, the prevailing view in both legal systems is that delegation of management tasks is a duty that must be carried out diligently and in cooperation with all organs of the corporation for efficient governance. Another common point in both legal systems is that the core management functions should remain

---

[99] § 77(2), sentence 3 of the AktG. Seibt in Schmidt and Lutter (2020), AktG, § 77, para. 25.

[100] § 77(2), sentence 1 of the AktG.

[101] § 77 (2) of the AktG: "*Unless the articles of association stipulates that it is incumbent on the supervisory board to establish rules of procedure, or the supervisory board so establishes rules of procedure for the management board, the management board may itself establish its rules of procedure…*".

[102] Seibt in Schmidt and Lutter (2020), AktG, § 77, para. 26; Link in Wachter (2022), AktG, § 77, para. 19.

[103] Seibt in Schmidt and Lutter (2020), AktG, § 77, para. 24.

[104] Weber in Hölters and Weber (2022), AktG, § 77, para. 27.

[105] Li (2022), p. 58.

outside the scope of delegation. Below, the core management tasks that should be excluded from delegation in both legal systems are evaluated under a separate title since this statutory and doctrinal distinction will be important to the scope of delegation when examining the possibility and potential obligation of delegating to AI systems.

3.4.2.2 The Scope and Substance of Delegable Authority

While boards generally possess discretion to delegate management as a part of their managerial autonomy, this authority is neither absolute nor unlimited. Corporate laws universally recognise specific core management tasks as non-delegable, though many jurisdictions fail to define these tasks clearly. Turkish law provides specific clarity through Article 375 of the TCC, which enumerates non-delegable board duties.[106] Article 375 of the TCC lists non-delegable duties and authorities of the board of directors as follows:

- *"Overall management of the corporation and issuance of all necessary directives.*
- *Determination of the corporation's management organisation.*
- *Accounting, financial control and, to the extent required for the corporation's management, setting up necessary systems for financial planning purposes.*
- *Appointment and dismissal of managers, and persons with the same function as the managers and authorised signatories.*
- *Overall supervision of the persons in charge of management, in particular to determine as to whether they comply with law, articles of association, internal directives and written instructions of the board.*
- *Keeping shareholder ledger, resolution book of the board and meeting and negotiation books of the general assembly; preparing annual report and corporate governance declaration and submitting the same to the general assembly and; [organisation of general assembly meetings and] implementing the general assembly resolutions.*
- *Notification to the court in the event that the corporation is over-indebted."*[107]

While these non-delegable duties and authorities are itemised individually, the provision's nature is not a *numerus clausus*.[108] Some other provisions of the

[106] Bora Çınar (2022), p. 191.

[107] Art. 375 of the TCC.

[108] Doğan (2011), p. 173 ff; Kırca in Kırca et al. (2013), p. 540; Akdağ Güney (2016), p. 146; Büyükatak (2019), p. 148; Tekinalp (2020), p. 248; Kalender (2024), p. 51 and 102; Şener (2026), pp. 303–304.

TCC, such as Articles 145, 147, 169, 185, 186, 199, 353, 376, 378, 379, 446, and 457, grant rights and authorities that may only be exercised by the board of directors, meaning they are non-delegable.[109] The board of directors may not delegate these rights and duties to the general assembly or to any committees to be established, either by the articles of association or by a resolution. The board of directors may not waive them either.[110]

Unlike the TCC, the AktG does not list the non-delegable core management duties of the management board. However, the prevailing doctrinal position in German corporate law fulfils this presumed legal gap by establishing criteria to maintain a fundamental distinction between executive management tasks (*Aufgaben der Geschäftsführung*) and core management tasks (*Aufgaben der Leitung*).[111] As it is derived from *a contrario* interpretation of Section 76 of the AktG's silence on delegation compared to Section 77 of the AktG's explicit provision,[112] executive management tasks may be delegated to individual board members or third parties, but core management tasks remain strictly non-delegable and must be exercised collectively by the full management board.[113] The essential criterion for classifying an activity as a core management task lies principally in its substantive connection to fundamental corporate governance functions,[114] such as corporate planning, oversight, senior appointments, and compliance.[115] Modern approaches categorise these responsibilities also as strategic planning and management, organisational design, financial responsibility, and information responsibility.[116] Moreover, core management tasks now explicitly

[109] Altay (2011), pp. 162–163; Kırca in Kırca et al. (2013), p. 540 and 591; Koç (2018), pp. 102–103; Büyükatak (2019), p. 147 ff.; Ayhan et al. (2022), pp. 270–271; Kalender (2024), p. 51.

[110] Preamble to Art. 375 of the TCC. Ayhan et al. (2022), p. 265; Pulaşlı (2022), § 36, para. 8, p. 1320.

[111] Möslein (2007), p. 37 ff.; Fleischer in Spindler and Stilz (2019), § 76, para. 12 ff.; Spindler in MünchKomm-AktG (2019), § 76, para. 16; Seibt in Schmidt and Lutter (2020), § 76, para. 14; Nowak (2022), p. 140; Windorf (2025), p. 124.

[112] Li (2022), p. 58.

[113] Fleischer in Spindler and Stilz (2019), AktG, § 76, para. 9; Seibt in Schmidt and Lutter (2020), § 76, para. 14.

[114] Spindler in MünchKomm-AktG (2019), § 76, para. 17; Weber in Hölters and Weber (2022), AktG, § 76, para. 10; Windorf (2025), p. 125.

[115] Spindler in MünchKomm-AktG (2019), § 76, para. 16 ff.; Dörrwächter in Kubis and Tödtmann (2022), § 4, para. 15; Weber in Hölters and Weber (2022), AktG, § 76, para. 10; Li (2022), p. 59; Telle (2023), p. 32.

[116] Fleischer in Spindler and Stilz (2019), AktG, § 76, para. 18.

include tasks of exceptional strategic importance or significant risk exposure,[117] such as responsibility for information technology systems and data protection requirements,[118] reflecting the digital transformation. The concrete non-delegable core management tasks can be inferred from provisions assigning specific responsibilities exclusively to the management board as a collegial body. These include Sections 83, 90, 91, 92, 110, 118, 121, 170 and 245 of the AktG.[119]

The emerging view in German legal doctrine increasingly questions the notion of an absolute, non-delegable sphere of management tasks[120] as it is seen as conceptually flawed and practically hard to discern.[121] Critics of this categorical distinction between delegable executive management tasks and non-delegable core management tasks advocate for a more nuanced, case-specific analysis[122] based on the fiduciary duty standard of section 93(1) of the AktG.[123] It is argued that even under the current doctrinal distinction, the classification of specific tasks requires case-by-case analysis.[124]

Determining the delegable management tasks also requires assessing the procedural scope of the tasks along the decision-making continuum. The decision-making process for management tasks involves the preparatory, substantive decision-making, and implementation phases.[125] It is widely accepted in German legal doctrine that the preparatory stages of corporate decision-making, including information gathering, data processing, analytical modelling, and the generation of recommendations or decision alternatives, may be delegated to individual board members, subordinate management levels, or external third parties.[126] However, Section 76(1) of the AktG requires the management board

[117] Fleischer in Spindler and Stilz (2019), AktG, § 76, para. 18; Nowak (2022), p. 152.

[118] See references in Li (2022), p. 59, fn. 218.

[119] Li (2022), p. 58.

[120] Kuntz (2020), AG, p. 805 ff.; Seibt in Schmidt and Lutter (2020), AktG, § 76, para. 14; Koch (2024), AktG, § 76 para. 10. Cf. Linnertz (2020), p. 59 ff. and 204 ff.

[121] Spindler in MünchKomm-AktG (2019), § 76, para. 17; Kuntz (2020), AG, p. 805 ff.; Nowak (2022), p. 144 ff.; Koch (2024), AktG, § 76, paras. 11 and 13.

[122] Seibt in Schmidt and Lutter (2020), AktG, § 76 para. 14.

[123] Seibt in Schmidt and Lutter (2020), AktG, § 76, para. 9, 14 and § 77 para. 1.; Langenbucher (2023a), ZHR, p. 726 ff.; Nowak (2022), p. 162 ff.

[124] Weber in Hölters and Weber (2022), AktG, § 76, para. 11; Windorf (2025), p. 126.

[125] Möslein (2018), ZIP, p. 208; Linnertz (2020), p. 28; Telle (2023), p. 33; Rolsing (2025), p. 325.

[126] Fleischer in Spindler and Stilz (2019), AktG, § 76, para. 20; Spindler in MünchKomm-AktG (2019), § 76, para. 18; Li (2022), pp. 60–61; Weber in Hölters and Weber (2022), AktG, § 76, para. 8 and 12; Link in Wachter (2022), AktG, § 76, para. 22.

to retain ultimate decision-making authority in the substantive decision-making phase for core management issues.[127] Likewise, Turkish legal doctrine accepts that the board may seek advisory support from committees or delegate operational tasks to third parties in the execution of non-delegable duties, provided that the ultimate decision-making authority remains exclusively with the full board.[128] Internal regulations can specify who will carry out these duties, and which phases of the decision-making process can be delegated. The crucial point is that the board itself must always make the final decision. For instance, the board may delegate operational tasks necessary to the overall management of the corporation, such as accounting, financial auditing, and planning, to delegates, committees, or external experts, while retaining ultimate authority for final decisions on these matters.[129] In the same vein, although the duty of overall monitoring, encompassing high-level compliance monitoring and systemic risk governance, is categorised by law as a non-delegable duty, the board has the discretion to delegate ancillary monitoring tasks to a specially formed committee or an individual.[130] For instance, daily auditing functions, such as operational checks and transaction-level verification, may be delegated.[131] In these two delegation examples, the board retains final decision-making authority for overall management and monitoring, even when delegating operational tasks to delegates.

3.4.2.3 Board's Duties Regarding the Delegates

It is widely accepted in Turkish legal doctrine that, following a delegation, the responsibilities of board members shift from active management to a supervisory role, as the duties and powers previously held by the board are removed

[127] Fleischer in Spindler and Stilz (2019), AktG, § 76, para. 20; Weber in Hölters and Weber (2022), AktG, § 76, para. 8 ff.; Windorf (2025), p. 128. It should also be considered that distinguishing between the non-delegable substantive decision-making phase and the delegable preparatory and implementation phases artificially reduces core management to a series of residual, isolated decision points. This approach may lead to disregarding the substantive and contextual work, inherent in preparation and execution, that gives strategic decisions their ultimate meaning and context. For a similar critical approach, see Nowak (2022), p. 155.

[128] Kırca in Kırca et al (2013). pp. 540–541; Çamurcu (2015), p. 23; Ayhan et al. (2022), p. 265; Çamlı (2024), p. 110; Kalender (2024), pp. 104–106.

[129] Özatlan (2023), p. 63; Kalender (2024), p. 112.

[130] Kalender (2024), p. 285.

[131] Çam (2017), İKÜHFD, p. 536.

in relation to the authority delegated.[132] Hence, after the delegation of management tasks, delegates assume full liability for the powers they exercise.[133] The legal responsibilities retained by delegating board members are limited particularly to three areas: overseeing the activities of the delegates,[134] providing them with instructions,[135] and diligently selecting[136] them in the first place. Hence, the delegating board members can avoid responsibility for the actions of delegates only if management is delegated in accordance with the TCC and the board exercises due diligence in these three key areas,[137] collectively representing facets of

[132] Arslanlı (1960), p. 123; Çamoğlu (2010), p. 196; Doğan (2011), p. 116; Ceylan (2015), TNBHD, p. 29; Hacımahmutoğlu (2015), BATİDER, p. 47 ff.; Koç (2018), p. 65; Tekinalp (2020), p. 259; Küçüktuncay (2023), p. 9; Özatlan (2023), p. 108; Şener (2026), p. 304.

[133] İmregün (1989), p. 218; Üçışık and Çelik (2013), pp. 452–453; Paslı (2013), İÜHFM, p. 332; Ceylan (2015), TNBHD, p. 33; Akdağ Güney (2016), p. 94; Kayar (2018), p. 443; Koç (2018), p. 65; Küçükgüngör (2018), p. 316; Büyükatak (2019), p. 286 ff.; Tekinalp (2020), p. 260; Bahtiyar (2024), p. 196; Kalender (2024), p. 61; Çamoğlu in Poroy et al. (2025), para. 536, p. 379; Şener (2026), p. 303.

[134] Ünal (1982), BATİDER, p. 86; Paslı (2005), p. 303 and 306; Pulaşlı (2009), BATİDER, pp. 39–40; Çamoğlu (2010), p. 197; Altay (2011), p. 130 ff.; Kırca in Kırca et al. (2013), p. 560; Paslı (2013), İÜHFM, pp. 332–333; Göktürk (2014), TBBD, p. 197; Çamurcu (2015), p. 34 and 135; Hacımahmutoğlu (2015), BATİDER, p. 47 ff.; Büyükatak (2019), p. 180; Çam (2017), İKÜHFD, p. 536; Küçükgüngör (2018), pp. 316–317; Cenkci (2018), p. 99 ff.; Kayar (2018), p. 466; Bora Çınar (2022), p. 192; Pulaşlı (2022), § 35, para. 283, p. 1284; Küçüktuncay (2023), pp. 127–128; Özatlan (2023), p. 44, 215 and 411; Turanboy (2023), BATİDER, p. 772; Bahtiyar (2024), p. 197; Kalender (2024), p. 118, 301 and 320; Çamoğlu in Poroy et al. (2025), para. 536, pp. 379–380; Varlı (2025), p. 158.

[135] Pulaşlı (2009), BATİDER, p. 40; Çamoğlu (2010), p. 197; Altay (2011), p. 137 ff.; Kırca in Kırca et al. (2013), p. 613; Çamurcu (2015), p. 34 and 135; Akdağ Güney (2016), p. 99; Büyükatak (2019), p. 182; Pulaşlı (2022), § 36, para. 14, p. 1322; Küçüktuncay (2023), pp. 127–128; Özatlan (2023), p. 243 and 414; Bahtiyar (2024), p. 197; Kalender (2024), p. 108, 118, 253 and 329 ff. Contrary, Doğan (2011), p. 239; Doğan (2012), MÜHF-HAD, p. 634.

[136] Ünal (1982), BATİDER, p. 86; Pulaşlı (2009), BATİDER, p. 40; Çamoğlu (2010), p. 197; Altay (2011), p. 132; Kırca in Kırca et al. (2013), p. 556; Paslı (2013), İÜHFM, pp. 332–333; Çamurcu (2015), p. 34 and 135; Kayar (2018), p. 443; Koç (2018), p. 66; Büyükatak (2019), p. 289; Tekinalp (2020), p. 440; Pulaşlı (2022), § 36, para. 176, p. 1421; Küçüktuncay (2023), pp. 127–128; Turanboy (2023), BATİDER, p. 772; Bahtiyar (2024), p. 197; Varlı (2025), p. 157. The possession of requisite knowledge, expertise, and experience constitutes a fundamental criterion in the selection of a delegate. Kalender (2024), p. 279. Depending on specific circumstances, such as the corporation's size, its field of activity, and operation within regulated sectors, the required qualifications for delegates may need to be of a higher standard. Altay (2013), p. 19.

[137] Akdağ Güney (2016), p. 101.

the overarching 'duty of care.'[138] The degree of care for selection, instruction and monitoring should be assessed within the framework of the 'prudent manager' criterion under Article 369(1) of the TCC.[139] As prudent managers, the board members cannot escape responsibility by claiming ignorance of the activities conducted by delegates.[140] This interpretation is based on the argument that Article 553(2)[141] of the TCC must be read in conjunction with the duties of care and overall monitoring.[142]

In German corporate law, there is still no clear answer regarding the specific individual duties of the board member towards the delegate.[143] However, board members are expected to maintain their exclusive control over the corporation by establishing a framework that enables them to retain ultimate decision-making authority even after delegating. Therefore, the prevailing view accepts that delegation does not absolve the board members of responsibility but shifts the focus from the actual management task to establishing a solid framework.[144] This framework must ensure careful selection of delegates based on task complexity, corporation-related assessments, and personal qualifications;[145] instruction covering all task aspects and necessary resources;[146] and monitoring proportional to

[138] Özatlan (2023), p. 420.

[139] Özatlan (2023), pp. 420–421; Kalender (2024), p. 279.

[140] Çamoğlu (2010), p. 197; Kalender (2024), p. 274 and 287.

[141] While the statutory text explicitly emphasizes care in selection as the foundation for liability, a teleological interpretation, considering the legislative intent and the preamble, demonstrates that board members retain an ongoing duty of monitoring that persists following a valid delegation. Ayan (2021), p. 72; Varlı (2025), p. 160.

[142] Çamoğlu (2010), p. 197; Altay (2011), p. 303; Kırca in Kırca et al. (2013), p. 612; Akdağ Güney (2016), p. 95; Küçüktuncay (2023), pp. 127–128; Varlı (2025), p. 160.

[143] Li (2022), p. 95. These duties can be derived from general principles of civil law regarding the transfer of tasks (i.e. §§ 823 and 831 of the BGB) and board's duty of care (§ 93 of the AktG). Rolsing (2025), p. 127.

[144] Seibt in Schmidt and Lutter (2020), AktG, § 76, para. 33; Rolsing (2025), p. 126.

[145] Seibt in Schmidt and Lutter (2020), AktG, § 76, para. 33; Link in Wachter (2022), AktG, § 93, para. 66; Nowak (2022), p. 166; Rolsing (2025), pp. 127–128.

[146] Spindler in MünchKomm-AktG (2019), § 76, para. 18 ff.; Seibt in Schmidt and Lutter (2020), AktG, § 76, para. 33; Nowak (2022), p. 166; Calabro (2023), p. 129; Rolsing (2025), p. 129.

task importance and delegate experience[147] by the board members.[148] The management board remain fully liable under Section 93(1) of the AktG for these three fundamental obligations which apply to both internal and external delegation. For external delegation, additional contractual safeguards to preserve the board's control rights and compliance with sector-specific regulations may be required.[149]

3.4.2.4 Interim Result

Turkish and German corporate law each distinguish between delegable executive management tasks and non-delegable core management tasks. The TCC provides a non-exhaustive schema for this distinction, while German law employs a similar doctrinal categorisation. Although such a general distinction provides functional benefits, a case-by-case assessment of delegation's scope and substance is necessary, either in conjunction with or in place of this distinction. Furthermore, under both legal systems, executive management tasks can be delegated in their entirety. In contrast, while the substantive decision-making phase of core management tasks cannot be delegated to anyone, the preparation and implementation phases of these tasks can be delegated to individual board members, employees, and third parties. Moreover, in both legal systems, boards are required to act as prudent managers in selecting, instructing, and monitoring those to whom they delegate management tasks.

3.4.3 A Comparative Analysis of the Board's Authority to Delegate to AI

3.4.3.1 In General

The preceding comparative analysis of traditional delegation systems revealed that both Turkish and German law establish a substantive distinction based on the nature of the task itself when determining its delegability. Under Turkish law, tasks explicitly listed as non-delegable in the TCC, including those related to the

---

[147] Spindler in MünchKomm-AktG (2019), § 76, para. 18 ff.; Seibt in Schmidt and Lutter (2020), AktG, § 76, para. 33; Link in Wachter (2022), AktG, § 93, para. 66; Nowak (2022), p. 167; Calabro (2023), p. 135; Rolsing (2025), pp. 130–133.

[148] Fleischer in Spindler and Stilz (2019), AktG, § 93 para. 100; Seibt in Schmidt and Lutter (2020), AktG, § 76, para. 33; Li (2022), p. 64; Link in Wachter (2022), AktG, § 93, para. 66; Rolsing (2025), p. 126 ff.

[149] Fleischer in Spindler and Stilz (2019), AktG, § 76 para. 66; Li (2022), p. 65; Nowak (2022), p. 135 and 167.

corporation's overall management and monitoring, could not be delegated by the board of directors, while executive management tasks are delegable. In German law, although the AktG does not explicitly address the issue, the prevailing doctrinal view is that delegation of core management tasks is not possible. In contrast, executive management tasks could be delegated. Furthermore, both legal systems allow delegating the preparation and implementation of core management tasks. In the discussion concerning the legal possibility of delegation to AI systems, the question of whether the addressee of the delegation must have legal personality should be addressed before considering the distinction between core and executive management tasks. Consequently, assessing the permissibility of delegating management tasks to AI systems necessitates the evaluation of the personal scope (concerning the legal personality and liability of the AI), the substantive scope (on the nature and classification of the task), and the procedural scope (distinguishing between preparatory, substantive decision-making, and implementation phases).

3.4.3.2 Analysis Focusing on the Delegation's Personal Scope

It is essential to evaluate the personal scope of delegation permitted by relevant legal systems since the most fundamental difference between AI systems and traditional delegates lies in their legal personality. As mentioned above, AI systems in both the Turkish and German legal systems do not yet possess legal personality.[150] Therefore, the question is whether delegation to AI systems is possible despite their lack of legal personality.

While Turkish law does not explicitly state that delegation of management tasks must be made to an entity having legal personality, Article 367 of the TCC, which regulates delegation of management tasks, states that delegation can be made to "*one or more board members or a third person.*" This wording of the article might imply that the legislator's will dictates that delegation should be limited to natural or legal *persons.*[151] However, since the article's justification lacks any explanation on this matter, interpreting the legislator's will to determine the delegation's addressee through historical and teleological interpretation methods would also be instructive.[152]

From a historical perspective, when the TCC was being drafted in the early 2000 s, delegating any task to AI systems was not even a matter of debate, particularly within Turkish legal doctrine. Therefore, it cannot be concluded that the

[150] See 2.1.2.2.1.

[151] Bora Çınar (2022), p. 190; Varlı (2025), p. 249 ff.

[152] Bora Çınar (2022), p. 193.

legislator deliberately limited the scope of permitted delegation to natural or legal persons simply to exclude AI systems from the delegation system. Therefore, based on historical interpretation, it cannot be said that the legislator deliberately intended to prohibit the delegation of management tasks to AI systems. Consequently, it can be assumed that there is an unconscious (actual) gap in this matter. To fulfil this gap, a teleological interpretation may provide guidance.

A teleological interpretation, however, yields a different result because of the legal characteristics of delegation with respect to responsibility. Considering that the delegate is primarily responsible for the delegated tasks, and the board of directors that delegates the tasks are responsible only for the selection, instruction, and monitoring of the delegate, it can be derived that the legislator intended delegation to a legal subject, i.e. a natural or legal person, who could bear the legal responsibility arising from the delegated tasks. Indeed, what distinguishes delegation from receiving assistance during task execution is that, with delegation, primary responsibility for the delegated task also passes to the delegate, and the board of directors retains secondary responsibility only for the three subsidiary duties mentioned above. Therefore, without delegation, the board's use of assistance in its tasks does not alter its responsibility, and the board of directors retains primary responsibility. Considering the legislator's intention regarding the allocation of responsibilities in delegation, it can be concluded that the reason for limiting the scope of delegation to natural and legal persons is that these persons can be attributed responsibility. If the legislator's will, as revealed by the teleological interpretation, is that the delegate should bear responsibility for the tasks, delegating tasks to AI systems that do not yet have legal personality would be contrary to that will. Although the discussion on this issue is premature in Turkish legal scholarship, the current dominant view is that, because AI systems lack personality and therefore responsibility, the board cannot delegate management tasks directly to AI systems.[153]

In German corporate law, delegation of management tasks is not explicitly regulated, so the scope of delegation regarding the addressee lacks a statutory basis. Therefore, unlike Turkish law, there is no specific legal provision that must be interpreted in this regard when assessing the delegation of management tasks to AI. However, the issue has been subject to much more doctrinal debate in German legal doctrine than in Turkish legal doctrine. In these discussions, it has been argued that the delegation system is traditionally considered for human

[153] Dönmez Canseven (2021), pp. 107–108; Güçlütürk (2021), p. 459; Metin (2021), p. 523; Seçer (2025), pp. 97–98; Varlı (2025), pp. 249–251.

delegates[154] and that the management board's ability to delegate management tasks to AI may be evaluated in analogy to this system for human delegates.[155]

According to emerging views on the delegation to AI discussion, there is no requirement in current German corporate law that delegation can be made only to entities that have legal personality.[156] One manifestation of this is the vertical delegation of tasks to various departments within the corporation, even though these departments lack legal personality.[157] Moreover, Section 80(2) of the WpHG (*Wertpapierhandelsgesetz*, Securities Trading Act) is cited as an example of statutory authorisation for delegating trading decisions to algorithmic systems.[158] Furthermore, the legal doctrine acknowledges that when the management board delegates tasks to natural persons or legal entities, it is unclear whether these natural persons or legal entities covertly use AI systems to fulfil the delegated tasks.[159] At this point, it might also be argued that the delegates' hidden use of AI is irrelevant, as delegates, whether natural or legal persons, are primarily responsible for executing tasks and thus the liability gap is avoided. Therefore, apart from the hidden use of AI by the traditional delegates, direct delegation to AI systems risks creating a liability gap. The doctrine claims that this liability gap can be filled by holding accountable the natural or legal persons who produce, sell, and operate AI systems, or the management board within the framework of its selection, instruction, and oversight duties.[160] In light of these perspectives, the consensus in most scholarly works on the subject in German legal doctrine is that delegation of management tasks to AI systems is permissible[161] despite these systems' lack of legal personality. Therefore, certain management tasks can be delegated directly to AI systems.

One method for indirectly, if not directly, delegating management tasks to AI systems is to delegate to a natural person and have that person perform the tasks based on the AI's outputs. The board can ensure that a natural person (formal delegate) performs the delegated tasks based on AI outputs, through instructions,

---

[154] Möslein (2025a), p. 624.

[155] Möslein (2018), ZIP, p. 208; Möslein (2022), p. 76; Möslein (2025a), p. 623.

[156] Li (2022), p. 66; Nowak (2022), p. 174; Windorf (2025), p. 226.

[157] Fleischer in Spindler and Stilz (2019), AktG, § 76, para. 20; Spindler in MünchKomm-AktG (2019), § 76, para. 18; Li (2022), p. 66.

[158] Li (2022), p. 67; Calabro (2023), p. 87; Rolsing (2025), p. 141.

[159] Telle (2023), p. 42.

[160] Telle (2023), pp. 40–41.

[161] Li (2022), pp. 66–67; Lieder (2022), p. 336; Calabro (2023), p. 87 and 109; Telle (2023), p. 41; Nowak (2022), p. 174; Fleischer in BeckOGK (2025), AktG, § 76, para. 77; Rolsing (2025), p. 142; Windorf (2025), pp. 226–227.

internal regulations or contractual obligations. This way, the AI could become the indirect recipient of the delegation. Another way to bypass the legal personality and liability debate surrounding delegation and to make AI systems the addressee of delegation is to position the AI within a legal entity and ensure that the tasks delegated to that entity are performed by the AI. In this way, management authority could be indirectly delegated to this AI system, as the board's management authority can be delegated to legal entities under the law. To do so, the board may instruct or contractually mandate an 'AI housing' legal entity, as the formal delegate, to act in accordance with the outputs of the housed AI system. The 'AI housing' legal entity thus assumes liability as the original delegate and, if applicable, as the contractual party.

While these indirect models offer a technical pathway, they concurrently jeopardise the legal foundations of delegation. Although it is generally accepted that delegates receive instructions from the board, they are also expected to act independently as a requirement of their responsibilities. If a delegate, whether a natural person or a legal entity, performs a delegated task solely on the basis of AI output, the delegate will lose their independence and become a mere approver of AI outputs. Such a situation will undermine the very responsibility placed on the delegate. Therefore, while the methods described above may allow AI to become the addressee of the delegation indirectly, this could conflict with the existing delegation system and liability regime.

3.4.3.3 Analysis Focusing on the Delegation's Substantive and Procedural Scope

Although the preceding analysis concludes that delegation to AI is impermissible, due to the AI's lack of legal personality and attributable liability, under a strict interpretation of current Turkish law, this section adopts a forward-looking perspective. To construct a comprehensive evaluative framework to analyse the permissible substantive and procedural scope of delegation to AI, the following examination proceeds on the hypothetical premise that the delegation of management to AI is permitted under Turkish law.

In Turkish law, Article 367 of the TCC lists the non-delegable duties of the board of directors. These duties are core management tasks that the board of directors, as the executive body, must fulfil. Therefore, neither specific board members nor third persons can legally be delegated core management tasks. Given that these duties cannot be delegated to anyone, whether a natural or legal person, it can be concluded that the delegation of these tasks to AI systems is not legally possible, either. This conclusion regarding the substantive scope of delegation leads to the third and final element of the analysis, the procedural scope.

A complete evaluation requires analysing whether delegation to AI is permissible for the preparatory, substantive decision-making, or implementational phases of a core management task. While the law does not permit the delegation of core management tasks, the legal doctrine considers the board's decision-making processes as preparation, substantive decision-making, and implementation phases, and accepts that delegation of phases other than substantive decision-making is possible. In this case, delegating the preparation and implementation of core management tasks to AI systems would also be legally permissible under Turkish law. Within this framework, it can also be concluded that delegating all three phases of executive management tasks to AI is possible.

German legal doctrine argues that delegating management tasks to AI systems, despite their lack of legal personality, is possible.[162] However, the substantive scope of the tasks that can be delegated to AI must also be evaluated. Under this evaluation, it is clear that delegating executive management tasks to AI is permissible, as delegating them to any party is generally permissible. In contrast, core management tasks are those that the management board must fulfil and cannot therefore be legally delegated to either individual board members or third parties. Given that these core management tasks are inherently nondelegable, their delegation to AI systems is legally impossible as well.[163]

The concluding doctrinal step in German law is to examine the permissibility of delegating to AI within the procedural scope. Given that German legal doctrine permits the delegation of all three phases of executive management, it logically follows that delegating all three phases to AI is also possible.[164] While the doctrine considers the delegation of core management tasks absolutely prohibited, the preparation and execution phases of these tasks can be delegated. Consequently, only the preparatory and execution phases of core management tasks can be delegated to AI systems. Still, the substantive decision-making phase for core management tasks cannot be delegated to AI, as it is reserved for the management board.[165] Even if tasks such as data analysis, predictive forecasting, and specific action propositions are delegated to AI systems during the preparation phase, the management board retains final authority through the undelegated substantive decision-making phase.[166] It could be argued that managerial responsibility

[162] See 3.4.3.2.

[163] Rolsing (2025), p. 140.

[164] For particularly the preparatory stage, see Rolsing (2025), p. 387.

[165] Rolsing (2025), p. 422.

[166] Calabro (2023), p. 89 ff.

would be eroded if the board simply approved AI-generated recommendations.[167] However, such a risk relates not to the legal validity of the delegation, but to the information base the board must provide during decision-making. Therefore, a board that diligently selects, instructs, and monitors an AI can maintain control by reserving the right to withdraw the delegation or to verify the AI's recommendations through alternative means and its own collective judgment.[168] In this case, the ultimate decision-making authority regarding core management tasks remains with the board,[169] as mandated in law and doctrine.

Although the legal landscape currently lacks both judicial precedents and settled administrative practices concerning the delegation of decision-making authority to AI systems,[170] the German legal doctrine has gone a step further and examined whether substantive decision-making power can also be delegated to AI. In this context, it is discussed whether the management board may retain ultimate decision-making authority while delegating substantive judgment to AI systems through predefined parameters.[171] However, the legality of this proposal under German corporation law is criticised[172] on the grounds that such an approach would effectively constitute an impermissible surrender of core managerial responsibilities, which require continuous, active human oversight rather than static pre-programmed governance. Without the ability to verify alignment with its will before final execution of the decision, the board cannot ensure accountability. Thus, delegating substantive decision-making power to AI for core management tasks violates core tenets of directorial oversight.[173] Moreover, it is argued that such delegation deprives the board of meaningful oversight during the decision-making process since the board's intervention is limited to merely a completed AI decision, and such a structure prevents timely intervention when AI outputs deviate from intended parameters.[174] Hence, the lack of pre-execution oversight, coupled with the inability to meaningfully reclaim tasks mid-process because of the AI's operational opacity and execution speed, results in the board functionally ceding dynamic decision-making power to algorithmic processes,

[167] Kuntz (2020), AG, p. 808; Calabro (2023), p. 91.

[168] Kuntz (2020), AG, p. 811 ff.; Calabro (2023), p. 92 and 109.

[169] Li (2022), p. 67; Calabro (2023), pp. 89–90.

[170] Windorf (2025), p. 220.

[171] Weber et al. (2018), NZG, p. 1134; Becker and Pordzik (2020), ZfPW, p. 345; Calabro (2023), p. 110.

[172] Telle (2023), p. 43.

[173] Calabro (2023), pp. 111–112.

[174] Calabro (2023), pp. 112–113.

violating the statutory organisation of the corporation, the requirement of continuous, independent management and the requirement of the board's independent personal judgment.[175] As a result, the critics conclude that the board's statutory duty to exercise real-time personal judgment cannot be reconciled with any framework that replaces active human discretion with predetermined AI-driven decision rules, regardless of how carefully such parameters are initially established.[176]

German legal doctrine has also examined whether it should be possible to delegate core management tasks to AI, particularly in the context of a corporation's business field. It is discussed in the doctrine that whether complete delegation of management tasks to AI is permissible for highly specialised corporations, such as algorithmic trading firms, where AI-driven operations constitute the core business purpose and are fundamental to their *raison d'être*.[177] However, Section 76 of the AktG prohibits the delegation of core management tasks, regardless of the corporation's business type. Therefore, while high-technology use is inherent in some corporations, just as the management board in these corporations cannot delegate substantive decision-making power for core management tasks to human delegates, they should also not be able to delegate substantive decision-making power for core management tasks to AI, as the management board must carry out core management duties based on their own personal judgment.[178]

3.4.3.4 *De Lege Ferenda* Analysis

As seen in the comparative analysis of the *de lege lata*, the biggest obstacle to delegating management tasks to AI in both legal systems is AI's lack of legal personality and specific liability. German legal doctrine attempts to overcome this obstacle through a pragmatic interpretation of the law. While special regulations can be enacted to address this issue and ensure legal predictability and certainty, it is argued that existing legal rules, which position the management board as the master of decision-making processes, are sufficient to govern delegation to AI.[179] Although some authors argue that enacting specific legislation on AI delegation is not legally necessary,[180] it is essential to establish clear principles to guide

[175] Calabro (2023), pp. 113–114; Telle (2023), p. 43.

[176] Calabro (2023), p. 114; Telle (2023), p. 43.

[177] Zetzsche (2019), AG, p. 7; Calabro (2023), pp. 114–116. It is a critical interpretive point that while § 80(2) of the WpHG permits certain delegated functions in algorithmic trading, it does not override the fundamental corporate law principle that core management tasks are non-delegable.

[178] Cf. Calabro (2023), pp. 114–116.

[179] Kremer and Langenbucher (2024), p. 77, 3.14.

[180] Windorf (2025), pp. 269–270.

boards in delegating to AI and to ensure that legal predictability is not sacrificed to digitalisation.[181]

In Turkish legal doctrine, on the other hand, it is accepted that delegating to AI is legally impermissible because AI lacks personality and is not subject to attributable liability.[182] Since the TCC's general justification emphasises that the legislature aims to ensure that corporations benefit from current technological advancements, it would be prudent for the legislature to enact a regulation that provides legal certainty and predictability regarding the delegation of management tasks to AI. Such a development would shift the legal doctrine in an affirmative direction, away from an overly conservative stance that is grounded in a literal interpretation of the law towards technological developments and their use by corporations. In this context, enacting general risk-based legal rules regarding the use of AI systems and the obligations of those concerned, as in the EU AI Act, would be a good starting point. Then, a regulation that also allows delegating management tasks to AI systems would be appropriate to increase the benefits derived from AI systems in corporate management and mitigate risks arising from their *de facto* use. The liability gap that is feared to emerge from the delegation of management tasks to AI systems could be filled through the liability of the delegating board members whose liability arise from their obligations of selection, instruction, and monitoring, the liability of the manufacturers, vendors, operators, and users of the AI systems, and through the creation of new compensation systems such as insurance or compensation funds.

3.4.4 Interim Result

Currently, neither the Turkish nor the German corporate law systems have specific regulations governing the delegation of management tasks to AI. Therefore, for both legal systems, the delegation to AI may be examined under the current delegation regimes, with regard to the personal, substantive, and procedural scope of delegation.

---

[181] Möslein (2018), ZIP, p. 212.

[182] See 3.4.3.2. Because of this negative doctrinal opinion, no legal proposal has been found in Turkish legal doctrine on how to proceed on the issue of delegation to AI, and the limited number of general proposals only point to the need to re-evaluate corporation law and the delegation system in the face of technological developments. For these proposals, see Dönmez Canseven (2021), p. 108; Seçer (2025), pp. 97–98; Varlı (2025), p. 240 and 251.

An examination of the personal scope of delegation under Turkish law shows that Article 367 of the TCC is normatively silent on delegation to AI. This provision neither contains an express authorisation for delegation of management to AI nor establishes a categorical prohibition. The historical interpretation concludes that this situation represents an unconscious legal gap. A subsequent teleological interpretation of Article 367 TCC clarifies the legislative intent. By stipulating that delegation can be made to 'persons,' the provision implicitly requires the delegate to be an entity capable of bearing legal responsibility. Under this interpretation, Article 367 of the TCC excludes AI systems from delegation as they lack this essential attribute under current law. While there is no explicit prohibition, given the choice of the word 'person' in the Article 367 of the TCC and the presumed will of the legislator underlying that choice, delegation of management tasks to AI systems in Turkish law appears impermissible under the current legal framework due to AI's lack of legal personality and responsibility.

Considering that there is no precise determination in German statutory law regarding the personal scope of delegation, delegation can be made even to corporate departments that lack legal personality. Furthermore, Section 80(2) of the WpHG demonstrates the legislature's intent to allow delegation of (specific) decision-making authority to algorithmic systems that lack legal personality. Consequently, and in contrast to Turkish corporate law, the absence of legal personality in an AI system does not, *per se*, constitute a legal barrier to its appointment as a delegate in German corporate law.

With respect to the substantive and procedural scope of delegation, and assuming that delegation to AI is not precluded by AI's lack of legal personality under Turkish law, the preparatory, substantive decision-making, and implementation phases of executive management tasks can be delegated to AI systems in both legal systems. In terms of core management tasks, the preparatory and implementation phases can be delegated to AI, whereas the substantive decision-making phases cannot be delegated to AI in both legal systems.

From a *de lege ferenda* perspective, it would be prudent for the Turkish legislator to enact specific legislation to govern the delegation of management tasks to AI systems. In this way, the board of directors may leverage AI systems in a transparent, secure and legally predictable manner. Since the prevailing German legal doctrine is already in favour of delegating management tasks to AI systems, there is no immediate need for specific regulation in this regard in German corporate law. The German doctrinal discourse, in the interim, may provide boards with transitional guidance on delegating management tasks to AI. Nevertheless, enacting specific legislation on AI delegation in both legal systems would be beneficial for establishing clear principles for boards and for ensuring legal predictability.

3.5 Board's Potential Duty to Integrate AI into Corporation Management

3.5.1 In General

The legal permissibility for boards to use AI[183] and to formally delegate management tasks to AI[184] has been evaluated in the foregoing sections for both jurisdictions. As a next step, the question of whether corporate boards are obligated to integrate AI into corporation management requires a legal analysis under the doctrinal views, since there is no blanket mandate to adopt AI in corporation management in Turkish[185] and German[186] corporate law. However, given AI's capacity to process vast datasets and deliver predictive analytics that alternative methods cannot match, boards will likely face growing expectations to integrate AI into corporation management, particularly into the decision-making processes.[187] If such AI-generated predictions become the benchmark for comprehensive information gathering, a board's failure to obtain and consider these technologically advanced insights could itself be construed as a breach of their duty to act on an informed basis,[188] making the use of AI not just a strategic advantage but a legal necessity for sound governance. Therefore, under this title, whether boards are obligated to integrate AI systems into corporation management will be examined in light of their duty of care and the business judgment rule in Turkish and German law. The boards' duty of care in Turkish and German corporate law was investigated in the previous chapter.[189] As a complement to this investigation, the business judgment rule in both legal systems will be

[183] See 3.3.2.

[184] See 3.4.3.

[185] Güçlütürk (2021), p. 462; Metin (2021), pp. 524–525.

[186] Möslein (2018), ZIP, p. 209; Li (2022), p. 121; Calabro (2023), p. 176; Möslein (2023a), p. 182; Telle (2023), p. 79; Casper and Möslein (2025), ZGR, p. 886; Sanders (2025), NZG, p. 1406; Windorf (2025), p. 166.

[187] Töre (2025), SÜHFD, p. 902.

[188] Möslein (2025a), p. 626.

[189] Respectively see 2.1.1.3.1.1. and 2.1.1.3.2.1.

reviewed comparatively to base subsequent examination regarding the board's potential obligation to use AI systems.

3.5.2 Comparative Analysis of AI's Integration into Corporation Management as a Potential Duty under the Board's Duty of Care

Board members are obligated to exercise a certain level of care in performing their duties. Although the requisite standard is defined as that of a 'prudent manager' under Turkish law and a 'prudent and conscientious manager' under German law, the board's duty of care is not a static obligation, but a dynamic one. Hence, the increasing digital transformation of corporations necessitates modernising traditional due diligence standards to properly assess board members' duty of care.[190] One of the most fundamental requirements of this duty is that boards take the necessary measures to advance the corporation's interests and ensure the sustainability of its business amid changing market conditions and technological developments. In this context, just as boards are expected to constantly monitor market conditions from an economic perspective, it is also a requirement of their duty of care to keep up with technological developments relevant to corporate management.[191]

Given today's technological advancements, AI's progress is striking. AI enhances business efficiency by delivering superior administrative capabilities, executing tasks such as scheduling and reporting with unmatched speed, accuracy, and cost-effectiveness. Beyond streamlining operations, AI's real-time data processing and analytical capabilities enable optimised decision-making, enabling corporations to maintain strategic agility and a competitive edge in fast-moving markets.[192] It is possible to utilise these AI features across many of a corporation's activities.[193] AI, capable of collecting and processing vast amounts of data and generating analyses and predictions, can provide significant benefits, particularly in corporate management. Therefore, the question of whether the board

---

[190] Nowak (2022), p. 37.

[191] Telle (2023), p. 69.

[192] Dönmez Canseven (2021), p. 81; Karadeniz (2023), TAAD, p. 272; Ahern (2024), p. 411.

[193] For a systematic list and explanations of AI's practical benefits in terms of board's fiduciary duties, see Cowger, (2023), JOLTI, p. 158 ff.

members are obliged to integrate AI into corporation management within the scope of their duty of care must be answered.

There is no general obligation on boards to integrate AI systems into corporation management under their duty of care in both Turkish[194] and German[195] legal doctrine. In the latter, it is generally accepted that a management board can, in individual cases, where proven systems offer material advantages,[196] or where the corporation has a digitally savvy nature[197] or where AI outputs already exist as an information source,[198] be obligated to use AI.[199] According to these perspectives, the board must conduct a case-specific assessment to determine whether AI integration into corporation management is reasonable and necessary[200] in terms of the corporation's interests.[201] Likewise, Turkish legal doctrine argues that holding board members liable for failing to adopt AI is premature, given the technology's current developmental stage and lack of standardisation. However, the future advancements, such as proven AI reliability and widespread industry adoption, may establish a new duty of care benchmark for certain corporations.[202] Until then, assessments must be conducted on a case-by-case basis.[203]

Another view in Turkish legal doctrine argues that AI has become essential for economic survival, as corporations and individuals now depend on it. Hence, corporations must adopt cutting-edge technologies like AI to remain competitive, framing its use as a fiduciary obligation for boards under the duty of care.[204] Therefore, board members' duty of care requires them to select and implement

---

[194] Bahtiyar (2021), p. 49; Güçlütürk (2021), pp. 470–471; Helvacı (2021), pp. 49–50; Metin (2021), p. 525; Bora Çınar (2022), p. 216; Seçer (2025), p. 104.

[195] Noack (2019), ZHR, p. 122; Li (2022), p. 121; Calabro (2023), p. 176 ff.; Möslein (2023a), p. 182; Telle (2023), p. 79; Casper and Möslein (2025), ZGR, p. 886; Windorf (2025), p. 166.

[196] Noack (2019), ZHR, p. 122; Windorf (2025), p. 165.

[197] Nowak (2022), p. 91.

[198] Noack (2019), ZHR, p. 122 ff.; Telle (2023), p. 67.

[199] Möslein (2018), ZIP, p. 209; Lieder (2022), p. 339; Möslein (2023a), p. 182; Rolsing (2025), pp. 426–427; Windorf (2025), p. 166–167.

[200] Casper and Möslein (2025), ZGR, p. 886; Windorf (2025), p. 166–167.

[201] Rolsing (2025), pp. 516 ff.

[202] Bora Çınar (2022), p. 216.

[203] Bahtiyar (2021), p. 49; Metin (2021), p. 525; Seçer (2025), p. 104.

[204] Eroğlu (2021), pp. 475–477.

AI systems that are appropriately matched to their corporation's specific operational requirements and governance needs.[205] According to this view, when an industry establishes widely accepted standards for specific AI applications, boards using such systems may be deemed to have complied with their duty of care.[206] However, a practical argument for mandating AI systems, based on their increasing adoption in corporate practice, is criticised in German legal doctrine. It is argued that two fundamental requirements for the recognition of customary law are absent.[207] There is no judicial precedent confirming such an obligation, and the necessary longstanding, widespread practice, coupled with legal conviction, remains unproven.[208]

In both legal doctrines, it is accepted that the potential liability of corporate boards for failing to implement AI systems in corporation management depends on legal interpretation and case-specific circumstances, including the technology's proven effectiveness for particular tasks, industry standards, and foreseeable consequences of non-adoption. However, the defensibility of a board's decision to disregard these technologies diminishes over time, except in cases where a valid justification[209] can be established.[210] Hence, board members who choose not to implement AI systems must document and substantiate their reasoning,[211] as an unexplained rejection of demonstrably superior technological tools could constitute a breach of the fiduciary duty of care.

[205] Kaya (2024), p. 97.

[206] Cf. Varlı (2025), p. 258 and 279.

[207] Nowak (2022), p. 76.

[208] Nowak (2022), p. 76.

[209] A valid justification may be rooted in the organization's scale and financial capacity. Özer and Tomrukçu (2025), BATİDER, p. 260; Seçer (2025), p. 102.

[210] Spindler (2019b), ECFR, p. 136; Bora Çınar (2022), p. 216; Kaya (2024), p. 99; Özer and Tomrukçu (2025), BATİDER, p. 260; Seçer (2025), p. 102.

[211] Kaya (2024), p. 96. This reasoning must demonstrate that a prudent board member in a comparable corporation would reasonably take the same course of action. Özer and Tomrukçu (2025), BATİDER, p. 260.

3.5.3 Comparative Analysis of AI's Integration into Corporation Management as a Potential Duty under the Business Judgment Rule

3.5.3.1 A Brief Review: Business Judgment Rule in Turkish and German Law

The BJR[212] is a legal principle that provides a safe harbour for board members from personal liability for business decisions made in good faith, with due care, and without conflicts of interest, even if those decisions later prove harmful to the corporation.[213] The board members should not be liable for the economic outcomes (expediency) of their decisions, provided they exercised due diligence and made their best efforts in the decision-making process.[214] In this context, if the adequate research is made to gather necessary information and a decision is taken by safeguarding the interests of the corporation in compliance with the principle of honesty, even the corporation is damaged because of such decision, the liability of board members does not arise.[215] The judicial review should focus on whether the BJR's specific criteria were met in taking this decision, and whether the decision-making process was reasonable and non-arbitrary. However, when a court makes a ruling, it often highlights that the board's initial choice was mistaken and caused harm to the corporation. This realisation tends to seem much more apparent in hindsight than it did at the moment the decision was made,[216] a phenomenon known as hindsight bias.[217] Consequently, the BJR serves as a safeguard by mitigating the risk of hindsight bias when courts evaluate board decisions after the fact. It also allows boards a certain degree of discretion that is not subject to judicial review, provided the BJR's conditions are satisfied.[218]

---

[212] The business judgment rule was defined by the Delaware Supreme Court in its 1984 *Aronson vs. Lewis* decision as "...*The business judgement rule is a presumption that in making a business decision, the directors of a corporation acted on an informed basis, in good faith, and in the honest belief that the action taken was in the best interests of the company*..." Aronson v. Lewis, 473 A.2d 805, 812 (Del.1984).

[213] Helleringer and Möslein, (2025), U. Chi. L. Rev. Online, p. 1.

[214] Kırca (2004), BATİDER, p. 88; Çamoğlu (2010), p. 75; Göktürk (2011), İnÜHFD, p. 238; Sevi (2021), p. 288 ff.; Pulaşlı (2022), § 37, para. 158 g, p. 1581.

[215] Seyfarth (2016), § 23, para. 18 ff.; Link in Wachter (2022), AktG, § 93, para. 23.

[216] Kırca in Kırca et al. (2013), p. 660; Akdağ Güney (2016), p. 191.

[217] Link in Wachter (2022), AktG, § 93, para. 23.

[218] Akdağ Güney (2016), p. 190.

Turkish law currently lacks explicit statutory recognition of the BJR.[219] The preamble to Article 369 of the TCC indirectly recognises the BJR.[220] Hence, it is argued in Turkish legal doctrine that board members cannot be held to BJR standards solely because the concept is referenced in the preamble of the TCC.[221] Despite dissenting scholarly opinions, Turkish legal doctrine generally accepts that the BJR is fully applicable and legally valid within the framework of Turkish corporate law.[222] While the prevailing view holds that this rule aligns with Article 369 TCC's duty of care standards,[223] the Supreme Court of Appeals has maintained an ambiguous stance.[224] On the other hand, Turkish lower courts began to consider the BJR as a legal standard to determine whether board members should be held personally liable for damages in specific cases.[225]

In German law, the BJR was first adopted by the German Federal Court in 1997 in the *Arag/Garmenbeck* decision,[226] and it was integrated into corporation

---

[219] As the chairperson of the commission that prepared the draft of the TCC, Tekinalp states that the absence of an explicit codification of the BJR in the TCC stems from its undefined scope and unsettled elements. Hence, it is considered preferable for these elements to be settled and maturated through evolving case law. Tekinalp (2020), p. 444.

[220] Preamble to Art. 369 of the TCC: "*The prudent management principle recognizes that a board member can make a "business judgment" in accordance with corporate governance principles and is based on the principle that a member should not be held liable in cases where risks arise from this. According to the generally accepted rule, if appropriate research has been conducted, information has been received from the relevant parties and a decision has been made by the board of directors, even if developments are completely contrary and the corporation has suffered a loss, negligence cannot be considered.*"

[221] Güçlütürk (2021), pp. 466–468. For the view that BJR cannot be considered applicable in Turkish law given its current regulation under the TCC, see Özdemir (2017), pp. 152–161.

[222] Akdağ Güney (2016), p. 189 and 193; Pulaşlı (2022), § 37, para. 158 f., p. 1580; Kaya (2024), p. 72; Özer and Tomrukçu (2025), BATİDER, p. 245.

[223] Akdağ Güney (2016), p. 189 and 193; Pulaşlı (2022), § 37, para. 158 g, p. 1581; Bahtiyar (2024), p. 211; Çamoğlu in Poroy et al. (2025), para. 582, p. 426. As the chairperson of the commission that prepared the draft of the TCC, Tekinalp states that Art. 374 of the TCC also provides a legal basis for the application of BJR within the scope of Turkish corporate law. Tekinalp (2020), pp. 443–445.

[224] Sevi (2021), p. 284; Pulaşlı (2022), § 37, para. 194 ff., p. 1600 ff.; Kaya (2024), p. 72.

[225] For lower court decisions considering the BJR, see İstanbul 2nd Intellectual and Industrial Property Rights Court, Decision date: 12.12.2019, Case No: 2016/239, Decision No: 2019/515; Antalya 4th Commercial Court of First Instance, Decision Date: 21.06.2022, Case No: 2018/324, Decision No: 2022/544; Bakırköy 1st Commercial Court of First Instance, Decision Date: 17.03.2022, Case No: 2014/1099, Decision No: 2022/278 (This decision later uphold, see 12th Civil Chamber of İstanbul Regional Court of Appeal, Decision Date: 24.09.2025, Case No: 2022/1497, Decision No: 2025/1411).

[226] BGH, Judgment of 21 April 1997, "ARAG/Garmenbeck", BGHZ 135, p. 244 ff.

law in 2005[227] through the UMAG.[228] The BJR plays a crucial role in German corporate law by protecting management boards from liability arising solely from adverse outcomes when courts review decisions retrospectively.[229]

As the BJR lacks a statutory basis and specific high court decisions[230] in Turkish law, the main criteria for its application are developed in legal doctrine.[231] According to the legal doctrine, there must be a decision taken by the board to apply BJR. This decision must be a business decision.[232] The board members must conduct sufficient research to be informed regarding the decision.[233] In the scope of this research, an expert opinion must be obtained if necessary.[234] There must be no conflict of interest related to the board members, and they must make this decision in good faith.[235] Lastly, board members must act rationally and reasonably when making this decision. If these criteria are met cumulatively, board members can be protected under the BJR.

In German law, the main criteria for the application of BJR were developed in legal doctrine and case law based on Section 93(1) sentence 2 of the AktG.[236] These criteria are similar to the requirements set out in Turkish legal doctrine. Again, there must be a business decision.[237] This decision must be based on adequate information. The board members must be free from conflicts of interest

[227] Sailer-Coceani in Schmidt and Lutter (2020), AktG, § 93 para. 13; Link in Wachter (2022), AktG, § 93, para. 22.

[228] *Gesetz zur Unternehmensintegrität und Modernisierung des Anfechtungsrechts* (Act on the Implementation of the German Corporate Governance Code—UMAG) of 22.9.2005, BGBl. I 2005, 2802.

[229] Link in Wachter (2022), AktG, § 93, para. 23.

[230] Pulaşlı (2022), § 37, para. 194, p. 1600.

[231] Bozkurt Yaşar (2015), pp. 60–127; Akdağ Güney (2016), pp. 188–193.

[232] Pulaşlı (2022), § 37, para. 171, p. 1591.

[233] Pulaşlı (2022), § 37, para. 186, p. 1597.

[234] Pulaşlı (2022), § 37, para. 187, p. 1597.

[235] Bozkurt Yaşar (2015), p. 108; Pulaşlı (2022), § 37, paras. 188–189, pp. 1597–1598; Çamoğlu in Poroy et al. (2025), para. 582, p. 426; Varlı (2025), p. 126.

[236] § 93(1) sentence 2 of the AktG: "*No dereliction of duties will be given in those instances in which the member of the management board, in taking a business decision, was within their rights to reasonably assume that they were acting on the basis of adequate information and in the best interests of the corporation.*"

[237] Wirth et al. (2017), p. 111; Fleischer in Spindler and Stilz (2019), § 93, AktG, para. 67 ff.; Spindler in MünchKomm-AktG (2019), § 93, para. 43 ff.; Sailer-Coceani in Schmidt and Lutter (2020), AktG, § 93, para. 15.

regarding the decision,[238] and they must act in good faith.[239] If these criteria are met, a breach of duty is not established solely based on fault. Thus, the rule has meaningful legal implications in German corporate law, extending beyond the mere burden of proof.[240]

As it is accepted in both legal systems, the BJR applies specifically to business decisions. This doctrinal principle means the board must have the authority to choose among different actions.[241] Business decisions encompass key corporate actions, such as investing in new technologies, developing products or expanding markets, pursuing M&A transactions, approving major loans, and entering legal settlements.[242] Conversely, it is accepted that the BJR does not extend to legally binding decisions under corporate law -specifically TCC and AktG- and responsibilities arising from the other codes, the corporation's articles of association and lawful resolutions of the general assembly.[243]

Under the BJR, courts must analyse not the expediency of the board's business decisions.[244] On the contrary, the degree of care shown in the decision-making process must be considered when assessing whether board members acted as prudent managers. Hence, the negotiation process and the board members' access to necessary documents and information should be considered.[245]

Having an informed decision reflects the board's fulfilment of the necessary care under the BJR. Hence, objective criteria must be established for the *ex post* assessment of whether a board member is reasonably informed about

---

[238] Spindler in MünchKomm-AktG (2019), § 93, para. 69; Link in Wachter (2022), AktG, § 93, para. 24; Nowak (2022), pp. 92–93.

[239] Wirth et al. (2017), p. 111; Sailer-Coceani in Schmidt and Lutter (2020), AktG, § 93, para. 13; Link in Wachter (2022), AktG, § 93, para. 24.

[240] Seyfarth (2016), § 23, para. 19; Sailer-Coceani in Schmidt and Lutter (2020), AktG, § 93, para. 14; Link in Wachter (2022), AktG, § 93, para. 25.

[241] Sailer-Coceani in Schmidt and Lutter (2020), AktG, § 93, para. 15; Link in Wachter (2022), AktG, § 93, para. 26; Pulaşlı (2022), § 37, para. 159a, p. 1584.

[242] Fleischer in Spindler and Stilz (2019), AktG, § 93, para. 68; Spindler in MünchKomm-AktG (2019), § 93, para. 49.

[243] For Turkish law, see Göktürk (2011), İnÜHFD, p. 225; Bozkurt Yaşar (2015), p. 59; Pulaşlı (2022), § 37, para. 190, p. 1599; Varlı (2025), p. 126. For German law, see Seyfarth (2016), § 23, para. 21; Sailer-Coceani in Schmidt and Lutter (2020), AktG, § 93, para. 15; Link in Wachter (2022), AktG, § 93, para. 26.

[244] Çamoğlu (2010), p. 75; Akdağ Güney (2010), p. 82; Bozkurt Yaşar (2015), p. 170; Akdağ Güney (2016), p. 192; Çamoğlu in Poroy et al. (2025), para. 582, p. 427.

[245] Bozkurt Yaşar (2015), p. 170.

a decision.[246] Analysing alternative scenarios and probable risks may constitute objective criteria for assessing whether a board member was reasonably informed.[247] Moreover, the cost and utility of the information and the significance and urgency of the decision are expected to be considered together in assessing the board's decision under the BJR.[248]

The board can gather the necessary information for its decision-making by consulting both corporation employees and external experts. If the board does not have the required expertise, it is legally required to seek assistance in both legal systems.[249] Legal precedents[250] in German law have established specific standards for how the board should obtain legal advice, and these principles may also be applied to the procurement of other types of expert advice.[251] According to these legal precedents, the board must select a qualified advisor who can provide unbiased advice. Moreover, the board should ensure the advisor has sufficient information to complete relevant tasks effectively. Lastly, the board must subject the advice given to a plausibility check.[252]

Although there is no specific precedent in Turkish law, the legal doctrine holds that an expert report on the decision's subject should be provided to board members to support their understanding of the decision's prospective positive and negative effects on the corporation.[253] As an indication of their active participation in the informed decision-making process, board members are expected to study and criticise information and reports provided by the relevant committee or third-party experts.[254] In this regard, the Supreme Court of Appeals has recognised that board members who rely on expert reports when making significant business decisions, such as purchasing commercial raw materials, should

246 Bozkurt Yaşar (2015), p. 178.

247 Bozkurt Yaşar (2015), p. 178.

248 Bozkurt Yaşar (2015), p. 179.

249 For Turkish law, see Akdağ Güney (2010), p. 73; Kırca in Kırca et al. (2013), pp. 713–714; Bozkurt Yaşar (2015), p. 152; Çamurcu (2015), p. 74; Hacımahmutoğlu (2015), BATİDER, p. 35; Sevi (2021), p. 148; Çamlı (2024), p. 210. For German law, see Hopt and Roth in Großkomm AktG (2015), AktG § 93, para. 108; Link in Wachter (2022), AktG, § 93, para. 34.

250 BGH, Judgment of 20.9.2011—II ZR 234/09 (Ision), ZIP 2011, p. 2097 ff.

251 Link in Wachter (2022), AktG, § 93, para. 34.

252 Link in Wachter (2022), AktG, § 93, para. 34.

253 Bozkurt Yaşar (2015), p. 182; Kaya (2024), p. 74.

254 Bozkurt Yaşar (2015), p. 183.

be shielded from liability for resulting damages, provided the expert consultation was duly conducted.[255]

The BJR applies only if the board diligently identify and prepare necessary information for decision-making.[256] The board cannot, and need not, exhaust every potential information source before making a decision.[257] According to both legal doctrines, the adequacy of information for business decisions depends on a contextual assessment weighing multiple factors[258] such as the decision's significance, complexity, urgency and time constraints, cost-benefit trade-offs of additional data collection, prior experience with similar decisions, and legal/practical limits on information access.[259] However, the debate regarding the appropriate information basis is ongoing in German legal doctrine. The requirement set by the Federal Court of Justice that management must explore "*all available sources of information of a factual and legal nature in the specific decision-making situation*"[260] is criticised as it extends the criteria beyond what is reasonable.[261] It is argued in German legal doctrine that such a petition would, in practice, essentially undermine the BJR[262] as being *contra legem*.[263] It is proposed that boards be given some discretion regarding the appropriateness of the information they use as a basis for their decisions.[264] However, the appropriateness of information serves as the critical yet inherently ambiguous foundation for applying the BJR, often termed its 'Achilles heel' due to the lack of precise legal standards governing what constitutes an appropriate information basis.[265] The Higher Regional Court of Cologne's ruling clarifies the management board's duty

---

[255] 11th Civil Chamber of Supreme Court of Appeals, Decision Date: 14.10.1982, Case No: 1982/3596, Decision No:1982/3884.

[256] Link in Wachter (2022), AktG, § 93, para. 31.

[257] Spindler in MünchKomm-AktG (2019), § 93, para. 55.

[258] Spindler in MünchKomm-AktG(2019), § 93, para. 55; Sailer-Coceani in Schmidt and Lutter (2020), AktG, § 93, para. 17.

[259] Bozkurt Yaşar (2015), pp. 172–173; Sailer-Coceani in Schmidt and Lutter (2020), AktG, § 93, para. 17; Li (2022), p. 38; Link in Wachter (2022), AktG, § 93, para. 31; Möslein (2025a), pp. 626–627.

[260] BGH, Judgment of 14.7.2008—II ZR 202/07, ZIP 2008, p. 1675 ff.

[261] Link in Wachter (2022), AktG, § 93, para. 31.

[262] Windorf (2025), p. 147.

[263] Fleischer in Spindler and Stilz (2019), AktG, § 93, para. 70 ff.; Sailer-Coceani in Schmidt and Lutter (2020), AktG, § 93, para. 17. Further, see references in Calabro (2023), p. 172, fn. 459.

[264] Link in Wachter (2022), AktG, § 93, para. 31.

[265] See references in Windorf (2025), p. 144, fn. 25.

to establish an appropriate information basis under BJR. According to this ruling, while boards must fundamentally exhaust all available information sources, this obligation is bounded by a proportionality test that weighs the costs and benefits of fact-finding,[266] which the board should balance.[267] The court clarifies that the standard applies prospectively rather than through retrospective perfectionism.[268] However, given the Federal Court of Justice's strict position and the criticism of the legal doctrine, the debate seems to continue.

3.5.3.2 Comparative Analysis

As established above,[269] the prevailing legal doctrine in both legal systems maintains that the duty of care does not require a general mandate for board members to employ AI systems. Instead, the potential necessity of AI integration must be determined through a contextual, case-by-case assessment of whether its absence would constitute a breach of the prudent management standard. This section, therefore, separately examines whether a *de facto* obligation to utilise AI arises from the application of the BJR. The main investigation is how the use of AI in the decision-making process interacts with the BJR's criterion of an 'appropriate information basis.' Specifically, the analysis will address two questions. First, whether the standard of care implicit in the BJR compels board members to use AI to establish an appropriate informational basis; and second, whether the mere utilisation of an AI system can, in the decision-making process, be considered as *prima facie* evidence that the appropriate informational basis criteria of the BJR have been satisfied.[270]

AI systems reduce uncertainty by analysing large datasets to generate actionable insights and accurate predictions, enhancing decision-making across various fields.[271] Turkish legal doctrine argues that as AI becomes integral to data-driven decision-making, the legal standard for informed business judgment, which inherently involves uncertainty, may increasingly require directors to consult AI-generated insights in fulfilling their fiduciary duties. Such an advancement could

---

266 Higher Regional Court of Cologne, Judgment of 1.10.2019—18 U 34/18, NZG 2020, p. 113, para. 78.

267 Spindler (2019b), ECFR, p. 135.

268 Higher Regional Court of Cologne, Judgment of 1.10.2019—18 U 34/18, NZG 2020, p. 113, para. 78.

269 See 3.5.2.

270 For a similar methodological approach, see Casper and Möslein (2025), ZGR, pp. 879–880.

271 Uğurerkan (2024), p. 50.

evolve into an implicit obligation to leverage AI.[272] Hence, it is argued that decisions on AI adoption should fall under the BJR.[273] Especially for high-stakes strategic decisions, leveraging AI as a strategic partner to analyse comprehensive data beyond human processing capacity is becoming a best practice.[274] Hence, AI use in board decisions is an indicator of whether the obligation to obtain sufficient information and make the best decision for the corporation is fulfilled.[275]

Section 93(1) of the AktG explicitly imposes a mandatory duty on board members to base their business decisions on 'appropriate information.' The legal doctrine argues that this longstanding legal standard demands a modern interpretation.[276] Given AI's demonstrable superiority in processing vast datasets, expectations for making informed business decisions have heightened,[277] and a decision made without its analytical support may now fail to meet the legal threshold of being 'reasonably informed.'[278] To fulfil their fundamental duty to act on an informed basis within the scope of BJR, it is becoming increasingly necessary for corporate decision-makers to integrate certain digital technologies into their decision-making processes. This foreseeable evolution in corporate law, which would mandate that boards utilise AI to meet their standard of care, is referred to as the 'AI Judgment Rule.'[279] This emerging doctrine represents a modern adaptation of the traditional business judgment rule, updating the benchmark for informed, prudent corporate leadership in the digital age. However, it is counter-argued that the existing legal framework strikes a balance between encouraging innovation and maintaining accountability, making a separate 'AI Judgment Rule' unnecessary.[280] According to this view, a novel 'AI Judgment Rule' should not be codified since Section 93(1) of the AktG already provides the necessary legal basis to govern board's liability risks regarding the business decisions informed by AI.[281]

---

[272] Töre (2025), SÜHFD, p. 903.

[273] Seçer (2025), p. 103.

[274] Bora Çınar (2022), p. 213.

[275] Varlı (2025), p. 279.

[276] Helleringer and Möslein, (2025), U. Chi. L. Rev. Online, p. 5.

[277] Möslein (2018), ZIP, p. 209; Sailer-Coceani in Schmidt and Lutter (2020), AktG, § 93, para. 17. Also see Spindler in MünchKomm-AktG (2019), AktG, § 93, para. 56.

[278] Helleringer and Möslein, (2025), U. Chi. L. Rev. Online, p. 6.

[279] Helleringer and Möslein, (2025), U. Chi. L. Rev. Online, p. 5.

[280] Kremer and Langenbucher (2024), pp. 84–86, 3.24–3.27.

[281] Kremer and Langenbucher (2024), p. 84, 3.24.

Aside from the theoretical debate on adopting a separate AI Judgment Rule, the use of AI in establishing an appropriate information basis for business decisions is also being examined as a new and specific phenomenon. Within this scope, German legal doctrine argues that the case for mandatory adoption of AI systems fails to account for critical qualitative limitations, as they lack essential human decision-making capabilities, particularly in evaluating moral, ethical, and intuitive factors that evolve with social norms. Therefore, their inability to handle evaluative aspects of decision-making undermines arguments for compulsory use, especially for strategic choices that require human judgment beyond pure data analysis.[282] To overcome AI's such limitations, it is argued in the Turkish legal doctrine that for a decision supported by AI to qualify for protection under the BJR, board members must fulfil requirements that extend beyond merely researching and comparing the AI's recommendations. These essential requirements, which can only be met by the board members themselves, involve human judgment based on principles such as good faith, fairness, and the application of personal experience, factors that an algorithm cannot inherently consider.[283]

The BJR provides a framework in Turkish law for evaluating board decisions on AI adoption, with standards that vary by corporation size and resources. For well-capitalised firms, failing to implement AI, especially in critical functions such as audit and risk management, may breach the board's fiduciary duties, as AI tools have become industry-standard for operational efficiency and risk mitigation. Conversely, smaller corporations may justifiably forgo AI adoption under the BJR if implementation is demonstrably impractical or financially prohibitive.[284] Compliance with industry standards and pre-evaluation of an AI system's accuracy are other criteria considered in Turkish legal doctrine for assessing AI use under BJR. For instance, when a corporation implements an industry-accepted AI system with proven high accuracy after conducting proper due diligence, such adoption typically qualifies as reasonable business judgment. In these circumstances, board members should not face liability for breach of duty, even if a decision resulting from an AI-integrated decision-making process causes damages to the corporation.[285] As a result, Turkish legal doctrine accepts that the obligation to be sufficiently informed does not inherently require consultation

[282] Nowak (2022), pp. 75–76.

[283] When making business decisions, AI should be treated as one information tool among many since AI does not have all features of human judgment, including intuition and experience in interpersonal relations. Özer and Tomrukçu (2025), BATİDER, p. 265.

[284] For a similar reasoning, see Kaya (2024), p. 101.

[285] Güçlütürk (2021), p. 468.

with AI.[286] However, the board of directors' utilisation of AI in decision-making processes could create a pathway for liability avoidance.[287] Conversely, board members who choose not to utilise AI systems, despite their demonstrated superiority over human capabilities in boardroom decision-making, may risk violating their duty of care obligations[288] and fall outside the BJR protection.

In the German legal doctrine, another distinction is drawn between the business decision itself and the process of deciding how much information is required to make it. Unlike the final judgment, which is protected from judicial second-guessing under the BJR, this preliminary weighing of the costs and benefits of gathering information is subject to full judicial scrutiny.[289] However, it is essential to recognise that the board retains significant discretion in choosing and prioritising the information they utilise.[290] The selection of specific AI functions and datasets also typically falls within this discretionary realm, though legal frameworks such as data protection and anti-discrimination laws must be observed.[291] However, the management board's duty to secure an 'appropriate information basis' may increasingly require the use of AI systems when such tools are already available internally[292] and offer reliable solutions. This legal reasoning creates a dynamic standard. As AI tools become more affordable, accurate, and common in corporate practice, the justification for not employing them in significant decisions becomes increasingly difficult to assert[293] and is subject to plausibility check.[294] This view stems from the dynamic 'appropriate information basis' requirement, which evolves with technological progress.[295] Consequently, the emergence of a corporate law duty to make proper and reasonable use of available AI systems is a foreseeable legal development.[296] However, its precise parameters, validity, and intensity remain to be fully defined by legal doctrine,

[286] Özer and Tomrukçu (2025), BATİDER, p. 259.

[287] Çonkar in Karatepe Kaya et al. (2025), p. 78; İpekel Kayalı in Karatepe Kaya et al. (2025), p. 76.

[288] Kaya (2024), p. 96.

[289] Möslein (2020c), p. 813; Möslein (2022), p. 79; Möslein (2023b), p. 425; Helleringer and Möslein (2025), U. Chi. L. Rev. Online, p. 6.

[290] Sailer-Coceani in Schmidt and Lutter (2020), AktG, § 93, para. 17; Linke (2021), p. 206.

[291] Kremer and Langenbucher (2024), pp. 82–83, 3.23.

[292] Noack (2019), ZHR, p. 122 ff.; Telle (2023), p. 67; Rolsing (2025), p. 545.

[293] Möslein (2020b), p. 514; Möslein (2020c), p. 813; Möslein (2023b), p. 425; Helleringer and Möslein (2025), U. Chi. L. Rev. Online, p. 6; Roth (2025), SSRN, p. 8.

[294] Möslein (2018), ZIP, p. 209.

[295] Nowak (2022), pp. 72–73.

[296] Möslein (2020c), p. 813; Möslein (2022), p. 79.

courts and legislators.[297] This duty may not mandate AI use in every case, but would penalise the unreasonable rejection of a readily available, reliable, and relevant technological resource. Since the current AktG framework provides sufficient flexibility regarding AI use to meet the 'appropriate information basis' requirement, the doctrine holds that an obligation to use AI should not be codified in stock corporation law.[298]

In the debate over whether boards of directors are obliged to use AI when making business decisions, the resultative view in Turkish legal doctrine (although there is a lack of targeted legal analyses on this issue) is that a case-by-case analysis should be conducted rather than finding a categorical answer,[299] since boards are not obligated to use every available tool or technology and every decision requires a different informational basis. Expecting the same level of information and using all tools for board decisions impose an unrealistic burden.[300] Modern governance requires boards to balance thorough due diligence with real-world constraints such as the impracticality of pursuing every data source given finite time and resources. Hence, it is argued that exercising sound judgment means strategically selecting sufficient (not exhaustive) information while weighing investigation costs against decision quality.[301]

Similar to the views in Turkish legal doctrine, the prevailing opinion in German legal doctrine is that the question of mandatory AI adoption under the BJR cannot be answered categorically, but requires a nuanced, case-specific evaluation weighing costs, benefits, and contextual factors.[302] Key considerations include the significance and complexity of the decision, the maturity and reliability of available AI systems, operational constraints such as time sensitivity and cost, the legal and practical feasibility of obtaining information, industry standards[303] and the comparative advantage over human analysis.[304] For instance, the use of AI may be considered unnecessary when the board already possesses superior expertise.[305] Each application must be assessed individually to ensure the AI system

[297] Möslein (2022), p. 79.

[298] Kremer and Langenbucher (2024), p. 86, 3.28.

[299] Özer and Tomrukçu (2025), BATİDER, p. 259.

[300] Güçlütürk (2021), p. 470.

[301] Bora Çınar (2022), p. 214.

[302] Linke (2021), p. 206; Li (2022), pp. 52–53; Lieder (2022), p. 340; Helleringer and Möslein (2025), U. Chi. L. Rev. Online, p. 6; Windorf (2025), pp. 165–170.

[303] Casper and Möslein (2025), ZGR, p. 887; Rolsing (2025), pp. 557–548.

[304] Telle (2023), p. 70. Also see references in Telle (2023), p. 70, fn. 196.

[305] Li (2022), p. 39; Telle (2023), p. 68.

contributes meaningfully to the specific decision context.[306] As a result, it is widely accepted in the German legal doctrine that the BJR does not establish a blanket obligation to use AI in decision-making processes.[307]

The obligation to utilise AI systems to establish an appropriate information basis under BJR arises only in exceptional circumstances.[308] For instance, in data-intensive sectors where AI demonstrably outperforms human analysis, particularly for complex forecasting, large-scale data processing, or market-standard applications, its adoption may become necessary to meet the 'appropriate information' standard under the BJR.[309] Courts will assess whether the board's approach (including the non-use of AI) was reasonable based on case-specific factors such as the corporation's data reliance, economic proportionality, and prevailing industry practices.[310] While currently rare due to cost and implementation barriers, the threshold for mandatory AI adoption is expected to be lower as the technology becomes more accessible and its competitive advantages more pronounced.[311] Boards must therefore proactively evaluate AI's relevance to their decision-making processes. Hence, an explicit obligation to use AI would disregard the nuanced, context-dependent nature of these considerations. Instead, the flexible, fact-based assessment that considers diverse corporate needs inherent in existing law remains preferable.[312]

3.5.4 Interim Result

In contemporary Turkish and German corporate law, the integration of AI into corporation management remains a discretionary strategic choice for boards, not a legally compelled obligation. Instead of a blanket rule, a case-by-case evaluation of whether board members are required to integrate AI systems into corporation management under their duty of care is required in both legal systems. In this

---

306 Casper and Möslein (2025), ZGR, p. 880.

307 Möslein (2018), ZIP, p. 209; Weber et al. (2018), NZG, p. 1133 ff.; Lücke (2019), BB, p. 1991; Noack (2019a), ZHR, p. 122; Zetzsche (2019), AG, p. 9; Becker and Pordzik (2020), ZfPW, p. 347 ff.; Linke (2021), p. 206; Li (2022), p. 53; Calabro (2023), p. 176; Telle (2023), p. 62 ff.; Frey (2024), p. 150; Windorf (2025), p. 166.

308 Calabro (2023), p. 177; Windorf (2025), p. 165.

309 Lieder (2022), p. 340; Calabro (2023), p. 177.

310 Zetzsche (2019), AG, p. 9; Becker and Pordzik (2020), ZfPW, p. 347; Calabro (2023), pp. 176–178.

311 Möslein (2018), ZIP, pp. 209–210; Calabro (2023), p. 178.

312 Kremer and Langenbucher (2024), p. 86, 3.28.

evaluation, multiple factors, such as the technology's proven benefits, industry standards, and the corporation's size and resources, must be considered.

As AI systems become more reliable and widespread, they are raising the bar for what counts as prudent management. In this new reality, the number of cases in which boards are expected to use an AI system under their duty of care is increasing. Therefore, a board that chooses not to use a demonstrably beneficial and available AI system must provide and document a well-reasoned justification, grounded in the corporation's best interests. Failure to do so may increasingly be seen as a breach of their duty of care.

Under the BJR, both Turkish and German legal doctrines avoid establishing a categorical obligation for boards to use AI. The key legal question is whether the board members have based their decisions on an 'appropriate information basis,' a standard that must now account for modern technology. In a case-by-case assessment to answer this question, the decision's materiality, complexity, urgency, the board's prior experience with comparable decisions, the cost-effectiveness of gathering more data, and legal and practical constraints on data availability must be considered. Although using AI in corporation management is not a blanket requirement for the application of the BJR, it may be considered necessary in specific contexts. For instance, its use in data-intensive corporations or in scenarios where AI clearly offers a superior capability may be considered a requirement under the BJR. Therefore, a prudent board must continuously evaluate AI's applicability to management tasks. In this vein, the decision to forgo suitable AI must be documented with proportionate justifications. Otherwise, rejection of a reliable and available AI system without reasonable justifications may be considered as a failure to meet modern standards of prudent and informed management under the BJR.

Governing with AI: The Board's Evolving Duties

4

4.1 Proactive Framework Development: Board's Organisational Duties for AI Integration into Management

4.1.1 In General

Since the integration of AI into corporation management is still a nascent phenomenon, there are no specific statutory regulations directly governing such use in either Turkish or German[1] corporate law. For the same reason, judicial precedent has not yet emerged on this issue.[2] However, given the unique characteristics of AI systems and their increasing use in corporation management, board members' duties need to be modernised to account for AI's integration into corporation management processes.[3] Due to the lack of regulations and precedents, this task falls to legal doctrine.[4] Legal doctrine is already discussing the special organisational duties of board members regarding the integration of AI systems into corporation management,[5] by taking into account the general principles of corporate law,

---

[1] Möslein (2018), ZIP, p. 211; Li (2022), p. 15; Windorf (2025), p. 186.

[2] Möslein (2018), ZIP, p. 211; Windorf (2025), p. 186.

[3] Nowak (2022), p. 37; Zhao (2024), CLSR, p. 14.

[4] Möslein (2018), ZIP, p. 211.

[5] Möslein (2018), ZIP, p. 211; Lücke (2019), BB, p. 1993; Becker and Pordzik (2020), ZfPW, p. 348 ff.; Telle (2023), p. 87 ff.

S. T. İnce, *Artificial Intelligence and Corporation Management*, Juridicum – Schriftenreihe zum Wirtschafts-, Unternehmens- und Bankrecht / Series on Business, Corporate and Banking Law, https://doi.org/10.1007/978-3-658-52672-6_4

the balance of stakeholder interests, and the existing duties of board members.[6] In fact, when the classical development of law is taken into consideration, the legal rules to be applied to new situations should first be clarified through discussions to be held by the legal doctrine and then evolved into regulations, which will serve to produce more effective results in terms of the application of law to practical cases. When it comes to regulations related to AI, it becomes even more important to first engage in discussions within the legal doctrine rather than enacting rapid regulations. Because AI systems are developing dramatically, it is more likely that future regulations will fail to keep pace with these developments[7] and may even undermine technological advancements. For all these reasons, it is crucial to discuss the organisational duties that may be imposed on board members regarding the integration of AI into corporation management.

In this section, a comparative doctrinal analysis will be conducted to identify the organisational duties of boards integrating AI into corporation management. Scholarly discourse on the board's prospective organisational duties regarding the integration of AI into corporation management has made significant progress in German legal doctrine. In contrast, such discourse remains in an infancy stage within Turkish legal scholarship. Hence, this study will principally be informed by the mature German legal debate, supplemented by the emerging doctrinal perspectives in Turkish law. The duties revealed by this analysis will essentially be universal since the characteristics of AI systems, their benefits, and the risks they pose are universal, and the duties of board members, such as due diligence, management, and monitoring, are similar across modern corporate law systems, particularly in Turkish and German law. Using a comparative methodology, this study will also attempt to identify subject-specific differences between these two legal systems and explain how these differences will affect the results.

While identifying universal organisational duties for diligent board members in terms of AI integration into corporation management, it should also be noted that these duties should be evaluated case-by-case,[8] taking into account factors such as the legal system to which they apply, the type, scope and size of the corporation, relevant AI's prior operational deficiencies, transparency of AI logic and different characteristics of AI systems etc.[9] The duties identified here will

[6] For a 'smart regulation proposal' that prioritises the adaptation of existing board obligations and stakeholder participation in integrating AI into corporation management, see Zhao (2024), CLSR, p. 10 ff.

[7] Noack (2019), ZHR, p. 142; Windorf (2025), p. 267.

[8] Noack (2021), p. 951 ff.; Telle (2023), p. 102; Li (2022), p. 83.

[9] Telle (2023), pp. 102–103.

continue to change and evolve.[10] Therefore, this investigation will seek to contribute to the doctrinal debate by identifying general and abstract principles that can be interpreted and applied to specific cases.

This analysis adopts a unified framework for the organisational duties stemming from board-level AI integration, irrespective of whether it serves an advisory or a delegate function and whether it involves internal development or external procurement. Where different assessments are necessary, these functional distinctions and related consequences will be articulated separately. With this method, an attempt will be made to ensure analytical fluency by avoiding repeated similar evaluations.

4.1.2 Establishment of AI Policy

4.1.2.1 Comparative Review

AI's integration into corporation management introduces critical risks, including cybersecurity threats, data manipulation, algorithmic discrimination, and challenges to transparency and accountability.[11] Therefore, board members face heightened standards when relying on AI instead of a human specialist. Their oversight and auditing responsibilities become notably more stringent.[12] Hence, corporate boards must take precautions to mitigate these risks and ensure that AI integration into corporation management aligns with organisational values and long-term objectives.[13] For this purpose, boards must first develop a tailored AI policy that aligns with their overall business objectives.[14] It requires clearly defining AI's purpose[15] and ways of use[16] within the corporation's management while accounting for the corporation's unique culture, operational needs, strengths, and weaknesses. While stock corporations share fundamental traits, each requires

---

[10] Telle (2023), p. 103.

[11] Karadeniz (2023), TAAD, p. 273.

[12] Özer and Tomrukçu (2025), BATİDER, p. 258.

[13] Dönmez Canseven (2021), p. 105.

[14] Ustahaliloğlu (2025), CLGR, p. 131. Dan Byrne (n.d.). "Ten steps to creating an AI policy, Corporate Governance Institute." Available at: https://www.thecorporategovernanceinstitute.com/insights/guides/creating-an-ai-policy/?srsltid=AfmBOoqQA1VeZopdnHOcWG454ZjC2U7_sy5KXxmtNEt0dQr-VJGWbk-q. (Last accessed: 25.12.2025).

[15] Burgess (2018), pp. 91–94.

[16] Agnese et al. (2025), CG, p. 280.

a customised AI approach. Therefore, there is no universal AI policy solution suitable for all corporations.[17]

The adoption of an AI policy constitutes prudent corporation management,[18] particularly for corporations that extensively deploy AI systems. Such policies can clarify operational principles, determine responsibilities, and foster organisational trust in AI systems.[19] Under the AI policy, the boards may employ their strategic prioritisation by explicitly defining and balancing competing corporate objectives before implementation. Moreover, the board may then define the specific structure of the human-AI decision-making process. It involves determining the precise level of AI autonomy.[20] The policy framework may also include clear protocols for evaluating AI-generated recommendations, requiring a systematic assessment of their validity and relevance relative to other information sources.[21]

AI policies are becoming part of good corporate governance in Türkiye and Germany. It is increasingly common for large corporations to establish AI policies and share them publicly. In Türkiye, Sabancı Holding, one of the large holdings, recently disclosed its AI policy.[22] In Germany, SAP's Global AI Ethics Policy,[23] Allianz's Data Ethics and Responsible Artificial Intelligence Guideline,[24]

---

[17] Gözübüyük (2021), HHFD, p. 1204. General AI policy templates should be avoided. Bradford J. Kelley, Mike Skidgel and Alice Wang (2025, May 7). "Planning Your AI Policy? Start Here, Corporate Compliance Insights." Available at https://www.corporatecomplianceinsights.com/planning-your-ai-policy-start-here/. (Last accessed: 25.12.2025).

[18] Cowger (2023), JOLTI, p. 205; Rolsing (2025), p. 163.

[19] For the essential content of an internal corporate AI-guideline, see Ustahaliloğlu, (2025), CLGR, p. 131.

[20] Langenbucher (2024), EuZW, p. 858; Agnese et al. (2025), CG, p. 280; Varlı (2025), p. 261.

[21] Varlı (2025), p. 261. For a structured assessment protocol, see Dönmez Canseven (2021), pp. 103–105.

[22] Sabancı Holding Yatırımcı İlişkileri (n. d.) "Yapay Zeka Politikası (AI Policy)" (available only in Turkish). Available at: https://yatirimciiliskileri.sabanci.com/tr/surdurulebilirlik/detay/Yapay-Zeka-Politikasi/686/3263/0#:~:text=Sabanc%C4%B1%20Toplulu%C4%9Fu%20Yapay%20Zek%C3%A2%20Politikas%C4%B1,uygulanmas%C4%B1%20i%C3%A7in%20rehberlik%20sa%C4%9Flamay%C4%B1%20ama%C3%A7lar. (Last accessed: 25.12.2025).

[23] SAP. (n. d.). "Global AI Ethics Policy." Available at: https://www.sap.com/documents/2022/01/a8431b91-117e-0010-bca6-c68f7e60039b.html. (Last accessed: 25.12.2025).

[24] Allianz. (n.d.), "Data Ethics and Responsible Artificial Intelligence." Available at: https://www.allianz.com/en/about-us/strategy-values/data-ethics-and-responsible-ai.html#principles. (Last accessed: 25.12.2025).

and Deutsche Telekom's Guidelines for Artificial Intelligence[25] are examples of corporate AI policies. Beyond serving as a source of soft law, incorporating AI policies or guidelines into foundational documents, such as the articles of association, internal regulations, or employment contracts, can confer binding legal effect, thereby enabling their formal enforcement.[26]

4.1.2.2 Interim Result

AI policies tailored to corporations' characteristics and needs provide a useful framework for boards to guide the integration of AI systems into management structures. While their establishment may constitute an organisational obligation for boards under their duty of care, AI policies can also serve as documents outlining boards' other organisational obligations related to AI's integration into corporation management under both legal systems. For this purpose, these documents are expected to involve clear protocols and definitive criteria governing human-AI interactions throughout the AI's deployment, instruction and monitoring. As corporations increasingly integrate AI systems into their management, boards will be expected to develop and publicise AI policies as part of their prudent management duty in both legal systems. The fact that a corporation already has an 'AI Policy' in place can be considered a *prima facie* indication that its board has taken the first step to anticipate its organisational obligations regarding AI and make the necessary preparations to fulfil them. Incorporating AI policies into formal corporate documents and the employment contracts of management personnel would be a step toward ensuring their consistent and proper implementation.

4.1.3 Corporate Digital Responsibility as a Framework

4.1.3.1 Comparative Review

Digitalisation represents a more profound transformation than the mere adoption of digital tools or the automation of existing processes. At its core, it means a fundamental and comprehensive restructuring of entrepreneurial business models.[27] As a direct expression of ongoing digital transformation, the concept of Corporate

[25] Deutsche Telekom. (n. d.), "Digital Ethics Guidelines On AI." Available at: https://www.telekom.com/en/company/digital-responsibility/details/artificial-intelligence-ai-guideline-524366. (Last accessed: 25.12.2025).

[26] Rolsing (2025), p. 162.

[27] Möslein (2023b), p. 409.

Digital Responsibility (CDR) has recently[28] emerged as an evolution of Corporate Social Responsibility (CSR)[29] and has achieved substantial significance across various international jurisdictions.[30]

The truly distinctive characteristic of CDR (compared to the CSR) is its inherent and explicit connection to digitalisation. The CDR specifically addresses a corporation's responsibilities regarding the collection, use, and protection of data, as well as the impact of its digital technologies and processing activities.[31] By mandating transparency and accountability in digital practices, the CDR helps ensure that responsibility for technology-driven actions remains clearly defined and attributable within the corporate structure. CDR may also provide a normative grounding and operational guidance for the use of AI in boardrooms,[32] which is part of the digitalisation of corporations. Given the centrality of data governance to the effective and ethical deployment of AI, the CDR principles, particularly those related to data governance, will be beneficial for the prudent integration of AI into corporation management. Consequently, a board's demonstrable reliance on, and implementation of CDR principles for the integration of AI into corporation management will constitute *prima facie* evidence that they have fulfilled their obligations in this regard in accordance with their duty of care.

Despite its conceptual utility, there is no specific regulation underpinning CDR in Turkish and German law.[33] An attempt at detailed exploration and doctrinal development regarding its scope, principles and implications is still required[34] since the multifaceted nature of the CDR, with its complex and overlapping regulatory layers and their significant consequences, is poised to exert a transformative influence on corporate law.[35] While academic discussions on this specific subject are still in their infancy in Turkish legal doctrine, those in German legal doctrine are instructive for the comparative approach of this study.

[28] Noack (2019b), pp. 503–504; Möslein (2020c), p. 806.

[29] Möslein (2025b), ERA Forum, p. 639; Windorf (2025), p. 440.

[30] For more information regarding CDR developments in different jurisdictions see Möslein (2023b), pp. 419–420.

[31] Möslein (2020c), p. 805.

[32] Lieder (2022), p. 339; Möslein (2025b), ERA Forum, p. 637.

[33] For the German law perspective, see Möslein (2020c), p. 808; Möslein (2023b), p. 421.

[34] Möslein (2020c), pp. 805–806.

[35] Möslein (2023b), p. 432.

In Germany, the BMJV (*Das Bundesministerium der Justiz und für Verbraucherschutz*, the Federal Ministry of Justice and Consumer Protection) pioneered CDR efforts. In 2018, the BMJV launched an initiative for the human-centred digital transformation of corporations in collaboration with corporations and academia.[36] As a result of this initiative, the CDR Code emerged in 2021, and it became operational after the large German corporations participating in the initiative published their annual implementation reports.[37] However, the CDR has not yet achieved the same formal recognition as ESG (Environmental, Social and Governance) frameworks,[38] but is increasingly viewed as an essential element of compliance systems.[39] While the EU AI Act was expected to provide a legal basis in this regard, it has become clear that, due to its market-oriented approach and product-safety-first regulations, it can only provide an indirect legal basis for CDR.[40] Hence, German legal doctrine proposes that recommendations regarding CDR be included in the DCGK.[41] In addition to this proposal, the view that boards' obligations regarding CDR can be determined based on the duty of care under the AktG is prominent.[42] Nevertheless, it is also argued that DCGK Commission must establish the principles governing corporate AI use under the CDR by

[36] Möslein (2020c), p. 807. For more information, see Corporate Digital Responsibility Initiative, available at: https://cdr-initiative.de/en/code. (Last accessed: 25.12.2025).

[37] Windorf (2025), p. 442.

[38] Windorf (2025), pp. 440–441.

[39] Windorf (2025), p. 441.

[40] Möslein (2022), p. 82.

[41] Recommendation A.1 S. 1 could in future read: "*Der Vorstand soll die mit den Sozial- und Umweltfaktoren sowie mit datengetriebenen Unternehmenstätigkeiten verbundenen Risiken und Chancen sowie die ökologischen und sozialen Auswirkungen einschließlich der Auswirkungen des Umgangs mit personenbezogenen Daten der Unternehmenstätigkeit systematisch identifizieren und bewerten.*" (*The Management Board shall systematically identify and assess the risks and opportunities associated with social and environmental factors and data-driven business activities, as well as the ecological and social impacts, including the impacts of the handling of personal data in the business activities.*") Windorf (2025), p. 459. A new, targeted recommendation on AI transparency as *"Empfehlung: Zum Einsatz von Künstlicher Intelligenz soll Stellung genommen werden (Ergänzung zu A.5 DCGK—Lagebericht.)" (Recommendation: A statement should be made on the use of artificial intelligence (addition to A.5 DCGK—Management Report)."* is advised. Kremer and Langenbucher (2024), p. 89, 3.35.

[42] Casper and Möslein (2025), ZGR, p. 894.

issuing specific regulations, as CDR is decisively transitioning from a niche concern to an indispensable pillar of comprehensive corporate responsibility.[43] As data-driven decision-making becomes increasingly central to business operations, CDR principles are expected to gain greater significance.[44]

In the research conducted as part of this study, no significant administrative or market initiatives related to CDR were found in Türkiye. Corporations' voluntary establishment and publication of AI policies can be considered first steps in this path. As proposed in German legal doctrine, it may be recommended that boards' obligations regarding CDR be determined by reference to their duty of care under the TCC. Furthermore, the data governance obligations imposed on corporation management by the Personal Data Protection Law (KVKK) in Turkish law could provide guidance regarding CDR. Similarly, incorporating CDR principles into corporate governance principles, as recommendations, is another method that can provide a legal basis for these principles in Turkish corporate law as well.

4.1.3.2 Interim Result

Emerging CDR principles may provide a solid framework for boards' duties in technology-driven activities, particularly regarding transparency and accountability. In the context of AI's integration into corporation management, CDR principles, particularly regarding data governance, may serve as the board's guiding standards in Turkish and German corporate law. Commitment to these principles throughout the AI's integration into corporation management may not only guide boards but also assist them in demonstrating that they have acted prudently in discharging their duty of care. However, there is no coherent doctrinal foundation for conceptualised CDR in Turkish and German law to delineate its characteristic features, core principles, and legal contours. Detailed exploration and doctrinal development regarding its scope, principles and implications would have a transformative influence on the digitalisation of corporate law, including board-level AI use. After such doctrinal development, it would be beneficial first to transform CDR obligations into industry-led voluntary codes of conduct, then into recommendations in formal corporate governance principles, and later into binding regulations. Consequently, boards may derive significant strategic and legal benefits from the principles of CDR and from its anticipated regulatory

[43] Möslein (2019), Audit Committee Quarterly, p. 61; Möslein (2020c), p. 819.

[44] Möslein (2020c), p. 812; Windorf (2025), p. 441.

maturation, as this framework provides a structured guide for the prudent, risk-aware, and legally defensible integration of AI into corporation management in both legal systems.

4.1.4 Board Members' AI Literacy as a Fiduciary Expectation

4.1.4.1 Comparative Review

The integration of AI into corporate management has prompted scholarly debate in both Turkish and German legal doctrine over whether a board member's duty of care now requires functional literacy in AI systems. In neither legal system are board members expected to possess comprehensive expertise across all specialised domains. However, understanding AI systems is essential both to maximise their benefits and to identify the risks they pose and take precautions.[45] Furthermore, to ensure cognitive collaboration between AI systems and board members and to justify the board's reliance on AI outputs in compliance with their fiduciary duties,[46] board members must be familiar with the underlying operational logic and decision-making processes of the AI systems.[47]

Moreover, one of the significant risks posed by AI systems is humans' overconfidence in AI outputs. This risk manifests itself in the uncritical acceptance and application of AI outputs by board members when AI is integrated into management.[48] Especially if board members are unaware of AI systems' methodologies and their potential for errors, such as hallucinations, amplified discrimination, or unethical outcomes,[49] their blind trust in these systems' results and their likelihood of directly implementing them increases. However, in both legal systems, board members are expected to make independent decisions. Considering all these factors, the doctrine suggests that board members should have a

---

[45] Zhao (2022), Cath. U. L. Rev., p. 676; van Giffen and Ludwig (2023), MISQE, p. 260.

[46] Cowger (2023), JOLTI, p. 145; Ahern (2024), p. 425. A basic understanding of AI is also necessary for the fulfilment of board's duties of selection, instruction and monitoring duties regarding AI systems (as delegates). Rolsing (2025), p. 311 ff.

[47] Kremer and Langenbucher (2024), pp. 72–73, 3.7; Möslein (2025a), p. 626.

[48] Weber et al. (2018), NZG, p. 1133; Eryiğit (2021), pp. 117–118; Bora Çınar (2022), p. 176; Windorf (2025), p. 180.

[49] Casper and Möslein (2025), ZGR, pp. 878–879.

basic level of knowledge about AI systems.[50] It is stated that this level of knowledge, which does not constitute technical expertise[51] and requires delving into algorithmic intricacies,[52] should include an understanding of logic,[53] application parameters, risks, and management protocols for AI systems.[54]

Another view put forward in German legal doctrine holds that the 'basic technical understanding' of AI systems expected of board members will not make a meaningful contribution to illuminating algorithmic decision-making.[55] Furthermore, the board's control over these systems depends not on its technical understanding but on its monitoring of whether the AI operates within predetermined parameters.[56] Hence, it is sufficient for boards to possess the operational knowledge to initiate, monitor, and, if necessary, halt the operation of AI systems. Expecting a higher level of knowledge will either distort board composition[57] or unnecessarily deter AI adoption. Therefore, this view regards any ambiguous requirement for a basic technical understanding of AI as unreasonable and inefficient.[58]

It is generally accepted that current board members' knowledge of AI is inadequate, both technically and operationally.[59] There is currently no regulation in either legal system to address this inadequacy.[60] It is suggested that a

[50] For Turkish law perspective, see Dönmez Canseven (2021), pp. 85–86; Gözübüyük (2022), HBV-HFD, p. 155; Bora Çınar (2022), p. 126 and 194–195. For German law perspective, see Möslein (2018), ZIP, pp. 209; Möslein (2020c), p. 822; Dany (2022), BB, p. 2061; Li (2022), p. 150; Lasar (2023), pp. 174–177 (on the limited liability company 'GmbH'); Fleischer in BeckOGK (2025), AktG, § 76, para. 78; Sanders (2025), NZG, p. 1406; Windorf (2025), p. 215 and 255.

[51] Weber et al. (2018), NZG, p. 1132; Nowak (2022), p. 180; Özer and Tomrukçu (2025), BATİDER, p. 262; Adolff (2025), AG, p. 51; Windorf (2025), p. 215.

[52] Nowak (2022), p. 180.

[53] Zhao (2022), Cath. U. L. Rev., p. 676. For instance, board members must recognize that AI systems fundamentally detect correlations rather than establish causations. Adolff (2025), AG, p. 51; Windorf (2025), p. 168. For more information on the shift from causation to correlation in the context of AI, see Ebers (2020), pp. 45–46.

[54] Dönmez Canseven (2021), p. 103; Bora Çınar (2022), pp. 194–195; Gözübüyük (2022), HBV-HFD, p. 159; Lieder (2022), p. 336; Uğurerkan (2024), p. 81; Möslein (2025a), p. 626; Özer and Tomrukçu (2025), BATİDER, pp. 262–263.

[55] Telle (2023), p. 154.

[56] Calabro (2023), p. 103.

[57] Calabro (2023), p. 103.

[58] Calabro (2023), p. 96; Telle (2023), p. 153.

[59] Cowger (2023), JOLTI, p. 157.

[60] For German law, see Möslein (2020c), p. 822.

requirement for knowledge of AI systems be added to the articles of association as a board membership requirement,[61] particularly for corporations engaged in data-intensive business, to address this knowledge gap.[62] Furthermore, both legal doctrines suggest that board members be required to receive training on AI systems after their appointment.[63] Moreover, explainable AI systems with user-friendly interfaces that convert their outputs into conventional business and legal terminology[64] can be preferred to facilitate the board's understanding.[65] Furthermore, the establishment of an executive position, such as a Chief Digitalisation Officer (CDO) or Chief Artificial Intelligence Officer (CAIO),[66] specialised in AI to support the board, or a committee specialised in this field,[67] is discussed as a recommendation for corporations utilise AI in a holistic and permanent manner.

4.1.4.2 Interim Result

Despite the lack of explicit regulation in Turkish and German legal systems, boards that integrate AI into management bear an affirmative obligation under their duty of care to address the existing knowledge gap regarding such systems. A board that remains entirely uninformed about an AI system in operation cannot reasonably be expected to harness its benefits or exercise effective oversight. Given that the decision to integrate AI into corporation management is increasingly considered a strategic, core management decision in both legal doctrines, board members making this decision must possess a basic understanding of these systems, including foundational knowledge of these systems' capabilities, limitations, and operational implications. Otherwise, it may be claimed that board

---

[61] The articles of association may specify additional criteria for board membership; for Turkish law, see 2.1.1.2.1., and for the German legal framework, see 2.1.1.2.2.

[62] Metin (2021), p. 526. It is proposed in the German legal doctrine that an update to the DCGK, recommending that the supervisory board consider such expertise during appointments, would enhance corporate governance without requiring new legislation. Kremer and Langenbucher (2024), pp. 91–92, 3.37–3.38. For a restrictive approach foreseeing such specialized expertise only for digital savvy corporations with AI-focused field of operation, see Windorf (2025), p. 212.

[63] Möslein (2020c), p. 823; Gözübüyük (2022), HBV-HFD, p. 154; Lasar (2023), p. 177 (on the GmbH); Ahern (2024), p. 427; Erdem Aladağ (2024), Denetişim, p. 26; Agnese et al. (2025), CG, p. 281; Windorf (2025), p. 214.

[64] Bora Çınar (2022), p. 153.

[65] Bora Çınar (2022), p. 151; Özer and Tomrukçu (2025), BATİDER, p. 262.

[66] Bora Çınar (2022), p. 126; Li (2022), p. 76 ff. and 150; Nowak (2022), pp. 180–181; Calabro (2023), p. 142; Telle (2023), p. 160 ff. Cf. Noack (2019b), p. 503.

[67] Möslein (2020c), p. 823; Eryiğit (2021), p. 115; Möslein (2023b), p. 431; Erdem Aladağ (2024), Denetişim, p. 27.

members acted in breach of their duty of care and may be held liable, as they made their decision on this matter without sufficient information and were unable to properly fulfil their duties of overseeing the system's operation.

Within the both legal system's duty of care framework, the level of knowledge that board members are expected to have on AI systems and the measures they need to take to ensure this level of knowledge across the board should be calibrated on a case-by-case basis, depending on factors, such as the characteristics of the relevant AI system, magnitude and nature of the risks it may create, and how much the corporation's subject matter requires data-driven management.

4.1.5 Appointing a Specialised Executive and/or Establishing a Dedicated AI Department

4.1.5.1 Comparative Review

Appointing a dedicated executive, such as a CDO or CAIO, may provide comprehensive governance benefits in terms of addressing AI-related challenges and overseeing all aspects of AI integration into corporation management.[68] Under Turkish law, board members cannot evade their fiduciary responsibilities by simply delegating AI oversight to an executive.[69] However, boards may responsibly integrate AI systems into corporation management by appointing specialised executives for AI-related tasks while maintaining ultimate governance accountability. In practice, a board may assign AI implementation to this executive, who becomes responsible for preparatory work on technology selection, risk management, system deactivation when necessary,[70] and AI's alignment with the corporation's business goals, while the board retains oversight duties.[71] While there has been rapid growth in technology-related executive positions in Turkish corporations, their adoption still lags behind developed countries.[72]

The German corporation law does not mandate specific executive roles. Nevertheless, its core principles of effective management and a duty of care trigger a doctrinal discussion for formally establishing a CDO (or a CAIO) position to

[68] Bora Çınar (2022), p. 126; Lieder (2022), p. 339.

[69] See 3.4.2.3.

[70] Varlı (2025), p. 259, 270–271.

[71] Varlı (2025), pp. 270–271.

[72] Varlı (2025), p. 270.

support the management board.[73] Under section 77(1) sentence 2 of the AktG the delegation of AI-related tasks to specialised executives is permissible,[74] provided that core management responsibilities remain with the full board as per Section 76(1) of the AktG. However, strategic decisions about AI adoption remain the full board's collective responsibility.[75]

A specialised executive, i.e. CDO or CAIO, serves as both a technical expert[76] and a strategic bridge, advising the board on the integration of AI into corporation management and maintaining oversight to ensure all implementations serve the corporation's best interests. This executive's core duties include developing and implementing a digital strategy,[77] modernising information technology infrastructure, regularly checking integrated AI systems,[78] fostering cultural change through training and new work methods,[79] and managing external partnerships with tech providers and academia.[80] Such an executive must also monitor emerging technologies to identify opportunities for implementation.[81] Furthermore, this specialised executive must regularly report to board members on AI operations, so that all board members retain oversight responsibilities.[82] Consequently, this executive is required to support the board in coordinating and monitoring AI use.[83] The necessity of establishing such an executive position and the specific scope of this position vary significantly across corporations depending on their size, industry, financial capacity, and digital ambitions.[84] Hence,

---

[73] Armour and Eidenmüller (2019), ZHR, p. 178; Linardatos (2019), ZIP, p. 508; Lücke (2019), BB, p. 1993; Möslein (2020c), p. 823; Li (2022), p. 77; Nowak (2022), p. 180; Calabro (2023), p. 142; Möslein (2023b), p. 431; Telle (2023), p. 160.

[74] Li (2022), p. 84.

[75] Telle (2023), p. 160.

[76] Li (2022), p. 80. Although not explicitly characterized as a technical expert, it is implied that such an executive should be equipped with specialized expertise in AI. Rolsing (2025), p. 273.

[77] Li (2022), p. 78.

[78] Nowak (2022), p. 180.

[79] Li (2022), p. 79.

[80] Li (2022), pp. 78–79 and 88; Telle (2023), p. 160.

[81] Li (2022), p. 79.

[82] Telle (2023), p. 160.

[83] Frey (2024), p. 79; Rolsing (2025), p. 273.

[84] Li (2022), p. 79.

appointing a dedicated executive is neither a legal requirement nor a one-size-fits-all solution.[85] Such an appointment may be unnecessary for occasional or low-complexity AI use.[86]

To ensure responsible and effective AI adoption, corporations may also establish a dedicated AI department, preferably led by the CAIO or CDO.[87] This departmental structure allows specialised technical teams to handle operational complexities while transforming the board's role into monitoring.[88] This department should be tailored to the organisation's specific needs and tasked with securing high-quality datasets, training management on AI systems, monitoring algorithmic performance, and hiring specialised talent. While forming such a unit requires significant investment, it is a necessary safeguard given AI's inherent risks, ensuring reliable outcomes, mitigating operational and ethical risks, and maintaining alignment with business objectives.[89]

4.1.5.2 Interim Result

Boards integrating AI into corporation management are expected to undertake significant organisational reforms. These reforms include the creation of an executive position, staffed by an executive with expertise in AI, and the establishment of an internal AI department, managed by the specialised executive, to support the board in achieving the expected benefits of AI integration and in identifying and mitigating potential risks. For this purpose, such an executive or department may coordinate all phases of AI integration into management and provide regular reports to the board. Under the current legal frameworks of both legal systems, however, the appointment of an executive or the establishment of an AI department is not a mandatory requirement for boards. Such a strategic choice requires a contextual, case-by-case assessment. In particular, as the intensity of AI's integration into corporation management, the complexity of the AI systems deployed, and the potential operational, legal and reputational risks they pose increase, the board's strategic choice in this regard may evolve into an organisational duty.

---

[85] Möslein (2020a), § 13 para. 38; Telle (2023), p. 160; Kremer and Langenbucher (2024), p. 73, 3.8; Casper and Möslein (2025), ZGR, p. 896; Rolsing (2025), p. 274.

[86] Telle (2023), p. 161.

[87] Linardatos (2019), ZIP, p. 507; Lücke (2019), BB, p. 1993; Möslein (2020a), § 13 para. 38; Bora Çınar (2022), pp. 125–126; Telle (2023), p. 161.

[88] Becker and Pordzik (2020), ZfPW, p. 352 ff.; Telle (2023), p. 162.

[89] Gözübüyük (2021), HHFD, p. 1204.

4.1.6 Establishment of AI Committee

4.1.6.1 Comparative Review

With the integration of AI into corporation management, the board may need assistance to ensure the proper installation and ongoing oversight of AI systems. For board members who are not expected to be experts in a matter, seeking assistance from experts is not only a practical necessity but also a requirement of the duty of care.[90] As mentioned above, the board may appoint a specialised executive or establish a dedicated AI implementation department.[91] In corporate law, another way for the board to seek assistance on a matter requiring expertise is to establish committees composed of experts in the relevant field. In this context, a board that integrates AI into corporation management may employ an existing technology committee[92] or establish a specialised AI committee to receive support in the development of AI governance.[93]

Under Turkish corporate law, board members have a duty of care to establish necessary committees in line with management's needs.[94] These committees, which lack management authority,[95] consist of experts in relevant fields and serve as advisors to the board of directors.[96] In this context, an AI committee may assist the board of directors in integrating AI systems into corporate management, particularly by providing the board with information on the performance of these systems and the accuracy of AI outputs.[97]Although there is no statutory mandate, the establishment of an AI committee by the board is often cited as

[90] Hacımahmutoğlu (2015), BATİDER, p. 35; Pulaşlı (2022), § 37, para. 160, p. 1584.

[91] See 4.1.5.

[92] Montagnani and Passador (2022), J. Bus. Entrepreneurship & L., p. 6 ff. An empirical study concludes that existing technology committees in the European and North American corporations frequently fail to consider AI governance with adequate depth or specificity. Montagnani and Passador (2022), J. Bus. Entrepreneurship & L., p. 65.

[93] Enriques and Zetzsche, (2020), UCLJ, p. 92 ff.; van Giffen and Ludwig (2023), MISQE, p. 263; Yıldırım Soysal (2023), AÜHFD, p. 1825; Erdem Aladağ (2024), Denetişim, p. 27; Agnese et al. (2025), CG, pp. 281–282.

[94] Kaya (2014), DEÜHFD, p. 3269; Kalender (2024), p. 66.

[95] Arslanlı (1960), p. 118; Kırca in Kırca et al. (2013), p. 479; Demir (2016), p. 85; Koç (2018), pp. 139–141; Kalender (2024), p. 62; Çamoğlu in Poroy et al. (2025), para. 535, p. 379.

[96] Pulaşlı (2017), § 20, paras. 87–89; Gözübüyük (2021), HHFD, p. 1205.

[97] Gözübüyük (2021), HHFD, p. 1205; Gözübüyük (2022), HBV-HFD, p. 155.

a manifestation of the prudent management in Turkish legal doctrine.[98] However, a decision to establish such a committee should be made on a case-by-case basis, taking into account the specific corporation's needs, resources, and strategic goals. Since these committees do not have the authority to make management decisions, the board of directors is responsible for the decisions it makes after taking these committees' opinions into account.[99]

German corporate law also recognises the establishment of committees without decision-making authority to support the management board.[100] An AI committee would be considered as one of such committees. Since there is no legal mandate, establishing an AI committee is a discretionary decision and requires a case-by-case assessment. Such a specialised committee[101] could facilitate communication between AI providers and the management board, participate in the preparation of AI policies, and assist the board in identifying operational deficiencies while overseeing the AI integration into corporation management. However, it is emphasised that this committee has no decision-making authority. It can only provide information and consult, and the establishment of this committee does not relieve the board of its managerial obligations regarding AI systems.

4.1.6.2 Interim Result

In both legal systems, the establishment of an *ad hoc* or permanent AI committee composed of experts, acting in an advisory capacity without decision-making authority, is legally possible and advisable as a prudent governance measure to support the board in integrating AI into corporation management. While the establishment of a specialised AI committee is a strong indicator of good corporate governance in the digital age, it does not guarantee that board members have fulfilled their duty of care regarding AI's integration into corporation management. In the same vein, the mere absence of such a committee cannot be considered a breach of the duty of care. Accordingly, Turkish and German law do not impose a categorical duty to establish an AI committee. A case-by-case assessment must be conducted to determine whether the establishment of such a specialised committee constitutes an organisational duty under prudent management, taking into account the corporation's specific needs, available resources, and strategic goals.

---

[98] Eryiğit (2021), p. 115; Gözübüyük (2022), HBV-HFD, p. 155; İpekel Kayalı in Karatepe Kaya et al. (2025), p. 71; Özer and Tomrukçu (2025), BATİDER, p. 263.

[99] Demir (2016), pp. 85–86.

[100] Kubis in Kubis and Tödtmann (2022), § 1, para. 68; Telle (2023), p. 141.

[101] For the establishment of a committee specialised in digitalisation in general, see Möslein (2020c), p. 823; Möslein (2023b), p. 431.

4.1.7 Selection, Instruction and Monitoring Duties

4.1.7.1 In General

The integration of AI systems into corporation management requires board members to exercise care in selecting, instructing, and monitoring them. Since these obligations are not explicitly stipulated in either legal system, the existing law will be analysed to subsume this tripartite framework of care. Then, the board's 'modified duties of care'[102] within this framework will be investigated under this section.

4.1.7.2 Comparative Review

4.1.7.2.1 Legal Sources

4.1.7.2.1.1 In General

Within the scope of this study, no analogical approach to determining the board's obligations for integrating AI systems into corporate management has been encountered in Turkish legal doctrine. The absence of such an approach in Turkish legal doctrine may be attributed to the prevailing view that AI systems are merely auxiliary tools and not yet recognised as valid addressees of delegation. From the same perspective, Turkish legal doctrine generally rejects liability for AI systems within the scope of employer liability.[103] If such an assessment were possible, an employer's obligations to select, instruct, and monitor an employee would be analogously applied to AI systems. This doctrinal stance regarding AI's legal status and liability has hindered further and more comprehensive discussions regarding the board's specific obligations regarding AI systems integrated into the corporation management. Instead, discussions about the board's particular obligations regarding AI systems continue to focus on concrete obligations arising from the board's duty of care, rather than on analogical approaches to existing legal regulations. Under this theoretical framework, it is argued that when leveraging AI systems, board members retain ultimate accountability, authority, and legal responsibility for corporate outcomes.[104] Hence, the 'prudent manager' standard requires corporate boards to exercise reasonable care when deciding whether to

---

[102] For the terminology, see Spindler (2019), p. 137.

[103] Bak (2018), TAAD, pp. 222–223; Akkurt (2019), UMD, pp. 48–49; Ercan (2019), TAAD, p. 39; Sarı (2020), TBBD, p. 271; Kapancı (2021), pp. 165–166; Karaca (2023), p. 74. For a legal review examining the responsibility for AI within the scope of employer liability and proposing legal changes, see Selanik (2022), TAAD, p. 356 ff.

[104] Bora Çınar (2022), p. 202.

implement AI, selecting appropriate AI applications,[105] implementing AI applications, including continuous monitoring for risks, and implementing safeguards.[106] It is also argued that board members must conduct an independent assessment of the AI's output to verify its reliability to fulfil their duty of care.[107] If they fail to exercise reasonable care in these phases, board members will bear the full liability for any potential breach of care.[108]

Furthermore, although Turkish legal doctrine does not yet recognise the delegation of management to AI systems, board members' obligations to select, instruct, and monitor delegates in the traditional sense may serve as a guide for their responsibilities regarding AI systems.[109] Even if the use of AI systems in corporation management does not legally qualify as a formal delegation, board members can be expected to treat AI systems more like delegates, given their systemic complexity and autonomy compared to other traditional auxiliary tools. This analogical framework, however, has not been previously developed in Turkish doctrinal discussions.

German legal doctrine, on the other hand, discusses the establishment of the board's obligations for the use of AI in corporate management through the interpretation of specific existing legal regulations. Initially, the use of the standards for technology integration in §80(2) of the WpHG, which regulates algorithmic trading, is discussed as an analogy to determine the management board's obligations regarding AI.[110] Such an analogy has been criticised on several grounds, including differences in the purposes and contexts of the regulations.[111] As a middle ground, it is stated that the standards regarding the use of algorithmic systems in §80(2) of the WpHG should not be directly applied to all corporations, however, they may provide guidance in determining basic organisational

[105] Akın (2022), TAÜHFD, p. 20; Seçer (2025), p. 102.

[106] Keskin (2024), p. 128; Uğurerkan (2024), p. 81; Varlı (2025), pp. 259–260.

[107] Özer and Tomrukçu (2025), BATİDER, p. 258 and 261 ff.

[108] Dönmez Canseven (2021), p. 109.

[109] For board's duties regarding delegates in Turkish corporate law, see 3.4.2.3.

[110] Möslein (2018), ZIP, p. 211; Weber et al. (2018), NZG, p. 1135; Möslein (2020b), p. 517; Li (2022), pp. 174–175; Nowak (2022), pp. 185–186; Calabro (2023), pp. 143–150; Lasar (2023), p. 134 (on the GmbH); Telle (2023), p. 94; Frey (2024), p. 69 ff.; Windorf (2025), pp. 187–189.

[111] Lücke (2019), BB, p. 1992 ff.; Zetzsche (2019), AG, p. 8; Becker and Pordzik (2020), ZfPW, p. 351; Li (2022), p. 175; Nowak (2022), p. 186; Calabro (2023), pp. 145–146; Telle (2023), p. 94; Frey (2024), p. 69 ff.; Rolsing (2025), p. 272; Windorf (2025), p. 189.

duties of the board.[112] It has also been discussed that §130 of the OWiG (*Gesetz über Ordnungswidrigkeiten*, Act on Regulatory Offences) could be applied analogously in determining obligations regarding the monitoring of AI systems.[113] However, such an analogy has not gained widespread support due to the significant adaptations it requires and the differences between humans and AI as the subjects of monitoring. Moreover, German legal doctrine argues that the delegation principles stipulated in tort law, i.e., §§ 823/831 of the BGB, cannot be directly transposed to corporate board duties regarding AI systems, but they may provide a valuable conceptual foundation.[114] Both frameworks share the core principle that delegators retain oversight responsibilities, requiring careful selection, proper instruction, and active supervision of delegates.[115] However, this proposal is criticised for a conceptual mismatch between the purpose of tort law principles, which provide an external mechanism for allocating liability after third-party harm has occurred, and AI use in corporate management, which requires a forward-looking standard focused on ensuring positive task fulfilment and responsible integration.[116]

Having assessed potential analogies, German legal doctrine argues that AI's unique technical and operational characteristics demand a specialised approach.[117] The duty of care regulated in Section 93 AktG, which applies to the management boards of all stock corporations, can provide a legal basis for determining the management board's obligations regarding AI systems.[118] Within the framework of duty of care, management boards are obligated to exercise the care expected of a prudent and conscientious manager in selecting, instructing, and overseeing AI systems.[119] The general nature of this standard does not define

---

[112] Weber et al. (2018), NZG, p. 1135; Noack (2019a), ZHR, p. 127; Becker and Pordzik (2020), ZfPW, p. 352; Calabro (2023), p. 146; Rolsing (2025), p. 272. For an assessment of §80(2) of the WpHG's guiding role after the AI Act, see Casper and Möslein (2025), ZGR, pp. 892–893.

[113] Calabro (2023), pp. 139–143.

[114] Li (2022), p. 103.

[115] Li (2022), p. 103.

[116] Li (2022), p. 102; Windorf (2025), p. 237.

[117] Windorf (2025), p. 200.

[118] Li (2022), p. 177; Nowak (2022), p. 67 ff.; Telle (2023), p. 89; Windorf (2025), p. 200. It is also argued that the board's tripartite obligations concerning delegates derive from the statutory duty of care (§ 93 AktG), with their precise content being specified by customary legal principles. Rolsing (2025), p. 135 ff.

[119] Li (2022), p. 119.

obligations in technical terms, allowing the board to contextually determine its obligations regarding the use of AI in line with evolving technology.[120]

As another manifestation of the duty of care, German corporate law's rules on management delegation can also guide boards in determining their obligations regarding AI systems.[121] Within the current delegation system, the obligations of board members regarding the selection, instruction, and monitoring of delegates[122] could also be adapted to AI systems.[123] Thus, just as board members in the delegation system are exempt from liability if they fulfil their obligations to select, instruct, and monitor delegates, they can also be exempt from liability in the use of AI if they fulfil adapted obligations toward AI. This framework would, on the one hand, encourage board members to fulfil these obligations to avoid liability and, on the other hand, address the liability ambiguity that could hinder the board's decision to use AI. However, the traditional delegation framework, built on a foundation of human agency, cognition, and accountability, is not directly transferable to the AI systems.[124] The established legal principles governing delegation are expected to be rigorously reevaluated and adapted to the novel context of AI systems.[125]

Moreover, as a statutory manifestation of the duty of care, Section 91(2) of the AktG is considered to provide the legal basis for management boards' obligations regarding AI systems in German corporate law.[126] However, this proposal has not gained general acceptance in the literature, as the purpose of this provision is to protect corporations against existential threats, and the situations in which AI could pose such threats are very limited. Hence, comprehensive obligations regarding AI systems cannot be derived from it.[127]

As a result, it is clear that AI's unique technical and operational characteristics necessitate a specialised approach to determining board members' duties

---

[120] Telle (2023), p. 89.

[121] Li (2022), p. 68; Calabro (2023), pp. 118–120; Telle (2023), p. 90; Frey (2024), pp. 82–83; Fleischer in BeckOGK (2025), AktG, § 76, para. 77; Windorf (2025), p. 238.

[122] For board's duties regarding delegates in German corporate law, see 3.4.2.3.

[123] Li (2022), p. 68; Telle (2023), pp. 90; Fleischer in BeckOGK (2025), AktG, § 76, paras. 77 and 78.

[124] Casper and Möslein (2025), ZGR, p. 875; Rolsing (2025), p. 134 ff.

[125] Möslein (2022), p. 76; Fleischer in BeckOGK (2025), AktG, § 76, para. 77; Rolsing (2025), p. 134 ff.

[126] Li (2022), p. 167 ff.; Frey (2024), pp. 83–84.

[127] Telle (2023), p. 93; Rolsing (2025), pp. 234–235. For the opinion that § 91(2) of the AktG may provide the minimum standards for the board's duties regarding AI integration into corporation management, see Frey (2024), p. 84.

regarding AI's integration into corporation management. These duties can be determined on a case-by-case basis through a duty-of-care assessment, eliminating the need for legal regulations for each new technological development. Consequently, AI governance standards for boards should be derived from the general duty of care, with tailored mechanisms aligned with the realities of managerial decision-making and characteristics of the AI. New and tailored obligations must be developed to fulfil the duty of care and demonstrate the diligence of a prudent manager. In this process, the guidance of existing regulations can be used to fill in the content of new obligations without ignoring the purposes and contexts of these regulations.

4.1.7.2.1.2 Adaptation of Ision Criteria for AI

4.1.7.2.1.2.1 In General

In the legal research conducted within the scope of this study, no specific high court decision in Turkish law was found that established principles illuminating the board of directors' duty of care and responsibility in obtaining expert opinions from third parties. While legal doctrine frequently states that obtaining expert opinions on matters outside the board's area of expertise is a requirement of the duty of care, it has been observed that the principles governing expert opinions are discussed only in the context of legal expert opinions. According to these doctrinal discussions, which are occasionally inspired by the German legal doctrine and precedents, the board of directors must exercise diligence in selecting the expert from whom they will obtain a legal opinion.[128] Furthermore, the expert providing the opinion must be competent and independent,[129] and the board must disclose all relevant information and documents to the legal expert.[130] Finally, the board of directors is expected, within the framework of the duty of care, to evaluate whether the legal opinion obtained is sufficient for decision-making.[131]

There is no doctrinal or statutory obstacle in Turkish law preventing the extension of the abovementioned criteria, developed for the board's consultation of legal experts, to the board's consultation of experts in other substantive domains, such as technology, finance, and environment, etc. The criteria mentioned above for legal expert opinions may guide the determination of the duty of care and the responsibility of board members when seeking expert opinions in non-legal areas.

---

[128] Çelikboya (2023), p. 438.

[129] Yaşar (2020), p. 638; Sevi (2021), pp. 314–315; Çelikboya (2023), p. 438.

[130] Yaşar (2020), p. 639; Sevi (2021), pp. 314–315; Çelikboya (2023), p. 440.

[131] Yaşar (2020), p. 639; Sevi (2021), pp. 314–315; Çelikboya (2023), p. 440.

Nevertheless, Turkish legal doctrine would benefit from expanding and deepening its discourse on this topic, following the precedent set by recent German judiciary and legal scholarship. In German law, the Ision decision and subsequent case law and doctrinal discussions may provide guidance on the board's obligations when AI is integrated into corporation management. Therefore, German law's Ision criteria are explained below, first in general and then in terms of their applicability to AI.

4.1.7.2.1.2.2 Ision Criteria

The management board can gather the necessary information for its decision-making by consulting both corporation employees and external experts. If the board does not have the required expertise itself, it is legally required to seek help.[132] In German law, the Federal Court's 2011 Ision decision[133] specifically established standards for the management board to seek information and opinions from third parties.[134] While this decision pertained to the management board's seeking expert opinions on legal matters, subsequent court precedent and legal doctrine have recognised that the standards set forth in this decision also apply to the management board seeking expert opinions on any matter, including business decisions.[135] In fact, the legal doctrine holds that the criteria set forth in the Ision decision are not new. These criteria are a streamlined and combined version of the requirements previously expressed based on the duty of care by court decisions and doctrine regarding the board's right to seek expert opinion.[136]

According to the criteria established in the Ision decision, when seeking expert opinions, the management board must first select an independent and competent person capable of providing an impartial opinion.[137] This chosen person must be provided with all necessary information and documentation to give an accurate

---

[132] Hopt and Roth in Großkomm AktG (2015), AktG § 93, para. 108; Link in Wachter (2022), AktG, § 93, para. 34.

[133] BGH, Judgment of 20.9.2011—II ZR 234/09 (Ision), ZIP 2011, p. 2097 ff.

[134] Link in Wachter (2022), AktG, § 93, para. 34.

[135] Link in Wachter (2022), AktG, § 93, para. 34. On extending the Ision framework to external expert consultations generally, see Higher Regional Court of Hamm, Judgment of 6.4.2022—8 U 73/12, BeckRS 2022, 7579 para. 249 as cited in Windorf (2025), p. 184, fn. 315.

[136] Li (2022), p. 104.

[137] Wirth et al. (2017), p. 110; Fleischer in Spindler and Stilz (2019), § 93, AktG, para. 35c; Sailer-Coceani in Schmidt and Lutter (2020), AktG, § 93, para. 34; Link in Wachter (2022), AktG, § 93, para. 34.

opinion on the requested matter.[138] Finally, the management board must subject the expert opinion to a plausibility test.[139] A management board that cumulatively meets these criteria, as defined in the Ision decision and accepted by the legal doctrine, will not be liable for any subsequent losses to the corporation caused by decisions made based on expert opinions.[140]

German legal doctrine also interprets these criteria for specific situations. For example, the doctrine argues that when seeking an expert opinion in the legal field, the 'professionally qualified person' criterion can be easily determined by considering the expert's formal professional title. However, when seeking an expert opinion in other matters, such as business management, the expert's formal professional title, if any, should be taken into account, and the expert's special expertise and experience in the requested subject should also be considered[141] in conjunction with the importance of the matter.[142]

As another special situation, the confidentiality of corporate information and documents is vital to providing the expert with the necessary materials. The doctrine states that confidential information and documents may be given to the expert if the corporation's interests require it,[143] but in this case, measures, such as taking into account professional secrecy obligations or signing a confidentiality agreement,[144] must be taken to ensure the confidentiality of this information and documents.[145]

Furthermore, within the scope of the plausibility test, the board should evaluate the expert opinion from both a formal and substantive perspective.[146] A formal review should assess whether the expert was provided with all necessary information and documents related to the matter, whether the expert utilised all

[138] Wirth et al. (2017), p. 110; Sailer-Coceani in Schmidt and Lutter (2020), AktG, § 93, para. 34; Link in Wachter (2022), AktG § 93 para. 34; Li (2022), p. 108.

[139] Wirth et al. (2017), p. 110; Sailer-Coceani in Schmidt and Lutter (2020), AktG, § 93, para. 34; Link in Wachter (2022), AktG § 93 para. 34; Li (2022), p. 110. The required intensity of the plausibility test should be determined by considering the risks, urgency and board's own knowledge of the requested matter. Li (2022), p. 110.

[140] Sailer-Coceani in Schmidt and Lutter (2020), AktG, § 93 para. 34.

[141] Nowak (2022), p. 122.

[142] Li (2022), pp. 105–106.

[143] Fleischer in Spindler and Stilz (2019), AktG, § 93, para. 169; Sailer-Coceani in Schmidt and Lutter (2020), AktG, § 93, para. 27.

[144] Fleischer in Spindler and Stilz (2019), AktG, § 93, para. 171.

[145] Sailer-Coceani in Schmidt and Lutter (2020), AktG, § 93, para. 27; Li (2022), pp. 109–110.

[146] Li (2022), p. 111.

the information and documents provided, and whether the expert opinion adequately covers the subject for which the opinion is sought.[147] A substantive review should assess whether the expert opinion contains contradictions, gaps in its reasoning, and compare the conclusions reached in the expert opinion with the board's practical experience.[148]

Finally, within the framework of the Ision decision, an important point to be taken into consideration by boards is the need to document the process of obtaining the opinion, the opinion itself and the negotiations regarding the decision taken on the subject on which the opinion is given,[149] when taking a decision based on expert opinion.[150] Without such documentation, for instance, it cannot later be determined whether a verbal opinion has been subjected to a plausibility test.[151] Furthermore, documentation will be required to determine whether Ision's other required criteria have been met.

4.1.7.2.1.2.3 Applicability of Ision Criteria to AI

AI systems, like experts, provide information and analyses to the board. Therefore, whether the Ision criteria can also be applied to determining the board's obligations regarding the use of AI in corporation management is debated in German legal doctrine.[152] According to some scholars, the Ision criteria can also be applied to the process of information and analysis gathering from AI.[153] According to this view, the content of the Ision criteria should be redefined for AI.[154] In this respect, the characteristics of AI, such as its lack of professional responsibility, its black-box nature, and its dynamic learning capacity, must be considered.

The adaptation of the Ision's 'professional competence' criteria may necessitate the requirement for technical certifications or expert opinions for AI and

---

[147] Li (2022), p. 111.

[148] Li (2022), p. 113; Rolsing (2025), p. 438.

[149] Seyfarth (2016), § 8, para. 37; Link in Wachter (2022), AktG, § 93, para. 41.

[150] Seyfarth (2016), § 8, para. 37; Link in Wachter (2022), AktG, § 93, para. 40.

[151] Link in Wachter (2022), AktG § 93 para. 40.

[152] Weber et al. (2018), NZG, p. 1133; Linardatos (2019), ZIP, p. 504; Lücke (2019), BB, p. 1992; Zetzsche (2019), AG, p. 8; Thiel and Nazari-Khanachayi (2021), RDi, p. 141; Li (2022), p. 115 ff.; Nowak (2022), pp. 131–132; Lasar (2023), p. 145 ff. (on the GmbH); Adolff (2025), AG, p. 40–43; Rolsing (2025), p. 440 ff.; Windorf (2025), p. 184 and 189 ff.

[153] Weber et al. (2018), NZG, p. 1133; Li (2022), p. 120; Rolsing (2025), p. 441 ff.

[154] Nowak (2022), p. 132; Rolsing (2025), pp. 443–444.

its level of expertise,[155] rather than indicators of professional competence, such as diplomas, required of human experts, since the categorical refusal to utilise AI systems based solely on their lack of professional status would be unjustifiable.[156] Similarly, the 'independence' criterion for AI systems faces practical challenges in corporate settings.[157] Although AI operates on facts without conflicts of interest, risks persist, such as biased programming, flawed training data, or feedback-induced distortions[158] (e.g., AI adapting outputs to management preferences). This criterion, which is sought in human experts, can be adapted for AI by applying proactive methodologies to ensure that it is not affected by factors outside the corporation's interests.[159] Moreover, the requirement to 'provide all necessary information and documents' to the human expert may be interpreted as requiring the upload of all facts and data to the AI.[160] Furthermore, the content of the plausibility test applied to the human expert opinions should be adapted for AI.[161] The adapted plausibility test should involve methods to detect unique problems of AI systems, such cognitive cooperation issues,[162] programming flaws, data deficiencies, or concept and model drift.[163]

Despite all these adaptation solutions, some authors argue that applying the Ision criteria, established for obtaining opinions from human experts, to AI systems would create a misapplication rather than a valid legal adaptation.[164] According to this view, while the Ision criteria provide fundamental principles for proper data management and organisational governance, the board's obligations regarding obtaining information and analysis from AI systems should be

---

[155] Nowak (2022), p. 132; Rolsing (2025), p. 448 ff.

[156] Telle (2023), p. 110.

[157] Weber et al. (2018), NZG, p. 1133; Calabro (2023), pp. 159–162; Langenbucher (2023a), ZHR, pp. 733–734; Telle (2023), p. 112 ff.; Adolff (2025), AG, p. 42; Rolsing (2025), p. 456 ff.; Windorf (2025), p. 194.

[158] Li (2022), p. 126; Nowak (2022), p. 119; Telle (2023), p. 113; Rolsing (2025), p. 459.

[159] Nowak (2022), p. 132.

[160] Rolsing (2025), p. 462 ff.

[161] Langenbucher (2023a), ZHR, p. 734. For a detailed analysis, see Rolsing (2025), p. 465 ff.

[162] Langenbucher (2023a), ZHR, p. 735.

[163] Zetzsche (2019), AG, p. 8; Li (2022), p. 116. For more information on concept and model drift, see 1.2.4.2.

[164] Windorf (2025), pp. 197–198. Cf. Lasar (2023), pp. 145–147 (on the GmbH).

specifically defined,[165] based on the board's duty of care,[166] and taking into account the unique technical characteristics of AI systems.

4.1.7.2.2 Selection

4.1.7.2.2.1 In General

The board must exercise due diligence in selecting appropriate AI systems.[167] Hence, it is obligated to conduct technological 'market diligence,' which requires evaluating emerging technologies for suitability,[168] reliability, and riskiness.[169] To fulfil their fiduciary duty,[170] boards must carefully select systems with appropriate capabilities that match their corporation's specific needs[171] while addressing key risks.[172]

Due to the technical complexity of AI systems and the lack of an explicit legal basis for their assessment regarding integration into corporate management, the board's efforts to ensure quality in the selection process remain a case-by-case decision.[173] Boards may commission independent technical evaluations when procuring AI systems, as such due diligence informs selection.[174] Hence, the board is not required to micromanage the selection of specific AI systems. Preparatory work regarding the selection decision may be delegated to operational teams[175] or specialised experts.[176] The board must define binding governance frameworks to ensure alignment with corporate strategy and legal obligations. For this purpose, the board is obligated to define binding requirements for data quality,[177] security protocols, ethical safeguards, performance

---

[165] Adolff (2025), AG, p. 43; Windorf (2025), pp. 200–201.

[166] Windorf (2025), p. 200.

[167] Akın (2022), TAÜHFD, p. 20; Kaya (2024), p. 97; Keskin (2024), p. 50; Seçer (2025), p. 102.

[168] Langenbucher (2025), SSRN, p. 7; Rolsing (2025), p. 168, 297 ff. and 344 ff.

[169] Telle (2023), p. 69; Langenbucher (2024), EuZW, p. 857.

[170] Akın (2022), TAÜHFD, p. 20; Kaya (2024), p. 97; Seçer (2025), p. 102 and 105.

[171] Kaya (2024), p. 97; Rolsing (2025), p. 168 and 297.

[172] Kaya (2024), p. 94.

[173] Telle (2023), p. 126.

[174] Telle (2023), pp. 124–125; Frey (2024), p. 75.

[175] Windorf (2025), p. 139.

[176] Langenbucher (2023a), ZHR, p. 735; Rolsing (2025), p. 318 ff.

[177] Lieder (2022), p. 337.

standards, and permitted use cases, thereby ensuring the board's oversight of the issue.[178]

Although the board is responsible for selecting a technically sound and dependable system appropriate for its intended functions,[179] there are currently no formal assessment standards in place. Therefore, as part of their duty of care, boards are expected to determine case-specific criteria to select an AI system that aligns with the corporation's best interests, based on credible information.[180]

4.1.7.2.2.2 Selection of AI Source and Procurement Model

The integration of AI into corporate management requires a fundamental strategic choice about its sourcing. If outsourcing is selected, the board must further determine the appropriate outsourcing model and specific contractual design. How and under what conditions the AI system is provided plays a significant role in the board's organisational obligations within the framework of its duty of care.[181] The board must act in accordance with this duty of care when making this strategic decision,[182] because reversing the decision later would entail high financial and operational costs.[183] Such a strategic decision requires the combined evaluation of multiple factors,[184] including organisational priorities, resources, and risk appetite.

Developing AI systems internally will increase the board's control over them and protect the corporation's proprietary information from unauthorised disclosure. Furthermore, this method allows the AI system to be designed directly to the corporation's needs[185] and, thanks to internal familiarity with the system, development, problem identification, and resolution processes can proceed more quickly and effectively. It will ensure a sustainable investment in the corporation's long-term digitalisation[186] and development of expertise.[187] Therefore, it is recommended that particularly large corporations should develop their AI

---

[178] Windorf (2025), p. 139.

[179] Keskin (2024), p. 50; Rolsing (2025), p. 168 and 297.

[180] Li (2022), p. 131; Langenbucher (2025), SSRN, p. 7.

[181] Telle (2023), p. 105.

[182] Lasar (2023), p. 138 (on the GmbH); Telle (2023), p. 86 ff.; Rolsing (2025), p. 188.

[183] Telle (2023), p. 87.

[184] Telle (2023), p. 86.

[185] Rolsing (2025), p. 188.

[186] Bora Çınar (2022), p. 137.

[187] Rolsing (2025), p. 188.

systems internally rather than outsourcing them.[188] However, developing AI systems internally is more costly. There is also a risk that investments in AI system development may not yield the desired results. Therefore, it may be more practical and cost-effective for corporations lacking sufficient technical knowledge and financial resources to cooperate with third parties for co-development[189] or to outsource their AI systems.[190]

Outsourcing AI can provide more specialised capabilities[191] and generally reduces the board's due diligence obligations, as purchasers can reasonably rely on vendor qualifications as initial proof of suitability and reliability.[192] However, it does not exempt the board from its strict duty of care in the face of the nature of AI systems. Furthermore, the involvement of vendors/operators adds further layers to the already black-box nature of the system. Therefore, the board must ensure direct oversight of the entire AI process to ensure auditability, rapid responsiveness, and the proper fulfilment of management responsibilities when AI systems are outsourced.[193] To achieve this, boards must exercise diligence in selecting a suitable outsourcing model, continuously evaluating potential providers, designing the outsourcing agreement, and constantly monitoring the performance of the AI system.[194]

Corporations typically acquire external AI systems through leasing or purchasing. Each option carries unique operational and legal implications.[195] The use of AI can require significant investments in specialised personnel, equipment, and maintenance infrastructure. Therefore, leasing is often preferred, as it minimises necessary investments. Flexible leasing arrangements offer corporations adaptable solutions for their evolving needs. It allows them to maintain the operational effectiveness of the systems while avoiding the burdensome liabilities associated with full ownership.[196]

As another approach to external AI procurement, purchasing AI systems differs from other product purchases because they require ongoing hardware upgrades, software updates, and maintenance. Consequently, when corporations

[188] Bora Çınar (2022), pp. 136–137.
[189] Li (2022), pp. 129–130; Rolsing (2025), p. 189.
[190] Li (2022), pp. 128–129; Telle (2023), p. 105.
[191] Telle (2023), p. 86.
[192] Telle (2023), p. 105; Calabro (2024), p. 124; Windorf (2025), p. 241.
[193] Gözübüyük (2021), HHFD, p. 1203.
[194] Telle (2023), p. 162.
[195] Bora Çınar (2022), p. 140.
[196] Bora Çınar (2022), p. 142.

purchase AI systems, they also enter into a service contract.[197] Such contracts must include mandatory, ongoing vendor support obligations due to the system's inherent complexity. It transforms AI procurement into a long-term service partnership rather than a simple purchase.[198]

Alternatively, AI can be integrated through a service-based outsourcing model.[199] Corporations can choose between cloud-based 'Software as a service',[200] which provides direct access and control via web interfaces, or 'Managed Services', where providers operate the AI system in-house and deliver only final outputs.[201] The former model maintains internal control over data inputs and system interactions. Hence, it is suitable for corporations that prioritise transparency and adaptability. The latter offers instant solutions that reduce operational burdens but limit control. The decision between these two models should be based on balancing the need for control with operational simplicity.

Recently, algorithm marketplaces,[202] pioneered by major cloud providers and specialised analytics firms, have emerged as a transformative model for AI deployment. By offering pre-built AI applications, development tools, and infrastructure-as-a-service, these marketplaces allow corporations to bypass internal development and rapidly deploy AI solutions at lower cost.[203] Given the significant technical and financial barriers to developing internal AI systems, a specialised market for third-party AI services for corporation management is likely to emerge.[204]

Boards deciding to outsource AI systems are responsible for selecting suitable third-party AI systems by evaluating providers' reputations, reliability, performance guarantees, past success metrics, proven track records with similar organisations, and confidentiality standards.[205] After selecting the outsourcing model and provider, drafting the outsourcing contract is crucial in AI outsourcing.[206] To ensure the board's control over AI systems, this contract serves as the

197 Bora Çınar (2022), p. 141.

198 Bora Çınar (2022), pp. 140–141.

199 Petrin (2024), Sing JLS, pp. 98–99.

200 Li (2022), p. 128; Telle (2023), p. 163.

201 Telle (2023), p. 163.

202 Li (2022), p. 128.

203 Li (2022), pp. 128–129.

204 Dönmez Canseven (2021), p. 112.

205 Dönmez Canseven (2021), p. 105; Telle (2023), p. 163.

206 Telle (2023), p. 164.

primary mechanism.[207] It should include the necessary rights and obligations to compensate for the board's lack of direct management authority over the external provider. Within this framework, the contract should consist of clear performance standards, audit rights and monitoring mechanisms, data security and privacy protocols, information transfer requirements, and termination provisions. Generally, a modular contract is utilised for outsourcing AI services.[208] Such a modular contract structure consists of a 'Master Agreement' that defines governance, liability, and termination terms, and customisable 'Service Level Agreements' that precisely define performance metrics, quality standards, and service scope.[209] This approach provides the flexibility to update technical requirements through changes to 'Service Level Agreements' while maintaining consistent legal and operational governance through the 'Master Agreement'.

4.1.7.2.2.3 Selection Criteria

The AI system to be integrated into corporation management must be suitable and reliable.[210] To achieve this, the board must first identify the tasks and processes where AI can be used to create added value.[211] In this context, data-intensive tasks and processes in which AI is more successful than humans should be identified. Meanwhile, the board should also check whether the corporation's information technology infrastructure and data volume and quality[212] are sufficient to enable the use of AI systems,[213] since without sufficient, high-quality data and the necessary information technology infrastructure, even the best AI systems will fail to deliver the expected results.[214] Following these internal checks regarding the corporation's suitability for AI systems, market research should be conducted to identify reliable AI systems that align with the corporation's specific operational requirements and strategic objectives.[215] To achieve its strategic goals and fulfil its duty of care, the board must ensure that the

[207] It is crucial that any legal relationship with supporting third parties be structured to preserve the board's ultimate control. Link in Wachter (2022), AktG § 76 para. 23.

[208] Telle (2023), p. 165.

[209] Telle (2023), p. 165.

[210] Weber et al. (2018), NZG, p. 1133; Lücke (2019), BB, p. 1986; Zetzsche (2019), AG, p. 8; Becker and Pordzik (2020), ZfPW, p. 349; Li (2022), p. 123; Telle (2023), p. 108.

[211] Bora Çınar (2022), p. 169; Langenbucher (2023b), p. 10. For concrete cases where AI systems may create added value, see Varlı (2025), pp. 251–252 and 277–278.

[212] Calabro (2023), pp. 125–126; Langenbucher (2025), SSRN, p. 8.

[213] Frey (2024), pp. 75–76; Kremer and Langenbucher (2024), p. 86, 3.28.

[214] Li (2022), p. 122.

[215] Kaya (2024), p. 94 and 97.

selected AI systems are state-of-the-art.[216] However, this does not mean using the most advanced technology[217] but rather ensuring fit-for-purpose suitability for the tasks[218] and reliability.

Within the scope of market research, the board should also assess the technical capabilities and expertise of the providers. After determining the provider's reliability, the relevant AI system's suitability and reliability should be verified. Certificates and conformity tests for AI systems can assist in this verification process.[219] However, certifications for AI systems have not yet been standardised and widespread.[220] Hence, there is an urgent need for industry-wide certification frameworks to ensure compliance and reliability in AI selection.[221] However, the dynamic nature of AI systems makes traditional certification approaches, such as 'Algorithm TÜV,'[222] impractical because they require constant reassessment[223] due to the nature of AI systems that evolve beyond initial approval requirements through self-learning.[224] Furthermore, the mere certification of an AI does not demonstrate that the board has exercised due diligence in AI selection.[225] For these reasons, corporations may also rely on the provider's information to assess a specific AI system's capabilities. Key assessment methods include reviewing the provider's technical documentation,[226] direct provider consultations, and

[216] Telle (2023), p. 53. For more elaboration on state-of-the-art criteria, see Rolsing (2025), p. 176 ff.

[217] Windorf (2025), p. 202.

[218] Weber et al. (2018), NZG, p. 1132; Armour and Eidenmüller (2019), ZHR, p. 177; Bora Çınar (2022), p. 150; Kaya (2024), p. 97; Keskin (2024), p. 50; Rolsing (2025), p. 168 and 178; Windorf (2025), p. 202.

[219] Telle (2023), p. 118. For the information regarding standardization and certification efforts across multiple governance levels, see Li, (2022), p. 124.

[220] Telle (2023), p. 112; Rolsing (2025), p. 179 ff.

[221] Telle (2023), p. 112.

[222] Lücke (2019), BB, p. 1992; Noack (2019a), ZHR, p. 128; Linardatos (2022), ZIP, p. 161; Windorf (2025), p. 192.

[223] Calabro (2023), p. 156.

[224] Möslein (2018), ZIP, p. 212; Dany (2022), BB, p. 2062; Rolsing (2025), pp. 180–181; Windorf (2025), p. 192.

[225] Telle (2023), p. 122.

[226] The instruction manual as legally mandated in the EU AI Act's Article 13 may serve as a critical tool for verifying AI system properties and ensuring responsible adoption. Article 13(3/a-f) of the EU AI Act contains a comprehensive catalogue of content requirements for the user manual for high-risk AI systems. For a similar analysis, see Telle (2023), pp. 123–124.

third-party reviews.[227] Although certifications and information provided by third parties can serve as preliminary indicators of system capabilities, these methods are not sufficient to fulfil the board's due diligence obligations. A comprehensive, diligent governance requires both upfront verification and ongoing operational oversight to ensure compliance with corporate standards. Therefore, the selected AI system should have features that enable continuous board oversight and anomaly detection during the implementation phase, to compensate for the lack of standardised pre-deployment evaluations.[228]

As an alternative to relying on third-party assessments, such as certificates and provider assurances, the relevant AI system may be subjected to a systemic functionality review by the corporation.[229] However, the board should not be expected to possess technical expertise in AI functionality.[230] Instead, testing should be designed for non-specialists, leveraging user-friendly interfaces or guided demonstrations by the AI provider, external experts, or qualified internal staff.[231] This review (e.g., software audits[232]) should test the AI system within the corporation's designated tasks and processes for AI use. The AI system must perform its functions without disruptions or errors.[233] It must have adequate processing capacity and demonstrate sufficient resilience against external interference. Thanks to this trial, the board may have the opportunity to evaluate the suitability and reliability of the AI system by using real data in real-world scenarios before making its final decision on the selection.[234]

Another consideration when selecting AI systems is whether the chosen system is explainable. The explainability feature of an AI system enables the board to identify key factors behind specific outputs.[235] The board's ability to monitor and control the AI system depends on understanding the rationales behind its recommendations.[236] In this informational interaction between the AI system and the board, the explanations provided by the AI system should be neither so detailed as to make it impossible to understand nor so superficial as to prevent

---

[227] Li (2022), p. 125.

[228] For the emphasis on the importance of post-deployment monitoring, see Li (2022), p. 126.

[229] Gözübüyük (2022), HBV-HFD, p. 159; Lieder (2022), p. 336; Telle (2023), p. 125.

[230] Becker and Pordzik (2020), ZfPW, p. 349; Telle (2023), p. 125.

[231] Telle (2023), pp. 125–126.

[232] Dönmez Canseven (2021), p. 85.

[233] Telle (2023), p. 108.

[234] Calabro (2023), p. 127.

[235] Li (2022), p. 149.

[236] Özer and Tomrukçu (2025), BATİDER, p. 250 and 262.

the board from making the necessary assessment.[237] Therefore, it is argued that a reasonable degree of explainability is required when selecting a system, as part of the board's duty of care.[238] Within this framework, the degree of explainability expected from the system is not uniform.[239] It should be determined by the risk level of the tasks for which it will be used. A low degree of explainability is sufficient for systems used in low-risk tasks, whereas a high degree of explainability is expected for systems used in high-risk tasks. This risk-based approach is also compatible with the EU AI Act, which prohibits the use of non-explainable AI systems in high-risk domains.[240]

In addition to the AI system's inherent explainability, specific methods later applied to the AI system may also provide the necessary justifications for AI outputs.[241] The board must diligently select appropriate explainability methods to achieve the required level of transparency in AI's operational processes.[242] Methods like LIME (Local Interpretable Model-agnostic Explanations)[243] and SHAP (SHapley Additive exPlanations)[244] may be used to learn what AI systems consider during their analytical process and how they arrive at their conclusions.[245]

---

[237] Özer and Tomrukçu (2025), BATİDER, p. 271.

[238] Dubovitskaya and Buchholz (2023), ECFR, p. 813 ff.

[239] AI outputs do not necessitate full explainability when they serve as a single informational input within a broader human decision-making process. The requirement for explainability is becomes obligatory only where such transparency would materially reduce the specific risk posed by a potentially erroneous prediction. Langenbucher (2023a), ZHR, p. 737.

[240] Langenbucher (2024), EuZW, p. 857.

[241] Rolsing (2025), pp. 218–219. Supplementing the AI's output with independent human analysis and contextual reasoning or obtaining and documenting an additional expert opinion from a qualified natural person are alternative means to compensate AI system's lack of necessary explainability. Telle (2023), p. 38.

[242] Rolsing (2025), p. 262.

[243] LIME method helps to understand how an AI makes a specific decision. It works by slightly changing the information provided to the AI and testing how its prediction changes. Based on these tests, LIME builds a simple, summary that shows which factors were most important in the AI's final output. For application examples and more information on LIME method, see Molnar (2019), p. 168 ff.

[244] SHAP is another method that explains an AI's decision by showing exactly how much each piece of information contributed to the final output. This method enable board to see which factors mattered most in AI's processing. For application examples and more information on LIME method, see Molnar (2019), p. 177 ff.; Dubovitskaya, and Buchholz (2023), ECFR, p. 817.

[245] Adolff (2025), AG, pp. 27–28; Özer and Tomrukçu (2025), BATİDER, p. 267 ff.; Rolsing (2025), p. 359. For a concise information on explainability methods, see Dubovitskaya, and Buchholz (2023), ECFR, p. 815 ff.

In any case, when selecting an AI system, the board should prioritise AI systems with sufficient explainability, taking into account the areas in which the AI will be used. At the current stage of AI systems' development, the explainability features of these systems are increasing, and add-on methods that provide explainability are becoming widespread and accessible.

4.1.7.2.3 Instruction

Instructing AI systems fundamentally differs from instructing human employees (including human delegates). Upon starting employment, the board's obligation to instruct human employees includes informing them of the corporation's scope of business, goals, and values, as well as the work processes and responsibilities within the employee's role. Furthermore, employees should be instructed, as necessary, throughout their employment on how to perform their assigned duties. On the other hand, instructing AI systems often involves pre-configuring[246] them to meet the corporation's needs. Once AI systems are in use, if they experience problems, the board must take action to implement post-deployment refinements. Unlike employees, AI systems cannot dynamically adapt to verbal or contextual post-deployment directives of the board.[247] Hence, the board can request the AI provider to process the board's instructions into the system, or, if the system's interface is suitable, the board or its designees may enter these instructions directly into the system.

Additionally, instruction of AI systems requires full disclosure of relevant corporate data,[248] as is the case with conventional expert advice. Providing accurate, sufficient,[249] and purposeful data to the AI system is critical for the board's instruction of AI systems. The specified data characteristics are crucial for the proper operation of AI systems.[250] Therefore, the board should create a digital nervous system,[251] collect the corporation's data,[252] and transfer the necessary

[246] Calabro (2023), pp. 131–132; Lasar (2023), p. 141.

[247] Calabro (2023), pp. 131–132; Windorf (2025), p. 250.

[248] Telle (2023), p. 134.

[249] Sanders (2025), NZG, p. 1407.

[250] Lücke (2019), BB, p. 1993; Li (2022), p. 132; Telle (2023), p. 134 ff.; Frey (2024), p. 77; Windorf (2025), p. 203.

[251] For the terminology of digital nervous system, see Gates (1999).

[252] Bora Çınar (2022), p. 149.

data to the AI system. This transfer can be accomplished through various methods, such as automated data extraction systems or manually by the corporation's staff.[253]

Especially when AI systems are trained on corporation-specific data, the board must ensure rigorous data governance to maintain data quality and legality[254] and to prevent bias.[255] Furthermore, if the AI system collects data from open sources,[256] the board's obligation to instruct and supervise also includes oversight of the quality and legal compliance of the data collected. Since the board cannot be expected to review the raw data directly, it may fulfil these obligations through transparency commitments in the contract with the provider, required certificates, or the establishment of pre-authorisation mechanisms.[257]

The board should provide AI systems with the same comprehensive corporation information required for human experts.[258] Human employees (including experts and delegates) are expected to report any deficiencies in the information provided to them by the corporation and obtain the missing information. AI systems, on the other hand, may not recognise that the data they need to deliver the expected outputs is incomplete. Therefore, the board or its designated experts should monitor and document the scope and quality of the data to be transferred to AI systems for potential deficiencies.[259] If existing technological advancements allow, AI systems should include automated verification protocols to identify and flag insufficient or missing input data for assigned tasks.[260] Because the quality of data provided to an AI system significantly impacts its results, the board is expected to exercise due diligence in data management to ensure the system serves the corporation's objectives. This diligence, just as expected from the instructional obligations for human employees, will ensure that the processing and output of AI systems align with the corporation's mission, vision, and long-term goals.[261] Otherwise, AI systems may produce results that contradict the corporation's strategic objectives and operational focus.[262] As a result, the board

[253] Telle (2023), pp. 134–135.

[254] Li (2022), p. 142; Rolsing (2025), p. 202 ff.

[255] Windorf (2025), p. 204.

[256] Windorf (2025), p. 206.

[257] Windorf (2025), p. 204.

[258] Hoch (2019), AcP, p. 675; Calabro (2023), p. 152.

[259] Nowak (2022), p. 115.

[260] Calabro (2023), p. 153; Windorf (2025), p. 191.

[261] Bora Çınar (2022), p. 157.

[262] Bora Çınar (2022), p. 147.

should ensure the AI system receives accurate,[263] comprehensive,[264] ongoing, and governance-aligned data inputs throughout the system's operational lifecycle to fulfil the board's organisational instruction duty diligently.[265]

As seen in the assessment above, the board's obligation to provide AI-related instructions essentially involves configuring the system to meet the corporation's needs, providing the necessary data for the system's proper operation, and coordinating these processes with the AI provider or internal departments. Therefore, the board's obligation to provide data to AI can be characterised as an informational instruction duty, while its obligation related to fault detection and reconfiguration (under constant surveillance) can be characterised as an operational instruction duty.

4.1.7.2.4 Monitoring

Integrating AI systems into corporation management requires adapting the board's monitoring obligations to accommodate them. Although robust selection and instruction processes may reduce subsequent monitoring needs,[266] the board's monitoring obligation regarding AI is more comprehensive and burdensome than its oversight obligation of humans.[267] Within this obligation, the board is required to continuously monitor the entire AI pipeline.[268] This monitoring obligation for AI systems includes both oversight of the technical functionality of these systems[269] and checking the plausibility of system outputs.[270] Because the board is not expected to possess knowledge of the system's technical operation and functionality, it must carry out technical oversight through an internal organisation it establishes or through assigned experts.[271] This oversight can be achieved by

[263] Zhao (2022), Cath. U. L. Rev., p. 676; Adolff (2025), AG, p. 49.

[264] Rolsing (2025), pp. 193 and 199 ff.; Adolff (2025), AG, p. 49.

[265] These data-related obligations also constitute the core of the board's organisational duties in general. Lücke (2019), BB, p. 1993; Becker and Pordzik (2020), ZfPW, p. 350; Windorf (2025), pp. 242. The EU AI Act outlines strict data governance standards (e.g., representativeness, accuracy) for high-risk AI systems. However, these standards primarily target providers rather than corporate end-users. Telle (2023), pp. 136–137.

[266] Calabro (2023), p. 138.

[267] Özer and Tomrukçu (2025), BATİDER, p. 258.

[268] Bora Çınar (2022), p. 194; Lieder (2022), p. 336; Langenbucher (2023a), ZHR, p. 735; Özer and Tomrukçu (2025), BATİDER, p. 262; Rolsing (2025), p. 231 and 357; Seçer (2025), pp. 106–107.

[269] Lieder (2022), p. 336; Langenbucher (2023a), ZHR, p. 735; Telle (2023), p. 151.

[270] Telle (2023), p. 154.

[271] Frey (2024), p. 79; Rolsing (2025), p. 318 ff.

subjecting the AI system to periodic audits,[272] stress tests,[273] or by examining random samples, especially for bias detection.[274] The technical oversight obligation also includes oversight of the data used by the system to ensure it is sufficient and of the required quality,[275] since the quality of data, as the raw material of AI, is crucial to guaranteeing technical functionality.[276] Consequently, the application guidelines for overseeing the technical functionality of AI systems should be determined by experts, taking into account the characteristics of the relevant AI system and the required datasets.

Another aspect of the board's monitoring duty regarding AI is subjecting system outputs to a plausibility test to prevent their uncritical acceptance. Boards are expected to make decisions based on their own assessments,[277] and relying directly and solely on AI outputs when making decisions constitutes a breach of the duty of care and could lead to liability. Therefore, the board should subject AI outputs to a plausibility test, as it does for human expert opinions, before using them in its decisions.[278]

A plausibility test applied to AI outputs poses practical challenges compared to one applied to human experts' opinions.[279] As part of a plausibility test, human experts can provide justifications for their opinions and answer specific questions posed by the board. The black-box nature of AI systems and the complex algorithms they employ can hinder such communication between the board members and AI systems.[280] Therefore, the plausibility test applied should be adapted to AI systems. Applying the same scope and intensity of plausibility testing to every AI output could create unnecessary effort and time consumption, thereby eliminating the speed and efficiency expected from AI use.[281] On the other hand, reducing plausibility testing to a mere system functionality test would be insufficient to identify specific decision risks. Hence, the scope and intensity of this adapted

---

272 Dönmez Canseven (2021), p. 85; Calabro (2023), p. 150.

273 Telle (2023), p. 148.

274 Li (2022), p. 150 ff.

275 Zhao (2022), Cath. U. L. Rev., p. 676.

276 Dönmez Canseven (2021), p. 104; Rolsing (2025), pp. 237–238; Seçer (2025), p. 105.

277 Nowak (2022), p. 129.

278 Li (2022), p. 144 ff.; Langenbucher (2023a), ZHR, p. 733 ff.; Varlı (2025), pp. 250–251; Windorf (2025), p. 206 ff.

279 Weber et al. (2018), NZG, p. 1133; Thiel and Nazari-Khanachayi (2021), RDi, p. 141; Calabro (2023), p. 164; Langenbucher (2023a), ZHR, p. 734 ff.; Windorf (2025), p. 196 and 207.

280 Telle (2023), p. 115; Windorf (2025), p. 196 and 244.

281 Möslein (2018), ZIP, p. 211; Hoch (2019), AcP, p. 682; Windorf (2025), p. 197.

plausibility test, which the board must consider within the framework of their duty of care, must be determined by a case-by-case approach[282] considering many factors, including the significance of the relevant task to the corporation[283] and the potential risks it may pose,[284] and its compliance with legal regulations.[285]

Although the principles of the plausibility test applied to AI outputs should be determined on a case-by-case basis, the test must necessarily include an expediency review by the board.[286] As part of the expediency review, the content of AI outputs should be monitored for compliance with the corporation's purpose, core values, internal standards, and interests,[287] particularly its economic efficiency.[288] Additionally, it should be checked whether the AI's output specifically covers the topic for which the AI's opinion was requested,[289] since these outputs may be generic or abstract suggestions. The board must also scrutinise the logical consistency and completeness of the AI's reasoning, identifying any gaps, contradictions, or unsupported conclusions in its analytical process.[290] Moreover, a plausibility test of AI outputs may include counter-testing the system's underlying assumptions when technically feasible. Rather than directly evaluating the AI's final recommendation, this method involves querying and verifying the factual accuracy of key premises or decision-relevant prerequisites the AI used in its analysis.[291]

While the intensity of the board's monitoring duty for AI can be reduced for a while after the system's reliability is understood,[292] the dynamic nature of AI systems will prevent the oversight role from becoming too superficial or disappearing altogether. If the board believes that sufficient trust has been established in the AI

[282] Li (2022), p. 154; Calabro (2023), p. 135 (for monitoring obligations in general); Rolsing (2025), p. 244; Windorf (2025), pp. 209–210.

[283] Noack (2019), ZHR, p. 119; Li (2022), p. 154; Casper and Möslein (2025), ZGR, p. 885; Rolsing (2025), pp. 248–250.

[284] Li (2022), p. 154.

[285] Nowak (2022), p. 96.

[286] Windorf (2025), p. 249.

[287] Gözübüyük (2022), HBV-HFD, p. 159.

[288] Dönmez Canseven (2021), p. 103 and 105; Windorf (2025), p. 249.

[289] Calabro (2023), p. 163; Rolsing (2025), p. 467.

[290] Li (2022), p. 145; Rolsing (2025), p. 467; Windorf (2025), p. 208.

[291] Telle (2023), p. 157.

[292] Li (2022), p. 154; Telle (2023), p. 156; Windorf (2025), p. 209.

system, it may take a balancing approach by reducing the technical[293] and plausibility reviews, provided that they remain at a level that meets the requirements of the duty of care, and thus maintain the speed and effectiveness expected from AI at the optimum level.

4.1.7.3 Interim Result

Turkish and German legal doctrines have distinctive approaches to the legal basis for boards' selection, instruction, and monitoring duties in the context of AI's integration into corporation management. The contemporary Turkish legal doctrine does not adopt the analogous approach derived from the delegation or employer liability. Instead, it focuses on concrete obligations arising from the 'prudent manager' standard. In contrast, analogies with existing regulations, such as § 80(2) of the WpHG, § 130 of the OWiG, and tort law principles, are explored in the German legal doctrine. However, German legal doctrine acknowledges the limitations of such analogies and refocuses on adapting the board's duty of care to provide the legal basis for the above-mentioned duties.

Apart from exploring different analogical paths, the board's selection, instruction, and monitoring duties regarding the AI systems integrated into corporation management can be based on the board's duty of care in both legal systems. The duty of care's general and abstract characteristic provides the necessary flexibility to develop context-specific obligations. Therefore, an assessment that instrumentalises the implementation of the duty of care is necessary to reveal the board's specific selection, instruction, and monitoring duties regarding AI. Such an assessment across both legal systems reveals that boards are expected to perform these three duties as part of prudent management in the integration of AI into corporation management. Since the board's existing duty of care, which implicates management and monitoring duties as well, is codified in a general and abstract manner, the specification of the board's selection, instruction, and monitoring duties regarding AI does not require entirely new legislation for every technological development. These existing duties, which are also accepted as the board's fiduciary duties regarding delegates in both legal systems, can be adapted to new technological developments to determine the specific content of the board's selection, instruction, and monitoring duties regarding AI.

The board's duty of care in selecting the AI system primarily encompasses choosing the source of the AI system and, if procured from an external source,

---

293 A structured validation protocol should incorporate routine performance testing using simplified tasks on small datasets to verify the AI's baseline operational integrity, and immediate functionality checks conducted prior to its use in high-stakes board decisions. Dönmez Canseven (2021), p. 104.

strategically designing the procurement contract. Subsequently, managerial care must be taken in the specific selection of the AI system since the choice of the AI source, and specifically the system, will significantly affect the diligent fulfilment of instruction and supervision duties of the board and the achievement of the expected benefits from the AI. Whether to procure AI internally or externally, a case-by-case evaluation must be conducted, considering factors such as the corporation's resources and the cost of the AI use, the corporation's needs and control over the system, potential risks, and the suitability of existing AI systems. If the AI system is to be procured externally, the procurement method and the design of the procurement contract must be carefully determined, with the corporation's interests taken into account. When selecting a specific AI system, market research must be conducted to assess the provider's qualifications and evidence that the AI can reliably meet the corporation's needs (manufacturer assurances, certifications, etc.). Moreover, the board must ensure that the selected AI system is sufficiently explainable and that any deficiencies in its explainability can be addressed via add-on methods.

The board's instruction duty regarding AI systems differs from its duty to instruct human employees. Primarily, a pre-configuration of an AI system is necessary to ensure that its outcomes are consistent with the corporation's needs. Moreover, the board must have the opportunity to instruct the AI, particularly when the system malfunctions, during the deployment. Provision of all relevant data to the AI is another crucial part of the board's instruction duty. Furthermore, the integrated AI system is expected to flag insufficient data provision to enable the board to perform its instruction duty efficiently. In this framework, the board may fulfil its informational and operational instruction duty regarding AI systems prudently.

The board's monitoring duty regarding an AI system comprises technical monitoring of the system's functionality and oversight of the plausibility of its outputs. The board must establish an organisation to monitor the system's operationality, especially to detect operational interruptions. Moreover, the system's outputs must be subjected to a contextual plausibility test. The scope and intensity of this test must be calibrated on a case-by-case basis, considering different factors such as the strategic importance of the decision, previous experience with the system, and the magnitude of the probable risks. This test must assess the comprehensiveness of the outputs regarding the requested matter, their internal consistency, and their compatibility with the corporation's values, goals, and interests. Consequently, this monitoring framework must prevent the board from relying uncritically on AI outputs without applying its independent judgment.

4.1.8 Legality (Compliance) Duty

4.1.8.1 Comparative Review

4.1.8.1.1 In General

In both Turkish and German corporate law, the board's monitoring duty includes overseeing the legality of corporate operations and decisions.[294] The board must continuously monitor the compliance of both its own decisions and those of other delegates with mandatory legal rules, the corporation's articles of association, and internal regulations.[295] The integration of AI into corporation management imposes on the board the duty of overseeing the legality of both the operation of the AI and its outputs,[296] whether they are used as advisory informational sources or as direct (subsidiary) decision-makers as a result of delegation. Furthermore, the ever-increasing number of special laws related to digitalisation, along with the addition of digitalisation-related amendments to existing laws, provide new and more comprehensive legal foundations for the board's oversight duty regarding compliance.[297]

Although an AI system can be programmed to operate and produce outputs in compliance with legal rules from the very beginning of its creation, due to its dynamic nature, it may eventually begin to produce unlawful outputs.[298] Therefore, the board must ensure that the AI system delivers outputs in compliance with legal rules by taking necessary measures during both its creation and operation. In this context, the board should assess the risks of the relevant AI system and establish a compliance system to ensure the flow of information regarding AI in line with these risks.[299] Moreover, the board should ensure that these systems operate properly. Thus, by establishing a compliance system in accordance with the duty of care, the board can also delegate certain oversight responsibilities within this system, thereby indirectly fulfilling its oversight role to ensure the legal operation of AI systems. Directly fulfilling this oversight role would be inefficient both in terms of time and the board's level of technical and legal knowledge. Thus, by establishing a compliance system and ensuring its smooth operation, the board will have diligently fulfilled its legality duty.

---

[294] For Turkish law, see 2.1.1.3.1.3; for German law, see 2.1.1.3.2.3.

[295] Sailer-Coceani in Schmidt and Lutter (2020), AktG, § 93, para. 7; Yıldırım Soysal (2023), AÜHFD, p. 1823; Varlı (2025), p. 158; Windorf (2025), p. 251 and 283.

[296] Nowak (2022), pp. 96–97; Sanders (2025), NZG, p. 1408.

[297] Möslein (2023b), p. 427.

[298] Bora Çınar (2022), p. 158.

[299] Möslein (2023b), p. 426.

The possibility of unlawful AI outputs persists despite all reasonable precautions. Even if these unlawful outputs are in the corporation's best interest, both Turkish and German legal doctrine state that the board must disregard unlawful AI outputs and make lawful decisions.[300]

As a newly evolving part of the legality duty, this section analyses the board's duties under specific hard and soft law rules governing AI.

4.1.8.1.2 Compliance with the EU AI Act

The EU AI Act has introduced a new dimension to the set of legal rules that boards integrating AI into corporation management must comply with under German law.[301] However, the EU AI Act is not tailored for the use of AI in complex business environments, such as boardrooms,[302] and does not contain regulations primarily targeting internal AI use by corporations.[303] Therefore, the board's responsibilities regarding integrating AI into corporate management will continue to be primarily governed by corporate law.[304] However, the EU AI Act's general paradigm and specific principles, such as humans' ultimate responsibility,[305] may serve as benchmarks for determining the board's duties in integrating AI into corporate management.

The EU AI Act distinguishes between AI systems based on their riskiness. It establishes legal obligations for certain actors in the AI ecosystem, particularly regarding the use of high-risk AI systems. Annex III, as referred by Article 6 of the EU AI Act, stipulates in detail which AI systems fall into the high-risk AI systems category. In particular, systems related to corporations' employment processes, such as hiring, promotion, and dismissal, are designated as high-risk systems under Annex III (4). The EU AI Act stipulates the necessary features of high-risk AI systems, such as human oversight,[306] bias detection mechanisms, and explainability.[307]

---

[300] Li (2022), pp. 134–135; Varlı (2025), p. 126; Windorf (2025), pp. 289–290.

[301] Möslein (2025a), p. 614 and 633–634; Roth (2025), SSRN, pp. 8–9.

[302] Cowger (2023), JOLTI, p. 193; Zhao (2024), CLSR, p. 9.

[303] Möslein (2022), p. 82. Corporate law is not particularly addressed within the EU AI Act's framework. Roth (2025), SSRN, p. 8.

[304] Casper and Möslein (2025), ZGR, p. 871; Möslein (2025a), pp. 633–634. It is important to note that general regulations regarding AI, such as the EU AI Act, and regulations concerning the integration of AI into boardrooms differ in many respects, due to the unique nature of the latter. Zhao (2024), CLSR, p. 7.

[305] Roth (2025), SSRN, p. 8.

[306] Art. 14 of the EU AI Act. Langenbucher (2023b), p. 14.

[307] Art. 13 of the EU AI Act.

The responsibility for fulfilling obligations under the EU AI Act may fall to corporate boards. Under the EU AI Act's framework, corporations that professionally integrate AI systems into their management will be considered AI deployers and will be required to comply with the obligations imposed on deployers. In this context, the obligations of 'deployer' corporations regarding the high-risk AI systems are detailed in its Article 26. These obligations include taking the necessary technical and organisational measures, ensuring human oversight, ensuring that the data is sufficient, relevant to the desired outcome, and sufficiently representative, keeping and storing transaction logs, suspending the system in the event of a risk, and making the necessary notifications. To fulfil these obligations, the board must establish the necessary organisation. If corporations develop and use their own AI systems, they will have obligations not only as deployers but also as providers under the EU AI Act framework. Obligations of providers are explicitly regulated in Articles 16–22 of the EU AI Act. These obligations, which are more comprehensive than those imposed on the deployer, undoubtedly increase the provider corporation's board's responsibilities.

A board's failure to implement EU AI Act-mandated measures[308] could constitute a breach of its duty of care and of its legal compliance obligations. Hence, a board should first determine whether the AI system it will integrate into the corporation management falls within the high-risk AI category under the EU AI Act. For instance, AI systems that are integrated into corporate management for employment practices may be categorised as high-risk AI systems.[309] If the system falls into the high-risk AI category, the corporation's position according to the EU AI Act's framework must be determined. The corporation's position within the AI ecosystem will determine its obligations under the EU AI Act. While the board may receive technical and legal support in determining AI's risk level, the corporation's position within the AI ecosystem, and the specific obligations associated with that position, the board must retain ultimate decision-making authority and responsibility for the corporation's compliance with the EU AI Act.

If the relevant AI system does not fall into the high-risk AI category, the board will not have any specific obligations under the EU AI Act. However, when assessing the board's responsibilities arising from its obligations regarding these low-risk AI systems, the EU AI Act's general paradigm and principles may

---

[308] For an examination of whether the EU AI Act imposes organisational obligations on corporations and how to determine such potential obligations, see Casper and Möslein (2025), ZGR, p. 892.

[309] Cowger (2023), JOLTI, p. 193.

be taken into account. Therefore, even if the relevant AI system does not fall into the high-risk AI category, it would be beneficial for the board to consider the principles outlined in the EU AI Act regarding their obligations for AI systems to fulfil their duty of care.[310]

Turkish law does not yet have a legal regulation similar to the EU AI Act. However, the 'Medium-Term Program' for 2026–2028 indicates an intention to complete the harmonisation of Turkish law with the EU AI Act.[311] Until this work is completed and the necessary legal regulations are enacted, and given that Türkiye is an EU candidate country, the EU AI Act may serve as a guide in discussions of the board's obligations regarding AI systems in Turkish corporate law.

4.1.8.1.3 Compliance with Data Protection Laws

Given the data-driven operational structure of AI systems,[312] the integration of an AI system into corporate management triggers specific data protection obligations for the board.[313] These board-level obligations are grounded in the ever-increasing special legal regulations on data protection. As part of their legality duty, boards are expected to ensure the corporation's compliance with these special regulations.

The primary regulation regarding data protection in Turkish law is the KVKK (*Kişisel Verileri Koruma Kanunu*, Personal Data Protection Law),[314] modelled after the EU's GDPR (General Data Protection Regulation).[315] KVKK primarily imposes obligations on data controllers and processors. According to the KVKK, a data controller is the natural or legal person who determines the purposes and means of processing personal data and is responsible for establishing and managing the data recording system.[316] In this context, a corporation that uses an AI

[310] Telle (2023), p. 92.

[311] The Presidential Decision regarding 2026–2028 Medium-Term Plan, No. 10376, Official Gazette dated 07/09/2025 and numbered 33010-Duplicate Issue, p. 24 and 72.

[312] Lieder (2022), p. 337; Aksoy (2025), p. 192.

[313] Lieder (2022), pp. 337–338; Adolff (2025), AG, p. 39; Rolsing (2025), p, 204 ff. and 298–299; Ustahaliloğlu (2025), CLGR, p. 125.

[314] *Kişisel Verileri Koruma Kanunu* (Personal Data Protection Law), Law No. 6698, Official Gazette dated 07/04/2016 and numbered 29677.

[315] Regulation (EU) 2016/679 of the European Parliament and of the Council of 27 April 2016 on the protection of natural persons with regard to the processing of personal data and on the free movement of such data, and repealing Directive 95/46/EC (General Data Protection Regulation).

[316] Art. 3(1-ı) of the KVKK.

system to process personal data will be considered a data controller as a legal entity. It will be obligated to fulfil the obligations imposed on the data controller under the KVKK. Hence, the corporation must take all necessary technical and organisational measures to ensure an appropriate level of security to prevent the unlawful processing and unlawful access to personal data.[317] Since the board is responsible for ensuring the corporation fulfils its obligations under the KVKK, if the board integrates an AI system into management, it is responsible for ensuring compliance with the legislation governing AI's data processing.[318] The board bears responsibility for overseeing the entire AI training process. While the board is the ultimate decision-maker and responsible for data governance as a core management task,[319] it may seek support from within or outside the corporation to fulfil its duties. Even though the board is not expected to possess expertise in this area, securing the necessary support is a requirement of the duty of care. In this context, the board must draft an internal data protection strategy in line with the KVKK. Furthermore, the board may appoint an executive to support and manage operational processes, establish a department reporting to this executive, or appoint a committee to support the fulfilment of its organisational obligations with due diligence. When the board establishes an organisation for this purpose, it is also expected to oversee this organisation's proper functioning.

Under German law, the management board integrating AI into corporation management must ensure that this AI system complies with data protection laws.[320] If the corporation is a data controller, it must fulfil the obligations imposed on data controllers under Article 24 and other articles of the GDPR. The management board must take the necessary measures, within the framework of its duty of care and legality, to ensure the corporation fulfils its obligations under data protection regulations.[321] Given the growing importance of data protection, German legal doctrine recognises this issue as a core management task and, therefore, a non-delegable duty of the management board.[322] As with other core management tasks, the management board retains final decision-making authority and responsibility in this matter. The management board, which is not expected to be specialised explicitly in this area, may receive support to fulfil

[317] Seçer (2025), p. 117.

[318] Bora Çınar (2022), pp. 154–157; Töre (2025), SÜHFD, p. 899; Varlı (2025), p. 287.

[319] Eryiğit (2021), p. 114.

[320] Li (2022), p. 135; Nowak (2022), pp. 99–102; Telle (2023), p. 128; Frey (2024), p. 47; Rolsing (2025), p. 204 ff. and 298–299; Sanders (2025), NZG, p. 1408.

[321] Möslein (2020c), pp. 814–815; Möslein (2023b), p. 427.

[322] See references in Windorf (2025), p. 128, fn. 29.

its organisational duties in this domain. In this context, the management board may organise necessary support through various structural mechanisms. These include sourcing expertise from internal or external advisors, appointing a specialised executive officer, establishing a dedicated internal department, or forming a board-level committee to oversee and manage the relevant operational processes. While establishing these structural mechanisms, the management board should define binding governance frameworks to ensure compliance with legal obligations.[323] Beyond the mandatory provisions, the management board may also use the GDPR as a guide for its organisational obligations when integrating AI into corporation management. In particular, principles regarding privacy-by-design, transparency,[324] data minimisation[325] and the protection of sensitive data will guide the management board in acting diligently on data protection issues[326] in the process of AI's integration into corporation management.

Some provisions of the GDPR draw attention in terms of integrating AI into corporation management. For instance, the management board must be able to provide clear information on the core parameters of any AI system it employs, as these fall within the scope of Article 13 (2-f) of the GDPR on automated decision-making.[327] Moreover, Article 22 of the GDPR, which regulates automated individual decision-making, is crucial when integrating AI into corporation management.[328] This article governs fully automated decisions with legal or significant effects and requires meaningful human involvement in final determinations. Hence, boards must implement safeguards against 'rubber-stamp' approvals that could constitute *de facto* automated decision-making.[329] Unlike the GDPR, the KVKK does not contain such a specific provision regulating automated individual decision-making. However, Article 11 of the KVKK, which enumerates the rights of data subjects, provides a specific right to object to any result arising against the data subject from the analysis of processed data by exclusively automated systems.[330] Upon receiving such an objection under Article 11, the data controller is obligated to conduct a meaningful review of the contested automated

323 Lieder (2022), pp. 337–338.

324 Rolsing (2025), pp. 216–220.

325 Rolsing (2025), pp. 214–216.

326 Rolsing (2025), p. 213.

327 Möslein (2020c), p. 820.

328 Frey (2024), p. 47.

329 Nowak (2022), p. 102; Rolsing (2025), pp. 428–429.

330 Aksoy (2025), p. 194.

decision. Hence, boards are required to perform this review when an exclusively automated system is integrated into the management.

4.1.8.1.4 Compliance with Anti-Discrimination Laws

While AI systems reduce cognitive biases in human decision-making by providing more consistent and objective recommendations, they are not entirely free of bias.[331] Their data-driven nature, in particular, increases the likelihood of biased AI outputs, and their opaque nature makes it difficult to detect bias. AI systems can produce discriminatory results,[332] particularly due to biased programming, flawed training data, or feedback-induced distortions.[333] Therefore, boards integrating AI into corporation management should demonstrate proactive governance[334] and take the necessary precautions throughout AI processes to prevent biased AI outputs,[335] a requirement of both due diligence and legality. To this end, boards should implement structured impact assessment protocols[336] and conduct regular bias audits using specially developed tools[337] to identify potentially biased outputs.[338] Moreover, boards must implement rigorous safeguards and comprehensive documentation of decision pathways to mitigate liability risks[339] since corporations, and therefore their boards, that fail to exercise due diligence to mitigate the risk of biased AI outputs will be liable under anti-discrimination regulations in both Turkish and German law.

---

[331] Dönmez Canseven (2021), p. 84; İnce (2022), ANNALES, p. 271; Polat (2022), p. 34; Yıldırım Soysal (2023), AÜHFD, pp. 1827–1828. For more information on AI-related discrimination, see Ebers (2020), p. 76 ff.

[332] Nowak (2022), p. 97; Lasar (2023), p. 66; Frey (2024), p. 47; Möslein (2025b), ERA Forum, p. 632; Windorf (2025), p. 132. For concrete examples of AI-related discrimination in private sector, see İnce (2022), ANNALES, p. 276 ff.

[333] İnce (2022), ANNALES, p. 273; Telle (2023), p. 113.

[334] Li, (2022), p. 153.

[335] Telle (2023), p. 144.

[336] Dönmez Canseven (2021), pp. 103–105; İnce (2022), ANNALES, p. 287.

[337] For instance, The AI Fairness 360 toolkit provides a suite of open-source algorithms and metrics to enable systematic examination of unfair bias in AI models. For more information, see The AI Fairness 360. "AI Fairness 360: Understand and mitigate bias in ML models." Available at: https://ai-fairness-360.org/.(Last accessed: 25.12.2025).

[338] Dönmez Canseven (2021), p. 104.

[339] Nowak (2022), p. 98.

4.1.8.1.5 Compliance with Corporate Governance Rules

Corporate governance is designed to minimise issues arising from the separation of ownership and control in stock corporations.[340] It serves to structure and balance relationships between a corporation and its stakeholders, including shareholders, directors, creditors, employees, and financial markets,[341] by clearly defining their rights and obligations.[342] This framework enables efficient and effective participation in corporate processes.[343] It treats the stock corporation as a complete and highly significant economic unit throughout its entire lifecycle, from establishment to liquidation.[344] While corporate governance frameworks were initially developed for publicly traded stock corporations (with mandatory compliance under the capital markets laws), their best practices have become increasingly relevant for non-public corporations.[345]

Corporate governance is built on four core principles, i.e. transparency, fairness, accountability, and responsibility,[346] which are significantly impacted by AI integration into corporation management. AI enhances operational efficiency, decision-making, and profitability[347] since the absence of human ambition and vulnerability in AI can potentially minimise conflicts of interest between shareholders and management.[348] Hence, the integration of AI systems into corporate governance is transitioning from an emerging consideration to a standard element of sound governance.[349] However, its use also poses risks to the abovementioned core principles of corporate governance. Hence, corporations must place responsible AI implementation and operational transparency at the core of their governance strategy.[350]

Despite the growing importance of AI systems in corporate management, neither the Turkish nor the German corporate governance principles[351] contain

---

340 Demir (2016), p. 30.

341 Tekinalp (2008), p. 635 ff.; Eminoğlu (2014), p. 1.

342 Eminoğlu (2014), p. 1; Karatepe Kaya (2021), HBV-HFD, p. 90; Özatlan (2023), p. 150.

343 Eminoğlu (2014), p. 1; Kaya (2024), p. 91.

344 For a comprehensive legal analysis of the separation of ownership and control within the framework of corporate governance, see Paslı (2005), p. 30 ff.

345 Karasu (2013), İnÜHFD, p. 36.

346 Paslı (2005), pp. 69–83; Eminoğlu (2014), pp. 14–24; Demir (2016), pp. 34–38.

347 Kaya (2024), p. 93.

348 Altaş (2023), SÜHFD, p. 1373.

349 Windorf (2025), p. 465.

350 Kaya (2024), p. 93.

351 Windorf (2025), p. 452.

specific regulations on this matter. In particular, German legal doctrine suggests either adding new principles and recommendations regarding the use of AI to the corporate governance principles or revising some of those principles and recommendations for this purpose.[352] However, it is argued that the fundamental regulations governing the use of AI in corporate governance should be incorporated into general corporate law rather than into corporate governance principles, as issues such as delegation and the board's methods of obtaining information fall outside the scope of corporate governance principles.[353]

4.1.8.2 Interim Result

When AI is integrated into corporation management, the board is obligated under both legal systems to ensure the legality of the integration process and the decisions made based on AI outputs. This obligation requires compliance with general regulations and digitalisation-related regulations, including AI-specific regulations, data protection laws, anti-discrimination regulations, and corporate governance principles in both legal systems.

In German law, the EU AI Act imposes direct and indirect obligations on management boards regarding the use of AI in corporation management. While no such legal regulation currently exists in Turkish law, the proposal to develop a legal framework modelled on the EU AI Act is included in the Medium-Term Program. Therefore, the EU AI Act's regulations currently guide but do not impose any obligations on the boards of directors of Turkish corporations.

Under Turkish and German law, the board is the final decision-maker and is responsible for fulfilling the corporation's AI-related data protection obligations when integrating AI into management. The board must act within the framework of its duties of care and legality in fulfilling these obligations. In this context, determining the corporation's data protection policy, establishing a committee to support the board's decisions, appointing an executive to provide support and manage operational processes, and establishing a department reporting to this executive are organisational measures the board may take to fulfil its legality duty in terms of data protection regulations.

In both legal systems, anti-discrimination regulations require boards that integrate AI into management to take required measures throughout the lifecycle of AI systems to ensure that AI-based decisions do not cause direct or indirect discrimination. Boards that fail to take the necessary precautions under their

[352] Kremer and Langenbucher (2024), p. 88, 3.31, p. 89, 3.35, p. 91, 3.37; Windorf (2025), pp. 459–464.

[353] Windorf (2025), p. 463. Cf. Ahern (2024), p. 426.

duty of care and legality can be held liable for violations of anti-discrimination regulations.

Even though neither the Turkish nor the German corporate governance principles contain specific regulations on AI's integration into corporation management, boards are expected to comply with the core pillars of corporate governance (i.e. transparency, fairness, accountability, and responsibility) in this integration process. Because corporate governance principles in both legal systems exhibit a more dynamic structure than general corporate law legislation, incorporating certain principles and recommendations on the use of AI in corporate governance into these principles could serve as a valuable guide for corporations. However, such new regulations, incorporated into corporate governance principles, should be general and abstract to adapt to technological developments without hindering innovation. In the long term, necessary amendments should be incorporated into general corporate law rather than corporate governance principles, as the former address legal essentials that governance principles are neither designed nor empowered to address.

4.2 Board Members' Civil Liability Regarding the Integration of AI into Corporation Management

4.2.1 Comparative Review

4.2.1.1 Civil Liability of AI Board Members

It was established that, under both Turkish and German law, an AI system cannot serve as a board member due to current legal regulations.[354] The lack of AI's civil liability is itself considered one of the obstacles to AI board membership. The regulation of AI's civil liability for damages caused by an AI system is a separate, general topic beyond the scope of this study.[355] While the debate continues over who should be held responsible for damages caused by an AI board member, in practice, legal doctrine frequently recommends, as a transitional solution, that compensation liability arising from such damages be met through insurance or a compensation fund.

[354] See 2.1.2.3.1.

[355] For a comprehensive analysis of AI's civil liability based on the current liability regulations in Turkish law, see Akkurt (2019), UMD, p. 47 ff.; Sarı (2020), TBBD, p. 257 ff.; Dönmez (2025), AD, p. 957 ff.

The proposal to insure the liability of AI board members[356] is inspired by the non-mandatory 'directors and officers liability' insurance currently provided to board members under both Turkish[357] and German[358] corporate law.[359] According to this proposal, a mandatory liability insurance system for AI board members could distribute premium payments across multiple stakeholders: the AI itself (via dedicated assets), programmers (covering design risks), manufacturers (addressing production flaws), user corporations (for operational risks), and service providers (maintenance liabilities).[360] This model would efficiently allocate risk through market-based pricing by insurers.[361] Beyond insurance, the doctrine also argues that corporations may establish an internal liability pool[362] or an external compensation fund with other stakeholders in the AI ecosystem[363] to mitigate liability risks arising from AI board members.

4.2.1.2 Civil Liability of Human Board Members

The integration of AI systems into corporation management introduces significant risk for corporate losses. These losses may arise from technical failures within the AI systems themselves or from the board's failure to diligently discharge its organisational duties regarding the integrated AI system. If the liability arose from a technical malfunction in the AI system despite the board fulfilling its organisational obligations, the AI system may be held liable. However, because an AI system lacks legal personality, it is necessary to discuss who should be held accountable for the damages it causes. This issue has long been debated in legal scholarship, and different views have been put forward on whether individuals in the AI ecosystem, such as manufacturers, vendors, operators, and providers, can be held individually or jointly liable for damages caused by AI. This discussion of

---

356 Amour and Eidenmüller (2019), ZHR, p. 184 ff.; Bora Çınar (2022), p. 204; Calabro (2023), p. 79; Keskin (2024), p. 48.

357 Art. 361 of the TCC. For a critical analysis of the wording of Art. 361 of the TCC, see Sopacı Öztuna (2015), pp. 100–102.

358 AktG § 93 para. 2.

359 Karatepe Kaya (2021), HBV-HFD, p. 83; Altaş (2023), SÜHFD, p. 1376; Seçer (2025), p. 114; Sopacı Öztuna in Karatepe Kaya et al. (2025), p. 75.

360 Dönmez Canseven (2021), p. 115. Karadeniz (2023), TAAD, p. 280.

361 Amour and Eidenmüller (2019), ZHR, p. 186; Calabro (2023), p. 79.

362 Sopacı Öztuna in Karatepe Kaya et al. (2025), p. 75. For more information, see Windorf (2025), p. 396–397.

363 Bora Çınar (2022), pp. 206–207.

who and how can be held liable for damages caused by AI systems is beyond the scope of this study, so the analysis in this section is limited to whether the board (members) can be held liable for losses incurred from integrating AI systems into corporate management.

Currently, neither the Turkish[364] nor the German[365] legal system has a specific liability regime stipulating the standard of liability for boards integrating AI systems into corporation management. Therefore, the board's responsibility in this matter should be determined under the diligence of the 'prudent manager' standard of conventional board liability regimes.[366] In both legal systems, board members are considered liable for damages resulting from negligent acts that breach their duty of care. Although it is argued in Turkish legal doctrine that a board's fiduciary duties persist unchanged regardless of AI integration,[367] AI systems provide analytical insights, risk assessments, and scenario modelling that directly inform board members' decisions, necessitating a re-evaluation of liability frameworks.[368] In the context of AI integration, such breaches may manifest in several ways, such as the failure to utilise AI systems where prudent, the uncritical adherence to or absolute disregard of AI outputs, the improper delegation of management tasks to AI, or the neglect of the board's organisational duties related to AI.

The above analysis established that, under both Turkish and German law, there is no general obligation for boards to use AI in management.[369] Whether the duty of care[370] or the BJR[371] mandates AI use must be evaluated on a case-by-case basis. Therefore, the board's failure to integrate AI systems into corporation management or disregard AI outputs does not, in itself, entail liability on the board.[372] A case-specific analysis must be conducted to determine whether its use, or omission, ultimately serves the corporation's best interests and fulfils the

---

364 Bora Çınar (2022), pp. 200–201; Gözübüyük (2022), HBV-HFD, p. 156.

365 Casper and Möslein (2025), ZGR, p. 892.

366 Bora Çınar (2022), pp. 200–202; Varlı (2025), pp. 273–274.

367 Bora Çınar (2022), p. 202.

368 Dönmez Canseven (2021), p. 102.

369 See, 3.5.

370 See, 3.5.2.

371 See, 3.5.3.

372 Helvacı (2021), pp. 49–50.

board's duty of care.[373] To impose liability, it must be demonstrated that the resulting damage was a direct consequence of the board's failure to use an AI system, despite such use being an explicit requirement of prudent management under the specific circumstances. Conversely, if a case-specific assessment finds that the duty of care did not necessitate the use of AI, the board will not be liable for the ensuing loss.

A similar assessment is also required to determine the board's liability for damages arising from whether the board makes decisions in accordance with AI outputs. Both legal systems recognise that the board must make its own decisions independently. The board retains full discretionary authority under corporate law to disregard AI outputs,[374] as mandating that it bases its decisions on AI would violate the board's independence.[375] Therefore, the board need not be held responsible merely because it makes a decision contrary to the AI's output. Furthermore, making decisions by uncritically accepting AI outputs would violate the board's obligation to make independent decisions. The board will only be relieved of liability by making its own decisions, taking into account existing AI outputs, with the care expected of a prudent manager.[376]

A further ground for liability arises from the improper delegation of management tasks to AI systems.[377] Because both legal systems recognise that core management tasks cannot be delegated, a board that delegates them to an AI will be liable for any damages arising from the AI's performance of those tasks.[378]

Finally, the organisational obligations of a board integrating an AI system into corporation management, whether as a delegate or an assistant, have been examined above.[379] If the board fails to fulfil these organisational obligations when necessary under prudent management standards, it will be liable for damages

---

[373] Bahtiyar (2021), p. 49; Metin (2021), p. 525; Telle (2023), p. 70; Kaya (2024), p. 99; Özer and Tomrukçu (2025), BATİDER, pp. 258–260.

[374] Zetzsche (2019), AG, p. 7; Li (2022), p. 158; Telle (2023), p. 159; Rolsing (2025), pp. 488–489; Windorf (2025), p. 181.

[375] Windorf (2025), p. 181.

[376] Windorf (2025), p. 183.

[377] Lieder (2022), p. 338; Möslein (2022), p. 81; Casper and Möslein (2025), ZGR, p. 897; Rolsing (2025), p. 562 and 570; Windorf (2025), p. 302.

[378] In general, for liability related results of improper delegation, see Büyükatak (2019), p. 284; Kalender (2024), pp. 237–238.

[379] See, 4.1.

arising from the use of AI in management.[380] If the board fulfils all organisational obligations and AI-based errors still cause damage to the corporation, the board should not be held liable.[381]

In all scenarios described above, the board will be exempt from liability if it can prove it acted with the care of a prudent manager. Therefore, it is strongly advisable for boards to meticulously document all processes and the rationale[382] for using or forgoing AI in corporate management.[383] This documentation should include decisions on whether to adopt an AI system, whether to act on its outputs, the delegation of tasks, and the fulfilment of all organisational obligations. A board that maintains comprehensive records demonstrating its consistent adherence to the duty of care throughout its engagement with AI will be well-positioned to defend against potential liability claims.

4.2.1.3 Interim Result

Determining the civil liability of AI board members requires establishing a comprehensive regulatory framework that defines the liability of AI systems themselves. In the absence of such a regulatory framework in both the Turkish and German legal systems, this study limits its examination to the civil liability of human board members for the integration of AI into corporate management. Nevertheless, apart from the discussion of who will be held responsible for damages caused by AI board members, potential transitional redress could be facilitated through liability insurance, an internal liability pool or an external compensation fund involving stakeholders within the AI ecosystem.

There are no specific statutory provisions in either the Turkish or German legal systems governing the board's civil liability arising from the integration of AI into corporate management. Therefore, the board's traditional civil liability regime in both legal systems should be adapted to account for AI use in corporation management. Within this adapted framework, the board may be liable for damages arising from the non-use of AI in corporation management where a duty of care

---

[380] Möslein (2020b), p. 516; Dönmez Canseven (2021), p. 105; Möslein (2022), p. 81; Möslein (2023b), pp. 415–416; Telle (2023), pp. 176–177; Rolsing (2025), p. 563 ff.; Windorf (2025), p. 303.

[381] Möslein (2018), ZIP, p. 211; Lieder (2022), p. 338; Casper and Möslein (2025), ZGR, p. 898; Rolsing (2025), p. 377. Boards fulfil their duties of selection, instruction and monitoring towards delegates become exempt from liability. Akdağ Güney (2016), p. 95 and 101; Özatlan (2023), p. 400.

[382] Kaya (2024), p. 96.

[383] Lieder (2022), pp. 338–339; Telle (2023), p. 159; Rolsing (2025), p. 379 and 489; Windorf (2025), p. 182 and 185–186.

or the application of the BJR require its adoption, direct disregard of or uncritical reliance upon AI outputs, improper delegation to the AI system, and failure to fulfil board's organisational obligations regarding the use of AI in both legal systems. A general conclusion is not possible to determine the board's liability in these situations. Hence, a case-by-case analysis that considers all relevant factors is required for each case. In any event, the board must maintain documentation of all decision-making and operational processes related to the use of AI and its outputs to avoid liability. Such documentation serves as evidence that the board has fulfilled its corporate law obligations, particularly the duty of care expected of a prudent manager.

Results

5

1. AI is a field with scientific and philosophical foundations dating back to ancient times, which developed in its modern sense after World War II. Following two 'AI winters,' the most substantive advances have occurred in the last thirty years. After rule-based expert systems, the development of data-driven machine learning, particularly encompassing various techniques such as supervised, unsupervised, and reinforcement learning, has made AI systems more successful and efficient in different application areas. As its success and speed increase, the 'black box' characteristic, the difficulty in understanding how AI arrives at its results, has also increased. Despite this opacity, in recent years, the use and application areas of AI systems have expanded dramatically with the development of generative AI and large language models. Furthermore, agentic AI is advancing rapidly, and the first general examples of physical AI are emerging. Although various predictions have been made regarding the advancement of AI, its actual development has consistently differed from forecasts, as it is progressing at an unpredictable pace and in unforeseen directions.

   A comparative etymological inquiry demonstrates that the terminological construction for the term 'artificial intelligence' in Turkish, German, and English integrates two core components: artificial genesis (non-natural) and cognitive function (the capacity for deliberative selection), mirroring key attributes of human intellect. Notwithstanding these linguistic commonalities, there are many definitions of AI from various perspectives. These definitions are bound to change as technology advances. Nevertheless, for this study, the definition of an AI system provided by the EU AI Act has been adopted because of its legal-formal perspective, which offers a stable and normative

S. T. İnce, *Artificial Intelligence and Corporation Management*,
Juridicum – Schriftenreihe zum Wirtschafts-, Unternehmens- und Bankrecht / Series on Business, Corporate and Banking Law,
https://doi.org/10.1007/978-3-658-52672-6_5

framework under the EU AI Act's binding nature in German law and its prospective influence on Turkish law's expected harmonisation with EU law. This definition focuses on AI systems' machine-based architecture, varying levels of autonomy and subsequent adaptiveness as well as their core function of inferring outputs that influence environments in line with explicit or implicit objectives.

AI systems are classified as weak/narrow AI and strong/general AI based on the methods used to create intelligence and the breadth of their scope. Presently, as strong/general AI has not yet been achieved, deployed AI systems consist of weak/narrow AI systems that simulate human intelligence but produce results in limited domains. AI systems are also categorised as assistant, augmented, and autonomous AI systems based on the level of human-AI interaction within decision-making processes. Contemporary AI systems comprise heterogeneous systems that may exhibit characteristics across these three categories, depending on their technical capacity and the configuration choices of human operators. Today, each AI system possesses different capacities and capabilities as a result of the combined use of various methodologies, and this design singularity must be considered in legal evaluations. Therefore, while general evaluations of AI systems can be made, they need to be reviewed for each individual AI system regarding probable legal consequences. **(1.2.7.)**

2. While Turkish corporate law adopts a monist board structure and German corporate law a dualist one, the strict approach to articles of association, core fiduciary duties, and their pragmatic implementation are common for both legal systems. One of the most fundamental differences between these legal systems is the personal eligibility criteria for board membership. Under Turkish corporate law, legal entities may serve as board members, whereas this is not yet possible under German corporate law.

   The fundamental duties of the board members in both legal systems, primarily care (of prudent manager), management, monitoring, legality, and loyalty, bring these systems closer together and enable management that prioritises the balance of power, transparency, and accountability in accordance with modern corporate management principles. Furthermore, the explicit reporting obligations in German corporate law and the right to information and inspection in Turkish corporate law demonstrate the similar importance placed on the flow of information within and between bodies in both legal systems. These distinct yet parallel architectures of the Turkish and German corporation management systems serve as a natural test-bed. Hence, the comparative analysis of these management structures, highlighting both common principles and distinct models, provides a critical framework for predicting the legal challenges and opportunities of integrating AI into corporate boards. **(2.1.1.6.)**

3. Legal debates concerning the attribution of legal personality to AI and the establishment of a special civil liability regime for AI are expected to continue for a long time in Turkish and German law. Regulations regarding disruptive technologies such as AI should be enacted after lengthy doctrinal discussions. In this way, the right choices can be made in the law-making process. However, rapid progress and the spread of AI systems increase the risk of liability gaps. Therefore, transitional regulatory frameworks regarding AI systems must be implemented immediately to mitigate such risk. In the legislative process, lawmakers should balance the theoretical frameworks of the doctrine with practical realities. In this context, attribution of legal personality to AI constitutes a secondary problem. The real issue is determining a civil liability framework for the damages caused by AI systems, which are becoming more autonomous and unpredictable by the day. Consequently, the civil liability of actors in the AI ecosystem must be determined promptly to ensure legal certainty and predictability. **(2.1.2.2.2.)**
4. Under the current statutory frameworks of both Turkish and German corporate law, the direct appointment of an AI system as a corporate board member is legally impermissible because AI systems lack legal personality. If AI systems gain legal personality, this would pave the way for AI systems to become board members under Turkish law, which permits legal entities to serve as board members. However, under German law, only natural persons can become board members; therefore, granting AI systems legal personality would not be sufficient for these systems to become board members. Hence, to ensure AI systems become board members under German law, not only must AI systems be granted legal personality, but legal amendments must also be enacted to allow legal persons to become board members.

   An 'AI housing' legal entity can be operationalised to realise indirect board membership of an AI system. In this context, a legal entity eligible for board membership may be appointed to the board while an AI system is integrated into it. This formal board member legal entity may act on the directives of the 'housed AI'. However, such an indirect approach is only possible in jurisdictions that allow legal entities to serve as board members. Therefore, this alternative approach may be functional in Turkish corporate law, but it would not be viable in German corporate law.

   Given AI's rapid development and widespread use across various domains, it is likely that regulations to realise AI's board membership will be enacted in the near future. In such a legislative process, concerns discussed in the legal doctrine, such as independent personal judgment, collegial and uninterrupted governance, operational continuity, sector-specific suitability, internal and external trust relations, and mandatory disclosure requirements must be addressed. Mere permission of AI's appointment as a board member would not be enough to achieve the expected benefits of AI. Therefore, the current corporate frameworks designed for human board members must be comprehensively reformed to involve prospective AI board members and account for their characteristics. Otherwise, systematic incompatibilities may create risks, especially regarding liability structures. After the necessary comprehensive reform is implemented, a gradual process for appointing AI board members should be phased in through pilot applications, primarily in data-driven corporations, and an initial allowance for hybrid boards in which human and AI board members work together. Thus, unpredictable application risks may be addressed before they turn into actual aggravated damages. **(2.1.2.4.)**

5. Despite the absence of specific statutory provisions, the board of directors under Turkish law and the management board under German law retain the inherent managerial competence to decide on the integration of AI into corporation management. While Turkish law provides the board of directors with statutory protection over its competencies, the German dual-board model allows the supervisory board to intervene in the management board's decisions regarding the integration of AI into corporation management in a reasonable manner through rules of procedure or *ad hoc* decisions, without undermining the management board's right to autonomous management.

   The integration of AI into corporation management may constitute a core management task when it carries strategic implications for the corporation's direction and the board's fiduciary responsibilities. In such cases, the substantive decision-making authority regarding AI's integration into corporation management is non-delegable under Turkish and German corporate law. However, tasks related to the execution of preparatory and operational processes for AI's integration into corporate management can be delegated under both legal frameworks, provided the board retains ultimate authority.

   Neither Turkish nor German corporate law contains an explicit statutory prohibition on the integration of AI systems into corporation management. Doctrinal arguments for categorical exclusion of specific AI systems due to their black-box problem are diminishing in relevance, given the gradual decline in the explainability problem in AI systems. Moreover, boards' inherent discretionary authority over managerial structures and information-gathering methodologies renders such a categorical exclusion untenable. Consequently, boards in Turkish and German corporations may integrate AI systems into management, either directly or through committees established and instructed by internal regulations, provided boards conduct case-specific evaluations and implement necessary safeguards to fulfil their fiduciary duties. **(3.3.3.)**

6. Turkish and German corporate law each distinguish between delegable executive management tasks and non-delegable core management tasks. The TCC provides a non-exhaustive schema for this distinction, while German law employs a similar doctrinal categorisation. Although such a general distinction provides functional benefits, a case-by-case assessment of delegation's scope and substance is necessary, either in conjunction with or in place of this distinction. Furthermore, under both legal systems, executive management tasks can be delegated in their entirety. In contrast, while the substantive decision-making phase of core management tasks cannot be delegated to anyone, the preparation and implementation phases of these tasks can be delegated to individual board members, employees, and third parties. Moreover, in both legal systems, boards are required to act as prudent managers in selecting, instructing, and monitoring those to whom they delegate management tasks. **(3.4.2.4.)**
7. Currently, neither the Turkish nor the German corporate law systems have specific regulations governing the delegation of management tasks to AI. Therefore, for both legal systems, the delegation to AI may be examined under the current delegation regimes, with regard to the personal, substantive, and procedural scope of delegation.

   An examination of the personal scope of delegation under Turkish law shows that Article 367 of the TCC is normatively silent on delegation to AI. This provision neither contains an express authorisation for delegation of management to AI nor establishes a categorical prohibition. The historical interpretation concludes that this situation represents an unconscious legal gap. A subsequent teleological interpretation of Article 367 TCC clarifies the legislative intent. By stipulating that delegation can be made to 'persons,' the provision implicitly requires the delegate to be an entity capable of bearing legal responsibility. Under this interpretation, Article 367 of the TCC excludes AI systems from delegation as they lack this essential attribute under current law. While there is no explicit prohibition, given the choice of the word 'person' in Article 367 of the TCC and the presumed will of the legislator underlying that choice, delegation of management tasks to AI systems in Turkish law appears impermissible under the current legal framework due to AI's lack of legal personality and responsibility.

Considering that there is no precise determination in German statutory law regarding the personal scope of delegation, delegation can be made even to corporate departments that lack legal personality. Furthermore, Section 80(2) of the WpHG demonstrates the legislature's intent to allow delegation of (specific) decision-making authority to algorithmic systems that lack legal personality. Consequently, and in contrast to Turkish corporate law, the absence of legal personality in an AI system does not, *per se*, constitute a legal barrier to its appointment as a delegate in German corporate law.

With respect to the substantive and procedural scope of delegation, and assuming that delegation to AI is not precluded by AI's lack of legal personality under Turkish law, the preparatory, substantive decision-making, and implementation phases of executive management tasks can be delegated to AI systems in both legal systems. In terms of core management tasks, the preparatory and implementation phases can be delegated to AI, whereas the substantive decision-making phases cannot be delegated to AI in both legal systems.

From a *de lege ferenda* perspective, it would be prudent for the Turkish legislator to enact specific legislation to govern the delegation of management tasks to AI systems. In this way, the board of directors may leverage AI systems in a transparent, secure and legally predictable manner. Since the prevailing German legal doctrine is already in favour of delegating management tasks to AI systems, there is no immediate need for specific regulation in this regard in German corporate law. The German doctrinal discourse, in the interim, may provide boards with transitional guidance on delegating management tasks to AI. Nevertheless, enacting specific legislation on AI delegation in both legal systems would be beneficial for establishing clear principles for boards and for ensuring legal predictability. **(3.4.4.)**

8. In contemporary Turkish and German corporate law, the integration of AI into corporation management remains a discretionary strategic choice for boards, not a legally compelled obligation. Instead of a blanket rule, a case-by-case evaluation of whether board members are required to integrate AI systems into corporation management under their duty of care is required in both legal systems. In this evaluation, multiple factors, such as the technology's proven benefits, industry standards, and the corporation's size and resources, must be considered.

As AI systems become more reliable and widespread, they are raising the bar for what counts as prudent management. In this new reality, the number of cases in which boards are expected to use an AI system under their duty of care is increasing. Therefore, a board that chooses not to use a demonstrably beneficial and available AI system must provide and document a well-reasoned justification, grounded in the corporation's best interests. Failure to do so may increasingly be seen as a breach of their duty of care.

Under the BJR, both Turkish and German legal doctrines avoid establishing a categorical obligation for boards to use AI. The key legal question is whether the board members have based their decisions on an 'appropriate information basis,' a standard that must now account for modern technology. In a case-by-case assessment to answer this question, the decision's materiality, complexity, urgency, the board's prior experience with comparable decisions, the cost-effectiveness of gathering more data, and legal and practical constraints on data availability must be considered. Although using AI in corporation management is not a blanket requirement for the application of the BJR, it may be considered necessary in specific contexts. For instance, its use in data-intensive corporations or in scenarios where AI clearly offers a superior capability may be considered a requirement under the BJR. Therefore, a prudent board must continuously evaluate AI's applicability to management tasks. In this vein, the decision to forgo suitable AI must be documented with proportionate justifications. Otherwise, rejection of a reliable and available AI system without reasonable justifications may be considered as a failure to meet modern standards of prudent and informed management under the BJR. **(3.5.4.)**

9. AI policies tailored to corporations' characteristics and needs provide a useful framework for boards to guide the integration of AI systems into management structures. While their establishment may constitute an organisational obligation for boards under their duty of care, AI policies can also serve as documents outlining boards' other organisational obligations related to AI's integration into corporation management under both legal systems. For this purpose, these documents are expected to involve clear protocols and definitive criteria governing human-AI interactions throughout the AI's deployment, instruction and monitoring. As corporations increasingly integrate AI systems into their management, boards will be expected to develop and publicise AI policies as part of their prudent management duty in both legal systems. The fact that a corporation already has an 'AI Policy' in place can be considered a *prima facie* indication that its board has taken the first step to anticipate its organisational obligations regarding AI and

make the necessary preparations to fulfil them. Incorporating AI policies into formal corporate documents and the employment contracts of management personnel would be a step toward ensuring their consistent and proper implementation. **(4.1.2.2.)**

10. Emerging CDR principles may provide a solid framework for boards' duties in technology-driven activities, particularly regarding transparency and accountability. In the context of AI's integration into corporation management, CDR principles, particularly regarding data governance, may serve as the board's guiding standards in Turkish and German corporate law. Commitment to these principles throughout the AI's integration into corporation management may not only guide boards but also assist them in demonstrating that they have acted prudently in discharging their duty of care. However, there is no coherent doctrinal foundation for conceptualised CDR in Turkish and German law to delineate its characteristic features, core principles, and legal contours. Detailed exploration and doctrinal development regarding its scope, principles and implications would have a transformative influence on the digitalisation of corporate law, including board-level AI use. After such doctrinal development, it would be beneficial first to transform CDR obligations into industry-led voluntary codes of conduct, then into recommendations in formal corporate governance principles, and later into binding regulations. Consequently, boards may derive significant strategic and legal benefits from the principles of CDR and from its anticipated regulatory maturation, as this framework provides a structured guide for the prudent, risk-aware, and legally defensible integration of AI into corporation management in both legal systems. **(4.1.3.2.)**
11. Despite the lack of explicit regulation in Turkish and German legal systems, boards that integrate AI into management bear an affirmative obligation under their duty of care to address the existing knowledge gap regarding such systems. A board that remains entirely uninformed about an AI system in operation cannot reasonably be expected to harness its benefits or exercise effective oversight. Given that the decision to integrate AI into corporation management is increasingly considered a strategic, core management decision in both legal doctrines, board members making this decision must possess a basic understanding of these systems, including foundational knowledge of these systems' capabilities, limitations, and operational implications. Otherwise, it may be claimed that board members acted in breach of their duty of care and may be held liable, as they made their decision on this matter without sufficient information and were unable to properly fulfil their duties of overseeing the system's operation.

Within the both legal system's duty of care framework, the level of knowledge that board members are expected to have on AI systems and the measures they need to take to ensure this level of knowledge across the board should be calibrated on a case-by-case basis, depending on factors, such as the characteristics of the relevant AI system, magnitude and nature of the risks it may create, and how much the corporation's subject matter requires data-driven management. **(4.1.4.2.)**

12. Boards integrating AI into corporation management are expected to undertake significant organisational reforms. These reforms include the creation of an executive position, staffed by an executive with expertise in AI, and the establishment of an internal AI department, managed by the specialised executive, to support the board in achieving the expected benefits of AI integration and in identifying and mitigating potential risks. For this purpose, such an executive or department may coordinate all phases of AI integration into management and provide regular reports to the board. Under the current legal frameworks of both legal systems, however, the appointment of an executive or the establishment of an AI department is not a mandatory requirement for boards. Such a strategic choice requires a contextual, case-by-case assessment. In particular, as the intensity of AI's integration into corporation management, the complexity of the AI systems deployed, and the potential operational, legal and reputational risks they pose increase, the board's strategic choice in this regard may evolve into an organisational duty. **(4.1.5.2.)**
13. In both legal systems, the establishment of an *ad hoc* or permanent AI committee composed of experts, acting in an advisory capacity without decision-making authority, is legally possible and advisable as a prudent governance measure to support the board in integrating AI into corporation management. While the establishment of a specialised AI committee is a strong indicator of good corporate governance in the digital age, it does not guarantee that board members have fulfilled their duty of care regarding AI's integration into corporation management. In the same vein, the mere absence of such a committee cannot be considered a breach of the duty of care. Accordingly, Turkish and German law do not impose a categorical duty to establish an AI committee. A case-by-case assessment must be conducted to determine whether the establishment of such a specialised committee constitutes an organisational duty under prudent management, taking into account the corporation's specific needs, available resources, and strategic goals. **(4.1.6.2.)**

14. Turkish and German legal doctrines have distinctive approaches to the legal basis for boards' selection, instruction, and monitoring duties in the context of AI's integration into corporation management. The contemporary Turkish legal doctrine does not adopt the analogous approach derived from the delegation or employer liability. Instead, it focuses on concrete obligations arising from the 'prudent manager' standard. In contrast, analogies with existing regulations, such as § 80(2) of the WpHG, § 130 of the OWiG, and tort law principles, are explored in the German legal doctrine. However, German legal doctrine acknowledges the limitations of such analogies and refocuses on adapting the board's duty of care to provide the legal basis for the above-mentioned duties.

    Apart from exploring different analogical paths, the board's selection, instruction, and monitoring duties regarding the AI systems integrated into corporation management can be based on the board's duty of care in both legal systems. The duty of care's general and abstract characteristic provides the necessary flexibility to develop context-specific obligations. Therefore, an assessment that instrumentalises the implementation of the duty of care is necessary to reveal the board's specific selection, instruction, and monitoring duties regarding AI. Such an assessment across both legal systems reveals that boards are expected to perform these three duties as part of prudent management in the integration of AI into corporation management. Since the board's existing duty of care, which implicates management and monitoring duties as well, is codified in a general and abstract manner, the specification of the board's selection, instruction, and monitoring duties regarding AI does not require entirely new legislation for every technological development. These existing duties, which are also accepted as the board's fiduciary duties regarding delegates in both legal systems, can be adapted to new technological developments to determine the specific content of the board's selection, instruction, and monitoring duties regarding AI.

    The board's duty of care in selecting the AI system primarily encompasses choosing the source of the AI system and, if procured from an external source, strategically designing the procurement contract. Subsequently, managerial care must be taken in the specific selection of the AI system since the choice of the AI source, and specifically the system, will significantly affect the diligent fulfilment of instruction and supervision duties of the board and the achievement of the expected benefits from the AI. Whether to procure AI internally or externally, a case-by-case evaluation must be conducted, considering factors such as the corporation's resources and the cost of the AI use, the corporation's needs and control over the system, potential risks, and the suitability of existing AI systems. If the AI system is to be procured externally, the procurement method and the design of the procurement contract must be carefully determined, with the corporation's interests taken into account. When selecting a specific AI system, market research must be conducted to assess the provider's qualifications and evidence that the AI can reliably meet the corporation's needs (manufacturer assurances, certifications, etc.). Moreover, the board must ensure that the selected AI system is sufficiently explainable and that any deficiencies in its explainability can be addressed via add-on methods.

The board's instruction duty regarding AI systems differs from its duty to instruct human employees. Primarily, a pre-configuration of an AI system is necessary to ensure that its outcomes are consistent with the corporation's needs. Moreover, the board must have the opportunity to instruct the AI, particularly when the system malfunctions, during the deployment. Provision of all relevant data to the AI is another crucial part of the board's instruction duty. Furthermore, the integrated AI system is expected to flag insufficient data provision to enable the board to perform its instruction duty efficiently. In this framework, the board may fulfil its informational and operational instruction duty regarding AI systems prudently.

The board's monitoring duty regarding an AI system comprises technical monitoring of the system's functionality and oversight of the plausibility of its outputs. The board must establish an organisation to monitor the system's operationality, especially to detect operational interruptions. Moreover, the system's outputs must be subjected to a contextual plausibility test. The scope and intensity of this test must be calibrated on a case-by-case basis, considering different factors such as the strategic importance of the decision, previous experience with the system, and the magnitude of the probable risks. This test must assess the comprehensiveness of the outputs regarding the requested matter, their internal consistency, and their compatibility with the corporation's values, goals, and interests. Consequently, this monitoring framework must prevent the board from relying uncritically on AI outputs without applying its independent judgment. **(4.1.7.3.)**

15. When AI is integrated into corporation management, the board is obligated under both legal systems to ensure the legality of the integration process and the decisions made based on AI outputs. This obligation requires compliance with general regulations and digitalisation-related regulations, including AI-specific regulations, data protection laws, anti-discrimination regulations, and corporate governance principles in both legal systems.

In German law, the EU AI Act imposes direct and indirect obligations on management boards regarding the use of AI in corporation management. While no such legal regulation currently exists in Turkish law, the proposal to develop a legal framework modelled on the EU AI Act is included in the Medium-Term Program. Therefore, the EU AI Act's regulations currently guide but do not impose any obligations on the boards of directors of Turkish corporations.

Under Turkish and German law, the board is the final decision-maker and is responsible for fulfilling the corporation's AI-related data protection obligations when integrating AI into management. The board must act within the framework of its duties of care and legality in fulfilling these obligations. In this context, determining the corporation's data protection policy, establishing a committee to support the board's decisions, appointing an executive to provide support and manage operational processes, and establishing a department reporting to this executive are organisational measures the board may take to fulfil its legality duty in terms of data protection regulations.

In both legal systems, anti-discrimination regulations require boards that integrate AI into management to take required measures throughout the lifecycle of AI systems to ensure that AI-based decisions do not cause direct or indirect discrimination. Boards that fail to take the necessary precautions under their duty of care and legality can be held liable for violations of anti-discrimination regulations.

Even though neither the Turkish nor the German corporate governance principles contain specific regulations on AI's integration into corporation management, boards are expected to comply with the core pillars of corporate governance (i.e. transparency, fairness, accountability, and responsibility) in this integration process. Because corporate governance principles in both legal systems exhibit a more dynamic structure than general corporate law legislation, incorporating certain principles and recommendations on the use of AI in corporate governance into these principles could serve as a valuable guide for corporations. However, such new regulations, incorporated into corporate governance principles, should be general and abstract to adapt to technological developments without hindering innovation. In the long term, necessary amendments should be incorporated into general corporate law rather than corporate governance principles, as the former address legal essentials that governance principles are neither designed nor empowered to address. **(4.1.8.2.)**

16. Determining the civil liability of AI board members requires establishing a comprehensive regulatory framework that defines the liability of AI systems

themselves. In the absence of such a regulatory framework in both the Turkish and German legal systems, this study limits its examination to the civil liability of human board members for the integration of AI into corporate management. Nevertheless, apart from the discussion of who will be held responsible for damages caused by AI board members, potential transitional redress could be facilitated through liability insurance, an internal liability pool or an external compensation fund involving stakeholders within the AI ecosystem.

There are no specific statutory provisions in either the Turkish or German legal systems governing the board's civil liability arising from the integration of AI into corporate management. Therefore, the board's traditional civil liability regime in both legal systems should be adapted to account for AI use in corporation management. Within this adapted framework, the board may be liable for damages arising from the non-use of AI in corporation management where a duty of care or the application of the BJR require its adoption, direct disregard of or uncritical reliance upon AI outputs, improper delegation to the AI system, and failure to fulfil board's organisational obligations regarding the use of AI in both legal systems. A general conclusion is not possible to determine the board's liability in these situations. Hence, a case-by-case analysis that considers all relevant factors is required for each case. In any event, the board must maintain documentation of all decision-making and operational processes related to the use of AI and its outputs to avoid liability. Such documentation serves as evidence that the board has fulfilled its corporate law obligations, particularly the duty of care expected of a prudent manager. **(4.2.1.3.)**

Bibliography

Adolff, J. (2025). KI-Governance für unternehmerische Entscheidungen [AI governance for business decisions]. Die Aktiengesellschaft (AG), 1–20, 1–71.

Agnese, P., Arduino, F. R., & Di Prisco, D. (2025). The era of artificial intelligence: What implications for the board of directors?. Corporate Governance (CG), 25(2), 272–287.

Ahern, D. (2024). Corporate law, corporate governance and AI: Are we ready for robots in the boardroom? In P. D. J. Morgan & E. Lim (Eds.), The Cambridge handbook of private law and artificial intelligence (pp. 409–430). Cambridge University Press.

Akdağ Güney, N. (2010). Anonim şirket yönetim kurulu üyelerinin hukuki sorumluluğu [Civil law liability of board members of a stock corporation] (2nd ed.). Vedat Kitapçılık.

Akdağ Güney, N. (2016). Anonim şirket yönetim kurulu [Board of directors of the stock corporation] (2nd ed.). Vedat Kitapçılık.

Akın, İ. (2022). Dijital gelişmelerin şirketler hukuku üzerindeki etkisi [The impact of digital developments on corporate law]. Türk-Alman Üniversitesi Hukuk Fakültesi Dergisi (TAÜHFD), 4(1), 3–26.

Akkurt, S. S. (2019). Yapay zekânın otonom davranışlarından kaynaklanan hukuki sorumluluk [Legal liability arising from autonomous behavior of artificial intelligence]. Uyuşmazlık Mahkemesi Dergisi (UMD), 7(13), 39–59.

Aksoy, H. C. (2025). Yapay zekânın yol açtığı zararlardan hukuki sorumluluk [Civil law liability for harms caused by artificial intelligence.]. In F. Bilir (Ed.), Yapay zeka teknolojilerine akademik bakış [An academic perspective on artificial intelligence technologies] (pp. 179–198). Adalet Yayınevi.

Altaş, A. (2023). Yapay zekânın şirket yönetiminde yer almasının değerlendirilmesi [Evaluation of artificial intelligence in corporation management]. Selçuk Üniversitesi Hukuk Fakültesi Dergisi (SÜHFD), 31(3), 1357–1380.

Altay, S. A. (2011). Anonim ortaklıkta yönetim yetkilerinin devrinin sorumluluğa etkileri [The effects of delegating management authority in a stock corporation on liability] (1st ed.). Vedat Kitapçılık.

S. T. İnce, *Artificial Intelligence and Corporation Management*, Juridicum – Schriftenreihe zum Wirtschafts-, Unternehmens- und Bankrecht / Series on Business, Corporate and Banking Law, https://doi.org/10.1007/978-3-658-52672-6

Altay, S. A. (2013). Anonim ortaklıklarda gözetim yükümlülüğünün sınırlarının ve ölçütlerinin belirlenmesine yönelik düşünceler [Thoughts on determining the limits and criteria of supervisory obligations in stock corporations]. In E. Ulusoy (Ed.), Ersin Çamoğlu'na armağan [Festschrift for Ersin Çamoğlu] (pp. 3–20). Vedat Kitapçılık.

Ansay, T. (1975). Anonim şirketler hukuku [Stock corporations law] (5th ed.). Ankara Üniversitesi Hukuk Fakültesi Yayınları.

Arkoudas, K., & Bringsjord, S. (2014). Philosophical foundations. In K. Frankish & W. M. Ramsey (Eds.), The Cambridge handbook of artificial intelligence (pp. 34–63). Cambridge University Press.

Armour, J., & Eidenmüller, H. (2019). Selbstfahrende Kapitalgesellschaften [Self-driving corporations]. Zeitschrift für das gesamte Handelsrecht und Wirtschaftsrecht (ZHR), 183(2), 169–189.

Arslanlı, H. (1960). Anonim şirketler (II–III anonim şirketin organizasyonu ve tahviller) [Stock corporations (II–III Organization of stock corporations and bonds)]. Fakülteler Matbaası.

Ay Kaplan, Ü. (2017). Anonim şirketlerde yönetim kurulunun gözetim görevi [The monitoring duty of the board of directors in stock corporations]. Seçkin Yayıncılık.

Ayan, Ö. (2021). Anonim şirket yönetim kurulu üyelerinin sadakat yükümlülüğü ve bu yükümlülüğün ihlalinin sonuçları (2nd ed.) [The duty of loyalty of board members of stock corporations and the consequences of breaching this duty]. Adalet Yayınları.

Ayhan, R., Çağlar, H., & Özdamar, M. (2022). Şirketler hukuku genel esaslar [General principles of company law] (4th ed.). Yetkin Yayınları.

Bahtiyar, M. (2021). Tüzel kişilik penceresinden anonim ortaklık sempozyumu, soru—cevap [Symposium on stock corporations from the perspective of legal entities: Question and answer session]. In H. Karagöz, F. B. Özcanlı, & S. Palanduz (Eds.), Tüzel kişilik penceresinden anonim ortaklık sempozyumu [Symposium on stock corporations from the perspective of legal personality]. On İki Levha Yayıncılık.

Bahtiyar, M. (2024). Ortaklıklar hukuku [Company law] (17th ed.). Beta Yayınları.

Bainbridge, S. M., & Henderson, M. T. (2018). Board service providers: The basic idea. In Outsourcing the board: How Board Service Providers Can Improve Corporate Governance (pp. 87–103). Cambridge University Press.

Bak, B. (2018). Medeni hukuk açısından yapay zekânın hukuki statüsü ve yapay zekâ kullanımından doğan hukuki sorumluluk [The legal status of artificial intelligence with regard to civil law and the liability thereof]. Türkiye Adalet Akademisi Dergisi (TAAD), 9(35), 211–232.

Baruffaldi, S., van Beuzekom, B., Dernis, H., Harhoff, D., Rao, N., Rosenfeld, D., & Squicciarini, M. (2020). Identifying and measuring developments in artificial intelligence: Making the impossible possible (OECD Science, Technology and Industry Working Papers, No. 2020/05). OECD Publishing.

Bathaee, Y. (2018). The artificial intelligence black box and the failure of intent and causation. Harvard Journal of Law & Technology (JOLT), 31(2), 890–938.

Bayern, S., Burri, T., Grant, T. D., Häusermann, D. M., Möslein, F., & Williams, R. (2017). Company law and autonomous systems: A blueprint for lawyers, entrepreneurs, and regulators. Hastings Science and Technology Law Journal (UCLSTJ), 9, 135–162.

Becker, M., & Pordzik, P. (2020). Digitalisierte Unternehmensführung [Digitalized business management]. Zeitschrift für die gesamte Privatrechtswissenschaft (ZfPW), 6(3), 334–357.

Bertolini, A. (2025). Artificial intelligence and civil liability—A European perspective. European Parliament, Directorate-General for Citizens' Rights, Justice and Institutional Affairs. https://data.europa.eu/doi/10.2861/0075079.

Boden, M. A. (2014). GOFAI. In K. Frankish & W. M. Ramsey (Eds.), The Cambridge handbook of artificial intelligence (pp. 89–107). Cambridge University Press.

Boden, M. A. (2016). AI: Its nature and future. Oxford University Press.

Bora Çınar, S. (2022). Şirket yönetiminde yapay zekâ [Artificial intelligence in corporate management]. Seçkin Yayıncılık.

Borges, G. (2019). New liability concepts: The potential of insurance and compensation funds. In S. Lohsse, R. Schulze, & D. Staudenmayer (Eds.), Liability for artificial intelligence and the Internet of Things (pp. 145–164). Nomos.

Boucher, P. (2019). How artificial intelligence works (PE 634.420). European Parliamentary Research Service, Scientific Foresight Unit (STOA).

Bozkurt Yaşar, S. (2015). Anonim şirketlerde işadamı kararı ilkesinin (Business judgment rule) uygulaması [Application of the business judgment rule in stock corporations]. Beta Yayınları.

Bryson, J. J., Diamantis, M. E., & Grant, T. D. (2017). Of, for, and by the people: The legal lacuna of synthetic persons. Artificial Intelligence and Law (Artif Intell Law), 25(3), 273–291.

Buchanan, B., & Miller, T. (2017). Machine learning for policymakers. Belfer Center for Science and International Affairs, Harvard Kennedy School.

Burgess, A. (2018). The executive guide to artificial intelligence: How to identify and implement applications for AI in your organization. Palgrave Macmillan. (e-book)

Buxmann, P., & Schmidt, H. (2019). Grundlagen der künstlichen Intelligenz und des maschinellen Lernens [Fundamentals of artificial intelligence and machine learning]. In P. Buxmann & H. Schmidt (Eds.), Künstliche Intelligenz: Mit Algorithmen zum wirtschaftlichen Erfolg [Artificial intelligence: Using algorithms for economic success] (pp. 3–25). Springer Gabler.

Büyükatak, A. (2019). Anonim şirketlerde yönetim kurulunun yönetim ve temsil yetkisinin devri ve sınırlandırılması [Delegation and limitation of management and representation powers in joint stock companies] (Doctoral dissertation, İstanbul Kültür University). YÖK National Thesis Center.

Calabro, C. (2023). Künstliche intelligenz und corporate governance: Der einsatz von künstlicher Intelligenz im vorstand der börsennotierten aktiengesellschaft [Artificial intelligence and corporate governance: The use of artificial intelligence on the management board of a listed stock corporation]. Duncker & Humblot.

Casper, M., & Möslein, F. (2025). Künstliche intelligenz in der aktiengesellschaft [Artificial intelligence in the stock corporation]. Zeitschrift für Unternehmens- und Gesellschaftsrecht (ZGR), 54(6), 870–914.

Castelluccia, C., & Le Métayer, D. (2019). Understanding algorithmic decision-making: Opportunities and challenges. European Parliamentary Research Service.

Cenkci, E. (2018). Anonim ortaklıkta yönetim kurulunun temsil yetkisinin devri [Delegation of representation authority of the board of directors in a stock corporation]. Yetkin Yayınları.

Ceylan, N. (2015). Anonim şirketlerde yönetim ve temsil yetkisinin devrinin anlamı, sonuçları ve TTK m. 371 f.7 ile karşılaştırılması [The meaning and consequences of the transfer of management and representation authority in stock corporations, and a comparison with article 371, paragraph 7 of the Turkish commercial code.]. Türkiye Noterler Birliği Hukuk Dergisi (TNBHD), 2(1), 21–38.

Chesterman, S. (2020). Artificial intelligence and the limits of legal personality. International and Comparative Law Quarterly (ICLQ), 69(4), 819–844.

Chowdhary, K. R. (2020). Fundamentals of artificial intelligence. Springer.

Cowger, A. R., Jr. (2023). Corporate fiduciary duty in the age of algorithms. Case Western Reserve Journal of Law, Technology & the Internet (JOLTI), 14, 138–207.

Craglia, M. (Ed.), Annoni, A., Benczur, P., Bertoldi, P., Delipetrev, B., De Prato, G., Feijoo, C., Fernandez Macias, E., Gomez Gutierrez, E., Iglesias Portela, M., Junklewitz, H., Lopez Cobo, M., Martens, B., Figueiredo Do Nascimento, S., Nativi, S., Polvora, A., Sanchez Martin, J. I., Tolan, S., Tuomi, I., & Vesnic Alujevic, L. (2018). Artificial intelligence: A European perspective. Publications Office of the European Union. https://doi.org/10.2760/11251.

Çam, G. (2017). Anonim ortaklıkta yönetim kurulunun yönetim yetkisi ve yetki devri [The management authority of the board of directors and the delegation of this authority in a stock corporation]. İstanbul Kültür Üniversitesi Hukuk Fakültesi Dergisi (İKÜHFD), 16(2), 513–544.

Çamlı, Z. İ. (2024). Anonim şirketlerde yönetim kurulu iç yönergesi [Internal directives of the board of directors in joint stock companies] (Doctoral dissertation, Kırıkkale University). YÖK National Thesis Center.

Çamoğlu, E. (2010). Anonim ortaklık yönetim kurulu üyelerinin hukuki sorumluluğu (Kamu borçlarından sorumluluk ile) [Civil law liability of board members of stock corporations (Including liability for public debts)] (3rd ed.). Vedat Kitapçılık.

Çamurcu, E. (2015). Anonim ortaklıklarda farklılaştırılmış teselsül ilkesi uyarınca yönetim kurulu üyelerinin sorumluluklarının belirlenmesi [Determining the liabilities of board members in stock corporations according to the principle of differentiated joint and several liability]. On İki Levha Yayıncılık.

Çekin, M. S. (2021). Yapay zeka teknolojilerinin hukuki işlem teorisine etkileri [The effects of artificial intelligence technologies on legal procedure theory.]. On İki Levha Yayıncılık.

Çelikboya K. (2023). Yönetim kurulunun hukuki değerlendirmelerden dolayı sorumluluğu: Hukuki karar ilkesine yönelik bir öneri [The liability of the board of directors for legal assessments: A proposal regarding the principle of legal judgment]. In F. Yusufoğlu Bilgin, T. Ayoğlu, & S. A. Altay (Eds.). Prof. Dr. H. Ercüment Erdem'e armağan [Festschrift for Prof. Dr. H. Ercüment Erdem] (pp. 419–446). On İki Levha Yayıncılık.

Daeenabi, I. M. (2025). Beyond human oversight: Corporate law and the case for AI directors. UC Law SF Law Journal (UCLJ), 76(4), 1271–1306.

Dany, J.-C. (2022). Haftung beim einsatz von KI durch den vorstand [Liability of the management board when using AI]. Der Betriebs-Berater (BB), 2056–2065.

Davies, P. L., & Hopt, K. J. (2013). Corporate boards in Europe: Accountability and convergence. The American Journal of Comparative Law (AJCL), 61(2), 301–375.
de Laat, P. B. (2018). Algorithmic decision-making based on machine learning from big data: Can transparency restore accountability? Philosophy & Technology (Philos. Technol.), 31(4), 525–541.
Delipetrev, B., Tsinaraki, C., & Kostic, U. (2020). Historical evolution of artificial intelligence (EUR 30221 EN). Publications Office of the European Union. https://doi.org/10.2760/801580.
Demir, E. E. (2016). Anonim şirket yönetim kurulu bünyesinde oluşturulan komiteler [Committees formed within the board of directors of a stock corporation]. Adalet Yayınevi.
Demirel, D. (2017). Anonim şirketlerde yönetim yetkisinin devri [Delegation of management authority in stock corporations]. Hacettepe Hukuk Fakültesi Dergisi (HHFD), 7(2), 211–250.
Develi, E. (2016). Tüzel kişinin anonim şirket yönetim kurulu üyeliği [Legal entity's membership on the board of directors of a stock corporation]. Seçkin Yayıncılık.
DIN e.V. & DKE. (2020). German standardization roadmap on artificial intelligence.
Doğan, B. F. (2011). Anonim şirket yönetim kurulunun organizasyonu ve yönetim yetkisinin devri [Organization of the board of directors of a stock corporation and delegation of management authority.]. Vedat Kitapçılık.
Doğan, B. F. (2012). Yönetim kurulunun devredilemez yetkileri ve yönetim yetkisinin devri [Non-transferable powers of the board of directors and delegation of management power]. Marmara Üniversitesi Hukuk Fakültesi Hukuk Araştırmaları Dergisi (MÜHF-HAD), 18(2), 609–640.
Dönmez Canseven, Z. (2021). Yapay Zekanın Anonim Şirketin Yönetim Kurulunda Yer Alması Ve Bu Durumun Hukuki Sorumluluğa Etkisi [Deployment of artificial intelligence in joint-stock corporation's board of directors and its impact on civil liability]. On İki Levha Yayıncılık.
Dönmez, Z. (2025). Yapay zekânın hukuki gelişimi ve AB yapay zekâ yasası [Legal development of artificial intelligence and EU artificial intelligence act]. Adalet Dergisi (AD), (74), 947–975.
Dremliuga, R., Kuznetcov, P., & Mamychev, A. (2019). Criteria for recognition of AI as a legal person. Journal of Politics and Law (JPL), 12(3), 105–112.
Dubovitskaya, E., & Buchholz, A. (2023). The management and the advice of (un)explainable AI. European Company and Financial Law Review (ECFR), 20(5–6), 794–821.
Dural, M., & Öğüz, T. (2020). Kişiler hukuku [Law of persons] (21st ed.). Filiz Kitabevi.
Ebers, M. (2020). Regulating AI and robotics: Ethical and legal challenges. In M. Ebers & S. Navas (Eds.), Algorithms and law (pp. 37–99). Cambridge University Press.
Ekici, Ş. (2025). New proposed personality model for artificial intelligence: Integrated personality. Bilişim Hukuku Dergisi (BHD), 7(1), 311–363.
Eminoğlu, C. (2014). Türk ticaret kanunu'nda kurumsal yönetim [Corporate governance in the Turkish commercial code]. On İki Levha Yayınları.
Enriques, L., & Zetzsche, D. A. (2020). Corporate technologies and the tech nirvana fallacy. UC Law SF Law Journal (UCLJ), 72, 55–98.
Ercan, C. (2019). Robotların fiillerinden doğan hukuki sorumluluk: Sözleşme dışı sorumluluk hallerinde çözüm önerileri [Legal responsibility resulting from the actions of robots:

solutions for non-contractual liability]. Türkiye Adalet Akademisi Dergisi (TAAD), 11(40), 19–52.

Erdem Aladağ, M. T. (2024). Kurumsal yönetişim ve yapay zeka: Potansiyel fırsatlar ve zorluklar [Corporate governance and artificial intelligence: Potential opportunities and challenges.]. Denetişim, (15) 31, 18–32.

Eroğlu, M. (2021). Tüzel kişilik penceresinden anonim ortaklık sempozyumu, soru—cevap [Symposium on stock corporations from the perspective of legal entities: Question and answer Session]. In H. Karagöz, F. B. Özcanlı, & S. Palanduz (Eds.), Tüzel kişilik penceresinden anonim ortaklık sempozyumu [The symposium on stock corporations from the perspective of legal personality]. On İki Levha Yayıncılık.

Eroğlu, M., & Karatepe Kaya, M. (2022). Impact of artificial intelligence on corporate board diversity policies and regulations. European Business Organization Law Review (EBOR), 23, 541–572.

Eryiğit, H. (2021). Güncel tartışmalar ışığında yapay zekâ ve anonim şirket yönetim kurullarının yeniden şekillenmesi [Artificial intelligence and the reshaping of corporate boards of directors in light of current debates]. In Ş. Ekici, E. Solak, & M. E. Avşar (Eds.), Uluslararası bilişim ve teknoloji hukuku sempozyumu tebliğler kitabı [Proceedings of the International Symposium on Information and Technology Law] (pp. 99–126). Adalet Yayınevi.

Eryiğit, H. (2023). Anonim şirketlerin yönetim sözleşmesi kapsamında yönetimi ve sonuçları [Management of stock corporations within the scope of management agreement and its outcomes]. On İki Levha Yayıncılık.

European Commission (2019). Communication from the Commission to the European Parliament, the Council, the European Economic and Social Committee and the Committee of the Regions: Building trust in human-centric artificial intelligence (COM/2019/168 final). https://eur-lex.europa.eu/legal-content/EN/TXT/?uri=celex:52019DC0168.

European Commission's High-Level Expert Group on Artificial Intelligence. (2019). A definition of AI: Main capabilities and disciplines. European Commission. https://digital-strategy.ec.europa.eu/en/library/definition-artificial-intelligence-main-capabilities-and-scientific-disciplines.

Fleischer, H. (Ed.) (2006). Handbuch des vorstandsrechts [Handbook of management board Law]. C.H. Beck.

Fleischer, H. (2018). Algorithmen im aufsichtsrat [Algorithms in the supervisory board]. Der Aufsichtsrat (AR), 15, 121–128.

Franklin, S. (2014). History, motivations, and core themes. In K. Frankish & W. M. Ramsey (Eds.), The Cambridge handbook of artificial intelligence (pp. 15–33). Cambridge University Press.

Frey, N. (2024). Sorgfaltspflichten von geschäftsleitern beim einsatz künstlicher intelligenz in der unternehmensführung [Due diligence obligations of corporate managers in the use of artificial intelligence for corporate management]. Nomos.

Gama, J., Žliobaitė, I., Bifet, A., Pechenizkiy, M., & Bouchachia, A. (2013). A survey on concept drift adaptation. ACM Computing Surveys (CSUR), 46(4), 1–37.

Gates, B. (1999). Business @ the speed of thought. Warner Books.

Goette, W., & Habersack, M. (Eds.). (2019). Münchener kommentar zum aktiengesetz: AktG: Band 2: §§ 76–117, MitbestG, DrittelbG [Munich Commentary on the Stock

Corporation Act: AktG: Volume 2: §§ 76–117, Co-Determination Act, One-Third Participation Act] (5th ed.). C.H. Beck. (MünchKomm-AktG)

Gordon, J. S. (2021). Artificial moral and legal personhood. AI & Society (AI & Soc), 36(2), 457–471.

Göktürk, K. (2011). Amerikan, Alman, İsviçre ve Türk hukukunda işadamı kararı ilkesi [The principle of business judgment in American, German, Swiss, and Turkish law]. İnönü Üniversitesi Hukuk Fakültesi Dergisi (İnÜHFD), 2(2), 207–247.

Göktürk, K. (2014). Anonim şirket yönetim kurulunun özellikle yetki devri halinde gözetim sorumluluğu ve hukuki belirlilik sorunu [The issue of supervisory responsibility of the board of directors of a stock corporation and legal certainty, especially in cases of delegation of authority.]. Türkiye Barolar Birliği Dergisi (TBBD), 114, 179–200.

Gözübüyük, B. (2021). Yapay zekâ algoritmalarının anonim ortaklıkların kurumsal yönetimine sağlayabileceği olası katkılar [Potential contributions of artificial intelligence algorithms to the corporate governance of stock corporations]. Hacettepe Hukuk Fakültesi Dergisi (HHFD), 11(2), 1184–1212.

Gözübüyük, B. (2022). Yapay zekâ algoritmalarının anonim ortaklıklarda alınan stratejik kararlar bakımından yönetim kuruluna sağlayabileceği olası katkılar [Potential contributions of artificial intelligence algorithms to strategic decision-making by boards of directors in stock corporations]. Ankara Hacı Bayram Veli Üniversitesi Hukuk Fakültesi Dergisi (HBV-HFD), 26(1), 141–164.

Grace, K., Salvatier, J., Dafoe, A., Zhang, B., & Evans, O. (2018). Viewpoint: When will AI exceed human performance? Evidence from AI experts. Journal of Artificial Intelligence Research (JAIR), 62, 729–754.

Gramitto Ricci, S. A. (2020). Artificial agents in corporate boardrooms. Cornell Law Review (Cornell L. Rev.), 105(3), 869–908.

Grigoleit, H. C. (Ed.). (2020). Aktiengesetz: Kommentar [Stock Corporation Act: Commentary] (2nd ed.). C.H. Beck.

Gunning, D., Stefik, M., Choi, J., Miller, T., Stumpf, S., & Yang, G. Z. (2019). XAI-Explainable artificial intelligence. Science robotics (Sci. Robot.), 4(37). https://doi.org/10.1126/scirobotics.aay7120.

Güçlütürk, O. G. (2021). Anonim şirket yönetiminde yapay zekanın kullanılması ve sorumluluğa etkisi [The use of artificial intelligence in the management of stock corporations and its impact on liability]. In F. B. Özcanlı, S. Palanduz, & H. Karagöz (Eds.), Tüzel kişilik penceresinden anonim ortaklık sempozyumu [Symposium on stock corporations from the perspective of legal personality] (pp. 453–474). On İki Levha Yayıncılık.

Güner, C. (2020). Yapay zekânın verdiği zarardan doğan sözleşme dışı sorumluluğa uygulanacak hukuk [Applicable law to non-contractual liability arising from damages caused by artificial intelligence]. Uyuşmazlık Mahkemesi Dergisi (UMD), 8(15), 229–272.

Gürpınar, B. (2013). Anonim şirket yönetim kurulu toplantılarının şekli ve elektronik toplantı sistemi [Format of board of directors meetings in stock corporations and electronic meeting system]. Marmara Üniversitesi Hukuk Fakültesi Hukuk Araştırmaları Dergisi (MÜHF-HAD), 19(2), 1101–1125.

Habersack, M., Kort, M., & Foerster, M. (2015). Aktiengesetz: Großkommentar: Band 4/1, §§ 76–91 [Stock corporation act: Comprehensive commentary: Volume 4/1, §§ 76–91] (5th ed.). C.H. Beck. (Großkomm-AktG)

Habersack, M., Hopt, K. J., Roth, M. & Foerster, M. (2015). Aktiengesetz: Großkommentar: Band 4/2, §§ 92–94 [Stock corporation act: Comprehensive commentary: Volume 4/2, §§ 92–94] (5th ed.). C.H. Beck. (Großkomm-AktG)

Hacımahmutoğlu, S. (2014). The business judgment rule: İşadamı kararı mı yoksa ticari muhakeme kuralı mı? [The business judgment rule: Is it a businessman's decision or a commercial reasoning rule?]. Banka ve Ticaret Hukuku Dergisi (BATİDER), 30(4), 99–145.

Hacımahmutoğlu, S. (2015). Anonim ortaklığın yönetim kurulu üyelerinin özen yükümlülüğü: Fonksiyonel bir yaklaşım [The duty of care of board members of a stock corporation: A functional approach]. Banka ve Ticaret Hukuku Dergisi (BATİDER), 31 (3), 23–56.

Haddadin, S., & Knobbe, D. (2020). Robotics and artificial intelligence: The present and future visions. In M. Ebers & S. Navas (Eds.), Algorithms and law (pp. 1–36). Cambridge University Press.

Harari, Y. N. (2017). Homo deus: A brief history of tomorrow. Vintage. (E-book)

Helleringer, G., & Möslein, F. (2025). AI & The business judgment rule: Heightened information duty. The University of Chicago Law Review Online (U. Chi. L. Rev. Online). https://lawreview.uchicago.edu/online-archive/ai-business-judgment-rule-heightened-information-duty.

Helvacı, M. (2021). Tüzel kişilik penceresinden anonim ortaklık sempozyumu, soru—cevap [Symposium on stock corporations from the perspective of legal entities: Question and answer Session]. In H. Karagöz, F. B. Özcanlı, & S. Palanduz (Eds.), Tüzel kişilik penceresinden anonim ortaklık sempozyumu [Symposium on stock corporations from the perspective of legal personality]. On İki Levha Yayıncılık.

Henssler, M. (Ed.). (2025, February 1). Beck-online.Grosskommentar zum Aktienrecht [Beck-online.Grand commentary on Stock Corporation Law]. C.H. Beck. (BeckOGK)

Hilb, M. (2020). Toward artificial governance? The role of artificial intelligence in shaping the future of corporate governance. Journal of Management and Governance (J Manag Gov), 24, 851–870.

Hoch, V. (2019). Anwendung künstlicher Intelligenz zur beurteilung von rechtsfragen im unternehmerischen bereich [Application of artificial intelligence to assess legal issues in the business sector]. Archiv für die civilistische Praxis (AcP), 219, 646–702.

Hoerdemann-Napp, C., & Pauli, L. K. (2021). KI am steuer der aktiengesellschaft? [AI at the helm of the stock corporation?]. In A. Compes, R. C. Thümmel, & A. Winkler (Eds.), Festschrift für Alexander Reuter zum 65. geburtstag [Festschrift for Alexander Reuter on his 65th birthday] (pp. 127–140). Otto Schmidt.

Hoffmann-Becking, M. (Ed.). (2020). Münchener Handbuch des Gesellschaftsrechts: Band 4: Aktiengesellschaft [Munich Handbook of Company Law: Volume 4: Stock Corporation] (5th ed.). C.H. Beck.

Hopt, K. J. (2011). Comparative corporate governance: The state of the art and international regulation. The American Journal of Comparative Law (AJCL), 59(1), 1–73.

Hopt, K. J., & Roth, M. (2019). Der Aufsichtsrat: Aktienrecht und corporate governance: Sonderausgabe aus dem großkommentar zum aktiengesetz §§ 95 bis 116 AktG [The Supervisory board: Stock corporation law and corporate governance: Special edition from the grand commentary on the stock corporation act §§ 95 to 116 AktG]. De Gruyter.

Hölters, W., & Weber, M. (Eds.). (2022). Aktiengesetz: AktG Kommentar [Stock Corporation Act: Commentary]. C.H. Beck.
Hüffer, U., & Koch, J. (2021). Aktiengesetz: Kommentar zum AktG [Stock Corporation Act: Commentary on the Stock Corporation Act] (15th ed.). C.H. Beck.
Iafrate, F. (2018). Artificial intelligence and big data. ISTE- Wiley.
Ihrig, H.-C., & Schäfer, C. (2020). Rechte und Pflichten des Vorstands [Rights and duties of the management boards] (2nd ed). Verlag Dr. Otto Schmidt.
İlbasmış Hızlısoy, Ö., & Ağırbaş, G. (2025). Anonim şirket yönetim kurulunda yedek ve tamamlayıcı üyelik [Substitute and pro tempore membership in the board of directors of joint-stock companies]. Ticaret ve Fikri Mülkiyet Hukuku Dergisi (TFM), 11(2), 273–305.
İmregün, O. (1989). Anonim Ortaklıklar [Stock corporations] (4th ed.). Yasa Yayınları.
İmregün, O. (2001). Kara Ticareti Hukuku Dersleri [Commercial Law Lectures] (12th ed.). Filiz Kitabevi.
İnce, S. T. (2022). European union law and mitigation of artificial intelligence-related discrimination risks in the private sector: With special focus on the proposed artificial intelligence act. Annales de la Faculté de Droit d'Istanbul (ANNALES), 71, 265–307.
Kahneman, D. (2011). Thinking, fast and slow. Farrar, Straus and Giroux.
Kalender, S. (2024). Anonim şirketlerde yönetim veya temsil yetkisinin devri halinde yönetim kurulu üyelerinin hukuki sorumluluğu [Civil law liability of board members in cases of delegation of management or representation authority in stock corporations]. Adalet Yayınevi.
Kapancı, B. (2021). Özel hukuk perspektifinden bir değerlendirme: Yapay zekâ ve haksız fiil sorumluluğu [An assessment from a private law perspective: Artificial intelligence and tort liability.]. In E. E. Aksoy Retornaz & O. G. Güçlütürk (Eds.), Gelişen teknolojiler ve hukuk II: Yapay zekâ [Emerging technologies and law II: Artificial intelligence] (pp. 127–193). On İki Levha Yayıncılık.
Kaplan, J. (2016). Artificial intelligence: What everyone needs to know. Oxford University Press.
Karaca, U. (2023). Yapay zekanın haksız fiillerinden doğan hukuki sorumluluk [Civil liability arising from the torts of artificial intelligence]. On İki Levha Yayıncılık.
Karadeniz, S. (2023). Yapay zekânın anonim şirket yönetim kuruluna üyeliği ve üyelikten doğan sorumluluğunun değerlendirilmesi [Evaluation of the membership of artificial intelligence to the board of directors of the stock corporation and its responsibility arising from membership]. Türkiye Adalet Akademisi Dergisi (TAAD), 14 (54), 255–288.
Karasu, R. (2013). 6102 sayılı türk ticaret kanunu ile anonim şirketlerde kurumsal yönetim ile ilgili getirilen yenilikler [Innovations introduced by the Turkish commercial code no. 6102 regarding corporate governance in stock corporations]. İnönü Üniversitesi Hukuk Fakültesi Dergisi (İnÜHFD), 4(2), 33–60.
Karatepe Kaya, M. (2021). Yapay zekanın şirket yönetimine olası katkılarının Türk şirketler hukuku kapsamında değerlendirilmesi ve yapay zekanın hukuki statüsünün belirlenmesinde şirketler hukukundan çıkartılabilecek dersler [Evaluation of the potential contributions of artificial intelligence to corporate management within the scope of Turkish corporate law, and lessons can be drawn from corporate law in determining the legal status of artificial intelligence]. Ankara Hacı Bayram Veli Üniversitesi Hukuk Fakültesi Dergisi (HBV-HFD), 25(3), 69–106.

Karatepe Kaya, M., Erdem, F. B., Solak, E., Keskin, A., Aydın, B. Y., Kılıç, H. D., & Karadeniz, S. (Eds.). (2025). Anonim şirketlerin dijital dönüşümündeki belirsizliklerin değerlendirilmesi ve giderilmesi çalıştayı kitabı [Book of the workshop on assessing and addressing uncertainties in the digital transformation of stock corporations]. On İki Levha Yayıncılık.

Karslıoğlu, H. (2021). Anonim şirket yönetim kurulu üyelerine tanınan bilgi alma hakkı ve bu hakkın üyelerin görev ve sorumlulukları ile ilişkisi[Right to obtain information of the joint stock corporation's board of directors members and the relationship of this right with their duty and liability]. Akdeniz Üniversitesi Hukuk Fakültesi Dergisi (AkdHFD), 11(2), 377–398.

Kaşak, E. (2019). Anonim şirketlerde genel kurul ile yönetim kurulu arasındaki yetki dağılımına ilişkin temel esaslar [Basic principles regarding the distribution of authority between the general assembly and the board of directors in stock corporations]. On İki Levha Yayıncılık.

Kaya, B. C. (2024). Directors' duty of care in corporate governance: Legal, technological, and sustainability perspectives. Adalet Yayınevi.

Kaya, M. İ. (2014). Anonim şirket yönetim kurulunun denetim ve gözetim görevi [The auditory and supervisory duties of the board of directors of a stock corporation]. Dokuz Eylül Üniversitesi Hukuk Fakültesi Dergisi (DEÜHFD), 16, 3261–3286.

Kayar, İ. (2018). 6102 sayılı Türk Ticaret Kanunu'na göre ticaret hukuku [Commercial law according to the Turkish commercial code no. 6102] (5th ed.). Seçkin Yayıncılık.

Kayıhan, Ş. (2011). 6102 sayılı yeni Türk ticaret kanunu'na göre anonim şirketlerde üst gözetim [Supervision in stock corporations according to the new Turkish commercial code no. 6102]. Seçkin Yayıncılık.

Kendigelen, A. (2016). Yeni Türk ticaret kanunu: Değişiklikler, yenilikler ve ilk tespitler [New Turkish commercial code: Amendments, innovations and initial findings] (3rd ed.). On İki Levha Yayıncılık.

Keskin, A. (2024). The impact of digitalisation on company law. Adalet Yayınevi.

Kırca, İ. (2004). Anonim şirket yönetim kurulu kararlarında takdir yetkisi-özen borcu [Discretionary power and duty of care in the decisions of the board of directors of a stock corporation]. Banka ve Ticaret Hukuku Dergisi (BATİDER), 22(3), 85–97.

Kırca, İ., Şehirali Çelik, F. H., & Manavgat, Ç. (2013). Anonim şirketler hukuku cilt: 1 [Stock corporations law volume: 1]. Banka ve Ticaret Hukuku Araştırma Enstitüsü Yayınları.

Koch, J. (2024). Aktiengesetz: Kommentar [Stock Corporation Act: Commentary] (18th ed.). C.H. Beck.

Koç, H. (2018). Anonim şirketlerde iç yönerge ile yönetim ve temsil yetkisinin devri [The delegation of management and representation authority through internal directives in stock corporations]. Adalet Yayınevi.

Kortunay, A. (2015). Anonim şirketlerde yönetim kurulu üyelerinin bilgi edinme hakkı [The right of board members to obtain information in stock corporations]. On İki Levha Yayıncılık.

Kraakman, R., Armour, J., Davies, P., Enriques, L., Hansmann, H., Hertig, G., Hopt, K., Kanda, H., Pargendler, M., Ringe, W.-G., & Rock, E. (2017). The anatomy of corporate law: A comparative and functional approach. (3rd ed.) Oxford University Press.

Kremer, T., & Langenbucher, K. (2024). Einfluss von digitalizierung und KI auf das aktienrecht [Impact of digitalization and AI on stock corporation law]. In J. Vetter & M.

Habersack (Eds.), Reformbedarf im Aktienrecht [Reform need in stock corporation law] (pp. 70–92). Verlag Dr. Otto Schmidt.
Kubis, D., & Tödtmann, U. (2022). Arbeitshandbuch für vorstandsmitglieder [User manual for management board members] (3rd ed.). C.H. Beck.
Kuntz, T. (2020). Leitungsverantwortung des vorstands und delegation [Management responsibility of the management board and delegation]. Die Aktiengesellschaft (AG), 65(21), 801–819.
Küçükgüngör, M. A. (2018). Kurumsal yönetim ilkeleri bakımından halka açık anonim şirketlerde icrada görevli olmayan yönetim kurulu üyeleri [Non-executive board members of publicly traded stock corporations in terms of corporate governance principles]. Yetkin Yayınları.
Küçüktuncay, F. (2023). Anonim şirketlerde yetki devri ve yönetim kurulu üyelerinin sorumluluğuna etkisi [The delegation of authority in joint stock companies and its effect on the liability of the members of board of directors]. (Master's thesis, İstanbul Bilgi University). YÖK National Thesis Center.
Langenbucher, K. (2023a). Künstliche intelligenz in der leitungsentscheidung des vorstands [Artificial intelligence in the (core) management decision-making of the management board]. Zeitschrift für das gesamte Handelsrecht und Wirtschaftsrecht (ZHR), 187, 723–738.
Langenbucher, K. (2023b). KI in der leitungsentscheidung des vorstands der aktiengesellschaft [AI in the (core) management decision-making of the management board] (SAFE White Paper No. 96). SAFE.
Langenbucher, K. (2024). KI und aktienrecht [AI and stock corporation law]. Europäische Zeitschrift für Wirtschaftsrecht (EuZW), 18, 854–861.
Langenbucher, K. (2025). Ownership and trust—A corporate law framework for board decision-making in the age of AI (ECGI Law Working Paper No. 758/2024). Social Science Research Network (SSRN). https://doi.org/10.2139/ssrn.4746241.
Lasar, T. (2023). Künstliche Intelligenz in der GmbH [Artificial Intelligence in the limited liability company]. dfv Mediengruppe.
Laukyte, M. (2019). AI as a legal person. In Proceedings of the International Conference on Artificial Intelligence and Law, 209–213.
Li, Y. (2022). Künstliche intelligenz im rahmen unternehmerischer entscheidungen des vorstands der AG [Artificial intelligence in the context of corporate decisions by the management board of stock corporation]. Nomos.
Lieder, J. (2022). From corporate governance to algorithm governance: Artificial intelligence as a challenge for corporations and their executives. In S. Voeneky, P. Kellmeyer, O. Mueller, & W. Burgard (Eds.), The Cambridge handbook of responsible artificial intelligence: Interdisciplinary perspectives (pp. 331–346). Cambridge University Press.
Linardatos, D. (2019). Künstliche intelligenz und verantwortung [Artificial intelligence and responsibility]. Zeitschrift für Wirtschaftsrecht (ZIP), 40(11), 504–509.
Linardatos, D. (2022). Neue technologien im insolvenzrecht: Einsatzfelder von künstlicher intelligenz, blockchain und smart contracts [New technologies in insolvency law: Application areas of artificial intelligence, blockchain and smart contracts.]. Zeitschrift für Wirtschaftsrecht (ZIP), 43(4) 153–161.
Linke, C. (2021). Digitale wissensorganisation [Digital knowledge organization]. Nomos.

Linnertz, A. (2020). Die delegation durch den vorstand einer aktiengesellschaft [Delegation by the management board of a stock corporation]. Duncker & Humblot.

Lohsse, S., Schulze, R., & Staudenmayer, D. (2019). Liability for artificial intelligence. In S. Lohsse, R. Schulze, & D. Staudenmayer (Eds.), Liability for Artificial Intelligence and the Internet of Things (pp. 11–26). Nomos.

Loza de Siles, E. (2021). AI, on the law of the elephant: Toward understanding artificial intelligence. Buffalo Law Review (Buff. L. Rev.), 69(5), 1389–1469.

Lucci, S., & Kopec, D. (2016). Artificial intelligence in the 21st century: A living introduction (2nd ed.). Mercury Learning and Information.

Lutter, M., Krieger, G., & Verse, D. A. (2020). Rechte und pflichten des aufsichtsrats [Rights and obligations of the supervisory board] (7th ed.). Verlag Dr. Otto Schmidt.

Lücke, O. (2019). Der einsatz von KI in der und durch die unternehmensleitung [The use of AI in and by company management]. Der Betriebs-Berater (BB), 1986–1994.

Mainzer, K. (2020). Artificial intelligence: When do machines take over? Springer.

McCarthy, J. (2007). What is artificial intelligence? http://jmc.stanford.edu/articles/whatisai/whatisai.pdf.

McCorduck, P. (2004). Machines who think. A K Peters Ltd.

Metin, U. (2021). Şirketlerde yönetim kurulu krizleri ve çözüm yolları [Boardroom crises and solutions in corporations]. Seçkin Yayıncılık.

Molnar, C. (2019). Interpretable machine learning: A guide for making black box models explainable. Independently Published. (Leanpub) Available as an e-book at: https://originalstatic.aminer.cn/misc/pdf/Molnar-interpretable-machine-learning_compressed.pdf.

Montagnani, M. L., & Passador, M. L. (2022). Toward an enhanced level of corporate governance: Tech committees as a game changer for the board of directors. Journal of Business, Entrepreneurship & the Law (J. Bus. Entrepreneurship & L.), 15 (1), 1–80.

Möslein, F. (2007). Grenzen unternehmerischer leitungsmacht im marktoffenen verband: Aktien- und übernahmerecht, rechtsvergleich und uropäischer Rahmen [Limits of corporate management power in a market-oriented association: Stock corporation and takeover law, comparative law and the european framework]. De Gruyter.

Möslein, F. (2018). Digitalisierung im gesellschaftsrecht: Unternehmensleitung durch algorithmen und künstliche Intelligenz? [Digitalization in corporate law: Corporate management through algorithms and artificial intelligence?]. Zeitschrift für Wirtschaftsrecht (ZIP), 39(5), 204–212.

Möslein, F. (2019). Vertrauenswürdigkeit künstlicher Intelligenz und corporate governance [Trustworthiness of artificial intelligence and corporate governance]. Audit Committee Quarterly, 2019(2), 60–61.

Möslein, F. (2020a). KI im Gesellschaftsrecht [AI in corporate law]. In M. Ebers, C. Heinze, T. Krügel, & B. Steinrötter (Eds.), Künstliche Intelligenz und Robotik [Artificial Intelligence and Robotics] (pp. 461–483, § 13.) C.H. Beck.

Möslein, F. (2020b). Aktienrechtliche leitungsverantwortung beim einsatz künstlicher intelligenz [Corporate law management responsibility in the use of artificial intelligence]. In T. Braegelmann & M. Kaulartz (Hrsg.), Artificial Intelligence und Machine Learning (pp. 509–522). C.H. Beck.

Möslein, F. (2020c). Corporate digital responsibility: Eine aktienrechtliche skizze [Corporate digital responsibility: A legal outline under stock corporation law]. In S. Grundmann, H.

Merkt, & P. Mülbert (Hrsg.), Festschrift für Klaus J. Hopt zum 80. geburtstag [Festschrift for Klaus J. Hopt on his 80th birthday] (p. 805–823). De Gruyter.

Möslein, F. (2022). AI and corporate law. In L. A. DiMatteo, C. Poncibò, & M. Cannarsa (Eds.), The Cambridge handbook of artificial intelligence: Global perspectives on law and ethics (pp. 74–86). Cambridge University Press.

Möslein, F. (2023a). Künstliche intelligenz in der aktienrechtlichen organtrias [Artificial intelligence in the corporate law organ triad]. In I. Eisenberger, M. Wendland, & R. Niemann (eds.), Smart Regulation: Theorie- und evidenzbasierte Politik [Smart Regulation: Theory- and evidence-based policy] (pp. 177–202). Mohr Siebeck.

Möslein, F. (2023b). Towards corporate digital responsibility. In M. Petrin & T. Wittig (Eds.), Research handbook on corporate liability (pp. 409–433). Edward Elgar Publishing.

Möslein, F. (2025a). Robots in the boardroom: Artificial intelligence and corporate law. In W. Barfield & U. Pagallo (Eds.), Research handbook on the law of artificial intelligence (pp. 614–635). Edward Elgar Publishing.

Möslein, F. (2025b). European company law in the age of digital transformation: Artificial intelligence, data economy, and digital corporate governance. ERA Forum, 26(4), 629–646.

Müller, V. C., & Bostrom, N. (2016). Future progress in artificial intelligence: A survey of expert opinion. In V. C. Müller (Ed.), Fundamental issues of artificial intelligence (pp. 555–572). Springer.

Nilsson, N. J. (2010). The quest for artificial intelligence: A history of ideas and achievements. Cambridge University Press. Web Version: https://ai.stanford.edu/~nilsson/QAI/qai.pdf.

Noack, U. (2019a). Organisationspflichten- und strukturen kraft digitalisierung [Organizational duties and structures resulting from digitalization]. Zeitschrift für das gesamte Handelsrecht und Wirtschaftsrecht (ZHR), 183 (2–3), 105–144.

Noack, U. (2019b). Der digitale aufsichtsrat [The digital supervisory board]. In B. Grunewald, J. Koch, & J. Tielmann (Eds.), Festschrift für Eberhard Vetter zum 70. geburtstag [Festschrift for Eberhard Vetter on his 70th birthday] (pp. 497–508). Otto Schmidt.

Noack, U. (2021). Künstliche intelligenz und unternehmensleitung [Artificial intelligence and corporate management]. In G. Bachmann, S. Grundmann, A. Mengel, & K. Krolop (Eds.), Festschrift für Christine Windbichler zum 70. geburtstag [Festschrift for Christine Windbichler on her 70th birthday] (pp. 947–962). De Gruyter.

Nowak, M. (2022). Vorstand und digitalisierung: Intelligente assistenzsysteme, autonome entscheidungssysteme und virtual reality [Management board and digitalization: Intelligent assistance systems, autonomous decision-making systems and virtual reality]. Nomos.

Oğuzman, M. K., Seliçi, Ö., & Oktay-Özdemir, S. (2021). Kişiler hukuku [Law of persons] (20th ed.). Filiz Kitabevi.

Oran, O. (2021). Anonim şirketlerde yönetim kurulu iç yönergesi [Internal directive of board of directors in stock corporations]. On İki Levha Yayıncılık.

Organisation for Economic Co-operation and Development (OECD). (2020). Recommendation of the Council on Artificial Intelligence (OECD/LEGAL/0449). OECD Legal Instruments.

Özatlan, Y. (2023). Anonim şirketlerde yönetim kurulunun üst gözetim görevi ve yetkisi [The overall supervisory duty and authority of the board of directors in stock corporations]. Yetkin Yayınları.

Özdemir, S. S. (2017). İş adamı kararı ilkesi (Business judgment rule) ve Türk hukukunda uygulanabilirliği [The business judgment rule and its applicability in Turkish law.]. On İki Levha Yayıncılık.

Özer, I., & Tomrukçu, T. (2025). Anonim şirket yönetim kurulunda yapay zekanın kullanılması ve bu kullanımın iş adamı kararı ilkesi açısından değerlendirilmesi [The use of artificial intelligence in the boards of directors of stock corporations and its evaluation from the perspective of the business judgment rule]. Banka ve Ticaret Hukuku Dergisi (BATİDER), 41(2), 239–278.

Pagallo, U. (2018). Vital, sophia, and co.—The quest for the legal personhood of robots. Information, 9(9), 230, 1–11.

Pan, Y. (2016). Heading toward artificial intelligence 2.0. Engineering, 2(4), 409–413.

Parker, P. M. (2008). Webster's Turkish—English thesaurus dictionary. ICON Classics.

Paslı, A. (2005). Anonim ortaklık kurumsal yönetimi, Corporate Governance [Corporate governance of a stock corporation]. Çağa Hukuk Vakfı Yayınları.

Paslı, A. (2013). Compliance kavramının anonim ortaklıklar hukukundaki anlamı ve sorumluluk sistemine etkisi [The meaning of the concept of compliance in corporate law and its impact on the liability system.]. İstanbul Üniversitesi Hukuk Fakültesi Mecmuası (İÜHFM), 71(2), 317–334.

Patchipala, S. G. (2023). Tackling data and model drift in AI: Strategies for maintaining accuracy during ML model inference. International Journal of Science and Research Archive (IJSRA), 10(2), 1198–1209.

Petrin, M. (2019). Corporate management in the age of AI. Columbia Business Law Review (Colum. Bus. L. Rev.), 2019(3), 965–1030.

Petrin, M. (2024). The impact of AI and new technologies on corporate governance and regulation. Singapore Journal of Legal Studies, 2024(1), 90–106.

Polat, C. (2022). Sözleşme dışı sorumluluk hukukunda otonom sistemler [Autonomous systems in non-contractual liability law]. Yetkin Yayınları.

Poroy, R., Tekinalp, Ü., & Çamoğlu, E. (2025). Ortaklıklar hukuku I [Companies Law I] (16th ed.). Vedat Kitapçılık.

Pulaşlı, H. (2002). Yeni tüzük hükümlerine göre avrupa anonim şirketi [European stock corporation according to the provisions of the new regulation]. Bankacılık ve Ticaret Hukuku Dergisi (BATİDER), 21(4), 5–26.

Pulaşlı, H. (2009). Türk ticaret kanunu tasarısı'na göre anonim şirket yönetim kurulu üyelerinin özen yükümlülüğü ve müteselsil sorumluluğu [The duty of care and joint and several liability of board members of a stock corporation according to the draft Turkish commercial code]. Banka ve Ticaret Hukuku Dergisi (BATİDER), 25(1), 27–63.

Pulaşlı, H. (2017). Şirketler hukuku genel esaslar [General principles of company law] (5th ed.). Adalet Yayınevi.

Pulaşlı, H. (2019). Compliance kavramı ve yönetim organının compliance sorumluluğu [The concept of compliance and the compliance responsibility of the management organ]. Banka ve Ticaret Hukuku Dergisi (BATİDER), 35(2), 27–59.

Pulaşlı, H. (2022). Şirketler hukuku şerhi [Commentary on company law] (4th ed.). Adalet Yayınevi.

Rahman, A. A., Hamid, U. Z. A., & Chin, T. A. (2017). Emerging technologies with disruptive effects: A review. Perintis eJournal, 7(2), 111–128.

Rolsing, N. (2025). KI-Governance in der aktiengesellschaft: Vorstandspflichten und -haftung beim einsatz von künstlicher intelligenz [AI governance in stock corporations: Management board's duties and liabilities when using artificial intelligence]. Nomos.

Roth, M. (2025). Digitization and AI in the board room.—Germany [Working paper]. Social Science Research Network (SSRN). https://doi.org/10.2139/ssrn.5385484.

Russell, S., & Norvig, P. (2010). Artificial intelligence: A modern approach (3rd ed.). Prentice Hall.

Salman, A. (2024). Türk anonim şirketler hukukunda compliance kavramına ilişkin bir inceleme [An examination of the concept of compliance in the light of Turkish corporate law] (Doctoral dissertation, Bursa Uludağ University). YÖK National Thesis Center.

Samoili, S., López Cobo, M., Delipetrev, B., Martínez-Plumed, F., Gómez, E., & De Prato, G. (2021). AI watch. Defining artificial intelligence 2.0: Towards an operational definition and taxonomy of the AI landscape (EUR 30873 EN). Publications Office of the European Union.

Sanders, A. (2025). KI in der Vorstandstätigkeit von Aktiengesellschaft und Genossenschaft [AI in the management board activities of stock corporations and cooperatives]. Neue Zeitschrift für Gesellschaftsrecht (NZG), 2025, 1403–1410.

Sarı, O. (2020). Yapay zekânın sebep olduğu zararlardan doğan sorumluluk [Liability for damages caused by artificial intelligence.]. Türkiye Barolar Birliği Dergisi (TBBD), 147, 251–313.

Schmidt, K., & Lutter, M. (2020). Aktiengesetz: AktG [Stock Corporation Act: AktG] (4th ed.). Verlag Dr. Otto Schmidt.

Schubert, N. E. (2019). Digital corporate governance—Möglichkeiten für den einsatz neuer technologien im gesellschaftsrecht (Beiträge zum transnationalen wirtschaftsrecht) [Digital corporate governance—Opportunities for the use of new technologies in corporate law (Contributions to transnational economic law)]. Issue 166. https://opendata.uni-halle.de/bitstream/1981185920/80371/1/BeitraegeTWR_166.pdf.

Seçer, İ. S. (2025). Corporate compliance enhanced by artificial intelligence (Master's thesis, İstanbul Medeniyet University). YÖK National Thesis Center.

Selanik, A. A. (2022). Adam çalıştıranın sorumluluğu kapsamında yapay zekâ robotun sorumluluğu ve sigortalanması hususunun değerlendirilmesi [Evaluation of the liability and insurance of artificial intelligence robot within the scope of employer liability.]. Türkiye Adalet Akademisi Dergisi (TAAD), 13 (50), 335–364.

Sevi, A. M. (2021). Anonim ortaklıkta yönetim kurulu üyeleri ve yöneticilerin özen yükümlülüğü [Duty of care of board members and managers in a stock corporation]. Seçkin Yayıncılık.

Seyfarth, G. (2016). Vorstandsrecht [Management board law). Carl Heymanns Verlag.

Solaiman, S. M. (2017). Legal personality of robots, corporations, idols and chimpanzees: A quest for legitimacy. Artificial Intelligence and Law (Artif Intell Law), 25(2), 155–179.

Solum, L. B. (1992). Legal personhood for artificial intelligences. North Carolina Law Review (N.C. L. Rev.), 70(4), 1231–1287.

Sopacı Öztuna, B. (2015). Yönetici sorumluluk sigortası D&O-sigortası [Directors and officers liability insurance D&O insurance]. Vedat Kitapçılık.

Spindler, G. (2019a). User liability and strict liability in the internet of things and for robots. In S. Lohsse, R. Schulze, & D. Staudenmayer (Eds.), Liability for artificial intelligence and the internet of things (pp. 125–144). Nomos.

Spindler, G. (2019b). Digitalization and corporate law: A view from Germany. European Company and Financial Law Review (ECFR), 16(1–2), 106–148.

Spindler, G., & Stilz, E. (Eds.). (2019). Kommentar zum Aktiengesetz [Commentary on the Stock Corporation Act] (4th ed.). C.H. Beck.

Strohn, L. (2018). Die rolle des aufsichtsrats beim einsatz von künstlicher Intelligenz [The role of the supervisory board in the use of artificial intelligence]. Zeitschrift für das gesamte Handelsrecht und Wirtschaftsrecht (ZHR), 182, 371–377.

Stone, P., Brooks, R., Brynjolfsson, E., Calo, R., Etzioni, O., Hager, G., Hirschberg, J., Kalyanakrishnan, S., Kamar, E., Kraus, S., Leyton-Brown, K., Parkes, D., Press, W., Saxenian, A., Shah, J., Tambe, M., & Teller, A. (2016). Artificial intelligence and life in 2030: One hundred year study on artificial intelligence: Report of the 2015–2016 study panel. Stanford University.

Şener, O. H. (2026). Ortaklıklar hukuku [Company law] (6th ed.). Filiz Kitabevi.

Tekinalp, Ü. (2003). Anonim ortaklıklara ilişkin yeni hukuk politikalarının dinamikleri ve bunlar arasındaki ilişki [The dynamics of new legal policies regarding stock corporations and the relationships between them]. In Ş. T. Ansay (Ed.), Prof. Dr. Turgut Kalpsüz'e armağan [Festschrift for Prof. Dr. Turgut Kalpsüz] (pp. 227–252). Turhan Kitabevi.

Tekinalp, Ü. (2008). Türk ticaret kanunu tasarısının kurumsal yönetim felsefesine yaklaşımı [The draft Turkish commercial code's approach to corporate governance philosophy.]. In M. İnceoğlu (Ed.), Uğur Alacakaptan'a armağan [Festschrift for Uğur Alacakaptan] (635–652). İstanbul Bilgi Üniversitesi Yayınları.

Tekinalp, Ü. (2011). Yeni anonim ve limited ortaklıklar hukuku ile tek kişi ortaklığının esasları [The new law on joint stock and limited liability companies and the principles of single member companies.] (2nd ed.). Vedat Kitapçılık.

Tekinalp, Ü. (2020). Sermaye ortaklıklarının yeni hukuku [New law regarding capital companies]. Vedat Kitapçılık.

Telle, M. (2023). Einsatz künstlicher intelligenz zur vorbereitenden unterstützung von leitungsentscheidungen des vorstands einer AG [Use of artificial intelligence to provide preliminary support for management decisions of the management board of a stock corporation]. Duncker & Humblot.

The Federal Government of Germany. (2018). Artificial intelligence strategy of Germany. https://www.ki-strategie-deutschland.de/.

The Royal Society. (2017). Machine learning: The power and promise of computers that learn by example. The Royal Society.

The Royal Society. (2019). Explainable AI: The basics (Policy briefing DES6051). The Royal Society.

Thiel, S., & Nazari-Khanachayi, A. (2021). Digitalisierung aus gesellschaftsrechtlicher perspektive: Chancen und herausforderungen des einsatzes softwarebasierter tools [Digitalization from a corporate law perspective: Opportunities and challenges of using software-based tools]. Recht Digital (RDi), 134–142.

Töre, İ. (2025). An assessment of the possible contributions of artificial intelligence to corporate management within the scope of corporate governance. Selçuk Üniversitesi Hukuk Fakültesi Dergisi (SÜHFD), 33(2), 877–911.

Turanboy, A. (2023). Anonim şirketlerde yönetim kurulunun yönetim ve temsil yetkisini murahhaslara bırakması [Delegation of board of directors' management and representation authority to delegates in joint stock corporations]. Banka ve Ticaret Hukuku Dergisi (BATİDER), 39(4), 761–783.

Turner, J. (2019). Robot rules: Regulating artificial intelligence. Palgrave Macmillan.

Uğurerkan, Ç. S. (2024). Artificial intelligence impact on corporate law and management. Yetkin Yayınları.

Ustahaliloğlu, M. K. (2025). Artificial intelligence in corporate governance. Corporate Law & Governance Review (CLGR), 7(1), 123–134.

Üçışık, G. & Çelik, A. (2013). Anonim ortaklıklar hukuku I [Stock corporations law I]. Adalet Yayınevi.

Ünal, M. (1982). Anonim ortaklıklarda yönetim ve yönetim görevlerinin murahhaslara bırakılması [Management and delegation of management duties to delegates in stock corporations]. Banka ve Ticaret Hukuku Dergisi (BATİDER), 11(3), 49–90.

van Giffen, B., & Ludwig, H. (2023). How boards of directors govern artificial intelligence. MIS Quarterly Executive (MISQE), 22(4), Article 7.

Varlı, E. B. (2025). Anonim şirketlerde yönetim kurulu üyelerinin rekabet ihlallerinden doğan sorumluluğu [Liability of board members in stock corporations arising from competition violations]. Seçkin Yayıncılık.

Veziroğlu, C. (2021). Anonim ortaklıklar hukukunda esas sözleşme özgürlüğü ve sınırları [Contractual freedom in articles of association and its limits in joint stock company law]. On İki Levha Yayınları.

Wachter, T. (Ed.). (2022). Aktiengesetz: Kommentar [Stock Corporation Act: Commentary] (4th ed.). RWS Verlag.

Wagner, G. (2019). Robot liability. In S. Lohsse, R. Schulze, & D. Staudenmayer (Eds.), Liability for artificial intelligence and the Internet of Things (pp. 27–62). Nomos.

Wang, P. (2019). On defining artificial intelligence. Journal of Artificial General Intelligence (JAGI), 10(2), 1–37.

Weber, R., Kiefner, A., & Jobst, S. (2018). Künstliche Intelligenz und Unternehmensführung [Artificial intelligence and business management]. Neue Zeitschrift für Gesellschaftsrecht (NZG), 29, 1131–1136.

Windorf, M. (2025). Künstliche intelligenz in der aktiengesellschaft: Auswirkungen auf organisationsverfassung und unternehmensführung [Artificial intelligence in stock corporations: Impact on organizational structure and corporate management]. Mohr Siebeck.

Wirth, G., Arnold, M., Morshäuser, R., Carl, S., & Greene, M. (2017). Corporate law in Germany (3rd ed.). C.H. Beck.

Yanlı, V. (1997). İsviçre anonim ortaklıklar hukuku'nda "işbölümü ilkesi" ve yönetim kurulunun münhasır yetkileri [The "principle of division of labor" and the exclusive powers of the board of directors in Swiss corporate law.]. İstanbul Hukuk Fakültesi Mecmuası (İHFM), 55(3), 261–278.

Yaşar, T. N. (2018). Şirketler hukuku açısından 'compliance' kavramı ve borsaya kayıtlı şirketlerde uygulanması [The concept of 'compliance' in corporate law and its application to publicly traded corporations] (Doctoral dissertation, Ankara University). YÖK National Thesis Center.

Yaşar T. N. (2020). Anonim şirketlerde yönetim kurulu açısından "hukuki muhakeme kuralı" (Legal Judgment Rule) [The "legal judgment rule" from the perspective of the board of directors in stock corporations]. In E. Göztepe, U. Orhan, & M. E. Göka (Eds.). Bilkent Üniversitesi Genç Hukukçu Araştırmacılar Sempozyumu 2019 [Bilkent University Young Law Researchers Symposium 2019] (pp. 625–647). On İki Levha Yayıncılık.

Yıldırım Soysal, H. (2023). Kurumsal yönetimde dijital dönüşüm [Digital transformation in corporate governance]. Ankara Üniversitesi Hukuk Fakültesi Dergisi (AÜHFD), 72(4), 1785–1842.

Yünlü, S. (2019). Current developments on artificial intelligence and liability for robot caused damages. Yeditepe Üniversitesi Hukuk Fakültesi Dergisi (YÜHFD), 16(1), 189–213.

Zetzsche, D. (2019). Corporate technologies—Zur digitalisierung im aktienrecht [Corporate technologies—On digitalization in stock corporation law]. Die Aktiengesellschaft (AG), 1–17.

Zhao, J. (2022). Artificial intelligence and corporate decisions: Fantasy, reality or destiny. Catholic University Law Review (Cath. U. L. Rev.), 71, 663–698.

Zhao, J. (2024). Promoting more accountable AI in the boardroom through smart regulation. Computer Law & Security Review (CLSR), 52, 1–16.

Online Sources

Abu Dhabi Media Office (2024, February 27). "Artificial Intelligence board observer appointed by International Holding Board of Directors." Available at https://www.mediaoffice.abudhabi/en/economy/artificial-intelligence-board-observer-appointed-by-international-holding-board-of-directors/. (Last accessed: 25.12.2025)

Aliando (2025, August 26). "ALIANDO Elects World's First AI Board Member at London Meeting." Available at https://aliando.com/news/aliando-elects-worlds-first-ai-board-member-at-london-meeting. (Last accessed: 25.12.2025)

Allianz. "Data Ethics and Responsible Artificial Intelligence." Available at: https://www.allianz.com/en/about-us/strategy-values/data-ethics-and-responsible-ai.html#principles. (Last accessed: 25.12.2025)

Artificial Intelligence Strategy of the German Federal Government 2020 Update. Available at: https://www.ki-strategie-deutschland.de/files/downloads/Fortschreibung_KI-Strategie_engl.pdf. (Last accessed: 25.12.2025)

BBC (2014, May 16). "Algorithm appointed board director." Available at https://www.bbc.com/news/technology-27426942. (Last accessed: 25.12.2025)

Board Intelligence. Available at https://www.boardintelligence.com/ai. (Last accessed: 25.12.2025)

Brooks, R. (2017, September 7). "The Seven Deadly Sins of Predicting the Future of AI." Available at: http://rodneybrooks.com/the-seven-deadly-sins-of-predicting-the-future-of-ai/. (Last accessed: 25.12.2025)

Burgess, M. (2018, March 1). "UK police are using AI to inform custodial decisions—but it could be discriminating against the poor." Available at: https://www.wired.co.uk/article/police-ai-uk-durham-hart-checkpoint-algorithm-edit. (Last accessed: 25.12.2025)

Burridge, N. (2017, May 10). "Artificial intelligence gets a seat in the boardroom." Nikkei Asian Review. Available at https://asia.nikkei.com/business/artificial-intelligence-gets-a-seat-in-the-boardroom. (Last accessed: 25.12.2025)

Byrne, D. (n. d.). "Ten steps to creating an AI policy." Corporate Governance Institute. Available at: https://www.thecorporategovernanceinstitute.com/insights/guides/creating-an-ai-policy/?srsltid=AfmBOoqQA1VeZopdnHOcWG454ZjC2U7_sy5KXxmtNEt0dQr-VJGWbk-q. (Last accessed: 25.12.2025)

Cambridge Online German-English Dictionary. "Intelligenz." Available at: https://dictionary.cambridge.org/dictionary/german-english/intelligenz. (Last accessed: 25.12.2025)

Cambridge Online German-English Dictionary. "Künstlich." Available at: https://dictionary.cambridge.org/dictionary/german-english/kunstlich?q=k%C3%BCnstlich. (Last accessed: 25.12.2025)

Corporate Digital Responsibility Initiative. Available at: https://cdr-initiative.de/en/code. (Last accessed: 25.12.2025)

Deutsche Telekom. "Digital Ethics Guidelines On AI." Available at: https://www.telekom.com/en/company/digital-responsibility/details/artificial-intelligence-ai-guideline-524366. (Last accessed: 25.12.2025)

Dilligent Boards. Available at https://www.diligent.com/products/boards. (Last accessed: 25.12.2025)

Finextra (2016, October 18). "Tieto appoints bot to leadership team." Available at https://www.finextra.com/newsarticle/29606/tieto-appoints-bot-to-leadership-team. (Last accessed: 25.12.2025)

Griffith, K. (2025, October 7). "How To Effectively Use AI For Legal Research." Thomson Reuters Legal Solutions Blog. Available at: https://legal.thomsonreuters.com/blog/how-to-effectively-use-ai-for-legal-research/. Last accessed: 25.12.2025)

Horner, H. (2025, May 12). "How Engineers Use AI To Work Smarter, Prototype Faster, And Stress Less." Engineering Institute of Technology. Available at: https://www.eit.edu.au/how-engineers-use-ai-to-work-smarter-stress-less/. (Last accessed: 25.12.2025)

IBM (n. d.). "What is agentic AI?." IBM Think Topics. Available at: https://www.ibm.com/think/topics/agentic-ai. (Last accessed: 25.12.2025)

IBM (n. d.). "Unsupervised Learning." Available at: https://www.ibm.com/think/topics/unsupervised-learning. (Last accessed: 25.12.2025)

Ismailov, V. (2025, October 7). "Artificial Intelligence Joins Board of Directors at Samruk-Kazyna." The Times of Central Asia. Available at https://timesca.com/artificial-intelligence-joins-board-of-directors-at-samruk-kazyna/. (Last accessed: 25.12.2025)

Kelley, B. J., Skidgel, M. and Wang, A. (2025, May 7). "Planning Your AI Policy? Start Here." Corporate Compliance Insights. Available at https://www.corporatecomplianceinsights.com/planning-your-ai-policy-start-here/. (Last accessed: 25.12.2025)

Liptak, A. (2017, May 1). "Sent to prison by a software program's secret algorithms." The New York Times. Available at: https://www.nytimes.com/2017/05/01/us/politics/sent-to-prison-by-a-software-programs-secret-algorithms.html. (Last accessed: 25.12.2025)

Loomion. Available at https://loomion.ch/en/. (Last accessed: 25.12.2025)

Max Planck Society. (2025, June 20). "Human–AI Collectives Make The Most Accurate Medical Diagnoses." Available at: https://www.mpg.de/24908163/human-ai-collectives-make-the-most-accurate-medical-diagnoses. (Last accessed: 25.12.2025)

Merriam-Webster Dictionary. "Artificial." Available at: https://www.merriam-webster.com/dictionary/artificial. (Last accessed: 25.12.2025)

Merriam-Webster Dictionary. "Intelligence." Available at: https://www.merriam-webster.com/dictionary/intelligence. (Last accessed: 25.12.2025)

Meyer, D. (2018, January 2025). "An AI Bot Named Einstein Critiques Salesforce Execs Every Week." Fortune News Tech Section. Available at https://fortune.com/2018/01/25/salesforce-benioff-einstein-davos-ai. (Last accessed: 25.12.2025)

Nişanyan Etymological Turkish Dictionary. "Suni." Available at: https://www.nisanyansozluk.com/?k=suni. (Last accessed: 25.12.2025)

Nişanyan Etymological Turkish Dictionary. "Yapay." Available at: https://www.nisanyansozluk.com/?k=yapay. (Last accessed: 25.12.2025)

Nişanyan Etymological Turkish Dictionary. "Zekâ." Available at: https://www.nisanyansozluk.com/?k=zeka. (Last accessed: 25.12.2025)

OnBoard. Available at https://www.onboardmeetings.com/onboard-ai/. (Last accessed: 25.12.2025)

Reinsw (2024, May 30). "REINSW appoints Australia's first AI Board Advisor." Available at https://www.reinsw.com.au/Web/Web/News/Media_Releases/2024/05-May/ai-board-advisor.aspx. (Last accessed: 25.12.2025)

Republic of Türkiye Ministry of Industry and Technology, "2030 Industry and Technology Strategy." https://www.sanayi.gov.tr/assets/pdf/plan-program/2030IndustryAndTechnologyStrategyENG.pdf?1751241600107. (Last accessed: 25.12.2025)

Rowan, J., Gaus, T., Gilbert, F., & Brown, C. (2025, December 24). "AI goes physical: Navigating the convergence of AI and robotics." Deloitte Insights. Available at: https://www.deloitte.com/us/en/insights/topics/technology-management/tech-trends/2026/physical-ai-humanoid-robots.html. (Last accessed 25.12.2025)

Sabancı Holding Yatırımcı İlişkileri. "Yapay Zeka Politikası (AI Policy) [Sabancı Holding Investor Relations. Artificial Intelligence Policy (AI Policy)]" Available at: https://yatirimciiliskileri.sabanci.com/tr/surdurulebilirlik/detay/Yapay-Zeka-Politikasi/686/3263/0#:~:text=Sabanc%C4%B1%20Toplulu%C4%9Fu%20Yapay%20Zek%C3%A2%20Politikas%C4%B1,uygulanmas%C4%B1%20i%C3%A7in%20rehberlik%20sa%C4%9Flamay%C4%B1%20ama%C3%A7lar. (Last accessed: 25.12.2025)

SAP. "Global AI Ethics Policy." Available at: https://www.sap.com/documents/2022/01/a8431b91-117e-0010-bca6-c68f7e60039b.html. (Last accessed: 25.12.2025)

Sharma, B. (2023, February 9). "Youth organisation appoints ChatGPT AI bot as its CEO, calls it 'groundbreaking'." India Times. Available at: https://www.indiatimes.com/technology/news/organisation-appoints-chatgpt-bot-as-its-ceo-592620.html. (Last accessed: 25.12.2025)

The AI Fairness 360. "AI Fairness 360: Understand and mitigate bias in ML models." Available at: https://ai-fairness-360.org/.(Last accessed: 25.12.2025)

TPN/Lusa. (2023, April 28). "Portuguese entrepreneur creates viral company. The Portugal News." Available at: https://www.theportugalnews.com/news/2023-04-28/portuguese-entrepreneur-creates-viral-company/77089. (Last accessed: 25.12.2025)

Wang, A. (2025, May 7). "Planning Your AI Policy? Start Here, Corporate Compliance Insights." Available at https://www.corporatecomplianceinsights.com/planning-your-ai-policy-start-here/. (Last accessed: 25.12.2025)

Wolfgang P. et al. (1993), Etymologisches Wörterbuch des Deutschen (Digitalized Version in Digitalen Wörterbuch der deutschen Sprache), "Künstlich." Available at: https://www.dwds.de/wb/etymwb/K%C3%BCnstlich. (Last accessed: 25.12.2025)

MIX
Papier | Fördert gute Waldnutzung
FSC® C083411

Kolibri 360 GmbH
Ferdinand-Jühlke-Straße 7
99095 Erfurt, Deutschland
produktsicherheit@kolibri360.de